# EXERCISE
## AND
# AGING

*The Scientific Basis*

# EXERCISE AND AGING
## The Scientific Basis

Papers presented at the
American College of Sports Medicine
Annual meeting, May 28-30, 1980
Las Vegas, Nevada

## EVERETT L. SMITH

*Director of Biogerontology Laboratory*
*Department of Preventive Medicine*
*University of Wisconsin*
*504 Walnut*
*Madison, Wisconsin 53706*

*and*

## ROBERT C. SERFASS

*Director of Human Performance Laboratory*
*School of Physical Education, Recreation*
*and School Health Education*
*University of Minnesota*
*Minneapolis, Minnesota 55455*

*Editors*

Enslow Publishers
Bloy Street & Ramsey Avenue, Box 777
Hillside, New Jersey   07205

W. SUSSEX INSTITUTE
OF
HIGHER EDUCATION
LIBRARY

**Library of Congress Cataloging in Publication Data:**

American College of Sports Medicine.
 Exercise and aging.

 1. Aging—Congresses. 2. Exercise—Physiological
aspects—Congresses. 3. Aged—Rehabilitation—Congresses.
4. Exercise therapy—Congresses. I. Smith, Everett L.
II. Serfass, Robert C. [DNLM: 1. Aging—Congresses.
2. Exertion—In old age—Congresses.

QP86.A52 1980   612'.67    80-24700
ISBN 0-89490-042-0

Printed in the United States of America

10 9 8 7 6 5 4 3 2

# CONTENTS

# FOREWORD

Henry Poincare once observed, "It is by logic that we prove, but by intuition that we discover." For many years, the value of physical exercise and activity for improving the physical and mental well-being of the elderly has been recognized intuitively, but there has been a paucity of good research to prove this value and practical programs to demonstrate it.

*EXERCISE AND AGING: The Scientific Basis,* a well-edited, well-documented collection of papers presented at an annual meeting of the American College of Sports Medicine, remedies this situation.

This book presents authoritative data and observations on the cardiovascular, musculo-skeletal, respiratory, and other systems of the body, and the principles and limitations of exercise for the aging. The papers primarily explore the environmental component of the aging curve and the modification of lifestyle that may prevent and/or reverse those components of aging attributable to inactivity. They permit the reader to weigh for himself, his patients, and clients the risks and benefits of physical activity with the obvious risks and detriments of a sedentary lifestyle. They supply information about exercise and the aging process and draw attention to the less clear-cut relationships between exercise and the preservation of youthful physical and organ characteristics, and the preservation of mental well-being. The book identifies not only the structural and functional aging characteristics of the major physical systems that have considerable implications for the optimal development and maintenance of physical fitness in the elderly. It also supplies reliable information relative to current knowledge about the adaptation of these systems in response to chronic physical activity. Another feature of this volume is the attention given to the principles of development of prudent exercise programs for the diverse aged population.

This excellent book is a welcome and important contribution to the current literature on the scientific basis of exercise and aging. It should appeal to the increasing numbers of physicians, sports medicine specialists, physical educators, physiologists, gerontologists, physiatrists, and others who are interested in learning more about the logical, scientific basis of exercise and aging. Experts may find material with which they are familiar, but expert and novice alike will find in this book new insights into the relationships between exercise and aging. These insights transform intuitive observations of the value of exercise for aging into accepted proof and practical guidance. A voluminous bibliography provides adequate documentation and a solid foundation for research and for the establishment of practical programs of exercise for the elderly.

In all, *EXERCISE AND AGING: The Scientific Basis*, constitutes a reliable source book on the increasingly important interdisciplinary field of exercise and aging.

Raymond Harris, M.D.,
*President,*
  *Center for the Study of Aging*
*Medical Consultant,*
  *President's Council on Physical Fitness and Sports*
*Clinical Associate Professor of Medicine,*
  *Albany Medical College*

## PREFACE

Over the past several years there has been an encouraging
upswing in participation and interest in exercise by the older
adult. This trend seems to be nurtured by the realization
that the maintenance or restoration of an optimal level of
physical fitness can signifcantly effect the overall quality
of the later years of an individual's life. This phenomenon
of increased physical activity and exercise programs has cut
across the entire range of the elderly population from the
institutionalized to senior citizens who are engaging in
Masters' competitive athletics. Consequently, it is becoming
increasingly inaccurate to stereotype the elderly as sedentary
and non-responsive to lifestyle changes. In conjunction with
the rapid increase in the numbers of exercising elderly,
there has developed a significant need for the dissemination
of information on the effects of age related changes on work
capacity and physical performance, the effects of exercise on
the maintenance and/or improvement of physical fitness in the
elderly, and the principles related to the prudent development
of exercise programs for this diverse aged population.

The primary purposes for the symposium, Exercise and
Aging, at the 27th annual meeting of the American College of
Sports Medicine in Las Vegas, Nevada were (1) to provide a
forum for professional colleagues in the exercise and health
related services to share updated information about the effects of aging on relevant biophysical systems and, (2) to
survey current knowledge about the effects of chronic physical activity on the aging organism. The first portion of
these symposium proceedings deals primarily with aging of the

cardiovascular and musculoskeletal systems while the second portion considers the effects of organized exercise programs on these same systems. It is our hope that the information contained in this manuscript will provide an informative supplement to those who are already engaged in exercise programming and research related to the older adult. Further, it is hoped that these proceedings will stimulate those individuals who have demonstrated a peripheral interest in the elderly to become actively involved in the development of the body of knowledge germane to exercise programming for this population.

We extend our sincere appreciation to the administrative staff of the American College of Sports Medicine who supported and helped plan this symposium and to our colleagues who so willingly participated in the program. We wish to thank Miss Linda Johnson and Patricia E. Smith who assisted in the preparation of manuscripts for final printing, and to Cathy Gilligan for her hours of editorial assistance and final typing of the manuscripts.

Robert C. Serfass
Everett L. Smith

# AGE: THE INTERACTION OF NATURE AND NURTURE
## Everett L. Smith

The fact that man changes through time is as much a reality as birth and death. As man passes through time changes occur which limit his capability to adapt to his milieu. Thus, aging might be defined as the loss of man's ability to adapt to his environment. This decreased adaptability relates to the total phase of man's interaction with his environment, including the physical social, psychological, emotional and economic aspects of life. No one interactive process in the life of man can be totally separated from all the other aspects.

Each phase of a man's life has specific and unique characteristics that provide for maximum interaction with his environment. In the early years of development one is involved with the environment through experiencing as many things as possible with a brain designed to absorb all individual experiences. As one grows older the brain adapts by reducing the amount of material that it absorbs, in exchange for the integration of all experiences into a cohesive framework. Thus, in looking at the whole of life, one can say a life well lived today makes for an enjoyable memory of the past and provides for a hopeful future. Each chronological age of life is, in its own way, unique and beautiful. As a child I enjoyed those activities of freedom and play with my friends in experiencing the things of childhood. As a young adult I enjoyed those opportunities of sharing and the exuberance of youth and new experiences of marriage and family rearing. As an older member of society, I find myself enjoying new learning experiences but also having the adaptability of determining those ways I would desire life to go without the limitations of youth and inexperience. Thus, life at each age is an experience of joy that can provide complete satisfaction for living if the most is made of each day.

The text that follows is designed to define and make suggestions as to how one might help one's physical body to function at its optimal level. The first portion discusses those changes that occur as man ages. The second section deals with the effects of physical activity on the aging system and provides suggestions as to what one might be able to accomplish through a well-organized physical activity program toward preventing or retarding the declining functional capacity of the biological system.

Research in aging is most clearly expressed in terms of changes which relate to the activities of daily life. In order to define aging it is necessary to involve studies of both human populations and all other living organisms. These studies not only define the aging process, but also demonstrate the best way to maintain fitness and prevent early aging.

Studies on human aging have been carried out for many years, but there are difficulties in interpreting the results of this research because of variations in methods and techniques of measurement. An important point in studying the aging process and particularly in taking action so that the quality of life and possible life expectancy might be extended can be found in the differing rates of aging between individuals. These individual differences indicate that many factors, both genetic and environmental, play a role in aging. When it is known why some people age less rapidly than others, it may be possible to create similar conditions for all people that will minimize loss of functional cells and tissues, and thereby enable more people to live as long as those who live longest today.

In studying the aging process, the first general finding of biogerontologists is that the biological systems decline every day as the result of cell death (9,10,11). This death results in a decline in capacity and function which correlates directly with the progressive loss of body tissue. A loss of tissues has been shown to be associated with the disappearance of muscle, nerve and various cells of vital organ tissues. One of the most obvious manifestations of human aging is a decline in one's ability to exercise and do work (9,10,11). This decreased ability to exercise with advancing age is characterized by a reduced capacity of the body to exercise and a failure to return to normal levels of function as quickly as the young. This increased recovery time is one indication of the decreased ability of the aged to adapt to an ever changing environment.

There is a clear difference between chronological and physiological age. After the age of 65, chronological age plays a less important role in a person's continuance to interact and adapt to his environment. Physiological age is expressed by one's continued ability to adapt to his environment in either normal life situations or life crises. Within the broad spectrum of the population classified as old one may define two distinct groups of older adults. One group is defined as the young old (age 60 to 75) and the other the old old (age 75+). This categorization of the older population by chronological age is based on the general physiological observation that after the age of 75 many people have one or more chronic illnesses and have a greatly reduced ability to adapt. The Euro-American Curve (Figure 1) indicates this reduction in adaptability in general physiological function by man in the developed world. The values expressed by this curve exemplify average change in man over time. This curve shows that a person reaches his peak maturity at about age 30. After that time, he is often labeled as being "over the hill" as functional capacity declines at a rate of about .75% per year. This general rate of decline occurs in many of the organ systems of the body. The changes within the human body, while following a similar trend of about a .75 to 1% loss per year, vary from individual to individual and from organ to organ within an individual.

One's work capacity clearly follows this general aging trend. Work capacity declines by 30% between the ages of 30 and 70, with further decline after age 75 (10,11). Parallel to the work capacity decline is the decline of both muscular strength and muscle mass by 25-30% between the ages of 30 and

FIGURE 1

The Euro-American Curve

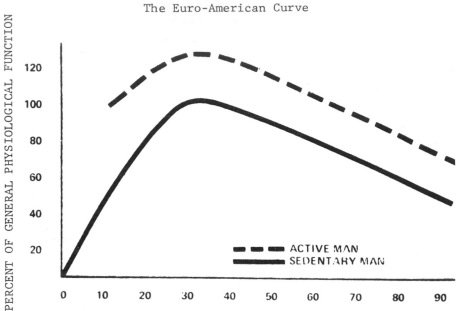

70 in both men and women (2,8). This results in a decreased ability to function within the environment, as well as a decrease in the basal metabolic rate of 10% (9). In conjunction with a decrease in muscle mass, general dehydration occurs in body cells. This overall decline of 15 to 20% is accounted for by decreased water in individual cells and by an overall increase in body fat between the ages of 30 and 70 (10,11). The result of this decline in body water is a greater probability of more rapid dehydration, or loss of water, in older individuals than in younger individuals exposed to adverse conditions of illness or extreme heat. In adverse conditions, such as burns, severe diarrhea or vomiting, an older individual is more susceptible to dehydration.

With advancement in age the cardiovascular system, both the heart and vascular bed, progressively declines in function. The maximum cardiac output (CO), which consists of two components--stroke volume (SV) and heart rate (HR)--declines by about 30% between ages 30 and 70 (6,11).

While cardiac output declines, blood pressure increases.

Both the systolic and diastolic blood pressures increase between the ages of 30 and 70 (6,11). On the average, the systolic blood pressure increases 10 to 15 mm of mercury and the diastolic pressure increases 5 to 10 mm of mercury over the same period of time.

In addition to decreased cardiac output and increased blood pressure, there is an increased resistance to blood flow. This increase may be related to the stiffening of the vessels and/or fatty deposits on the walls of the vessels.

Respiratory function declines with age. Vital capacity decreases by 40 or 50% between the ages of 30 and 70, while the lung residual volume increases by 40% (3,11).

The aging nervous system demonstrates two major changes. Cells within the brain die at a constant rate until about age 60. This death results in a decreased number of nerve cells in the brain. Whether this is good or bad is not yet clear. The rate of cell death does not appear to have any effect on one's intellectual capacity or the decision making process as one grows older. The only exception to this is in the extremely old individual where decreased nervous tissue function is directly related to a decreased blood flow to the brain tissue.

The nerve conduction velocity, or the speed that the nerve carries messages from one point to another, is also decreased (10,11). Research in this area has been done using measuring devices to monitor the rate of impulse speed from the shoulders to the wrists. This impulse rate is decreased over time, resulting in a slightly slower response to various activities in the environment by older individuals.

The support system of the body is the skeletal system, which loses bone at different rates depending upon sex and individual factors. In the average female, bone loss begins about age 35 or 40. By the time a woman is 70 years of age, she has lost as much as 30% of her bone (4,7). On the other hand, men lose bone starting at about age 55 and lose approximately 10-15% of their bone by the time they are 70 (4,7).

Two other vital organs that need to be referenced in this brief summary of changes with age are the liver and the kidney. Both organs lose about 40-50% of their function between the ages of 30 and 70. Although there is ample functional reserve, both organs are important in total body metabolism and are involved in the metabolisms of various drugs taken into the human body to fight disease or to help maintain body function. When the organs do not function at the fullest of their capacity, there is increased potential for drug toxicity. This toxicity could lead to side effects resulting in further medical complications. It is important for the older individual to be keenly aware of the possibility of side effects which could limit the function and the appropriateness of the drug they are taking.

Biological function clearly declines with age as expressed by the Euro-American curve. An identification of the proportions of the aging curve attributable to the genetics of aging and to environmental contributions to aging requires continued research.

Clearly the genetic components of age control the overall length of life, but the quality of life is controlled by how a person interacts with his environment. Some of the current research suggests that 50% of the decline frequently attributed to physiological aging is, in reality, disuse atrophy resulting from inactivity in an industrialized world.

The papers in this symposium primarily explore the environmental component of the aging curve and those modifications and lifestyle which may prevent and/or reverse those components of aging attributable to inactivity.

### REFERENCES

1. Bender, A.D. The effect of increasing age on the distribution of peripheral blood flow in man. J. Am. Geriat. Soc. 13:192-198, 1965.

2. Bourlière, F. Principes et méthodes de mesure de l'âge biologique chez l'homme. Bull. Mém. Soc. Anthropol. Paris XI(4):561-583, 1963.

3. Bourlière, F., H. Cendron and F. Clément. Le vieillissement individual dans une population rurale francaise. Etude de la commune de Plzevet, Finistere. Bull. Mém. Soc. Anthropol. Paris XI(10):41-101, 1966.

4. Garn, S.W., C.G. Rohmann and B. Wagner. Bone loss as a general phenomenon in man. Fed. Proc. 26:1729-1736, 1967.

5. Harris, R. The Management of Geriatric Cardiovascular Disease. Philadelphia: J.B. Lippincott, 1970.

6. Harris, R. Long-term studies of blood pressure recorded annually, with implications for the factors underlying essential hypertension. Trans. Assoc. Life Ins. Med. Dir. LI:30, 1968.

7. Mazess, R.B. and J.R. Cameron. Bone mineral content in normal U.S. whites. In: International Conference on Bone Mineral Measurements, edited by R.B. Mazess. Washington, D.C.: DHEW Publ. No. NIH 15-683, pp. 228-238, 1973.

8. Norris, A.W. and N. Shock. Science and Medicine of Exercise and Sports. New York: Harper, p. 466, 1960.

9. Shock, N.W. Metabolism and age. J. Chron. Dis. 2:687-703, 1955.

10. Shock, N.W. System integration. In: Handbook of the Biology of Aging, edited by C. Finch and L. Hayflick. New York: Van Nostrand Reinhold, pp. 639-655, 1977.

11. Shock, N.W. The physiology of aging. Scient. Am. 206(1):100-108, 1962.

# CARDIOVASCULAR LIMITATIONS IN THE AGED
## Roy J. Shephard

This section will review briefly changes in both the peripheral vessels and the heart with aging.

## PERIPHERAL VASCULATURE

### STRUCTURAL CHANGES

The age-related decline in the elasticity of the major blood vessels has been recognized for many years (34,49). Changes in connective tissue occur as elsewhere in the body--the elastic lamellae fray and atrophy, there is both diffuse and focal replacement by collagen in all the large vessels (21), and the average size of the aorta increases (11). In a young person, the collagen fibres function in parallel with the elastin, but after repeated cycles of elongation and contraction, they fail to resist distension until a substantial force is applied. Furthermore, elastin returns to its initial length once the distending pressure falls, but the collagen by which it is replaced shows substantial hysteresis, retaining as much as two thirds of its increase in length for a considerable time after the elongating force has passed.

Local atheromatous change, with secondary calcification, and ulceration in turn leads to rigidity of the vascular wall, with narrowing and occasional obstruction of vessels supplying both the heart and skeletal muscles.

There may be some reduction of the capillary/fibre ratio with aging (32), but because of associated wasting of muscle fibres, the diffusion pathway from the blood vessels to the

19

metabolic sites within the mitochondria remains relatively constant. The activity of many enzyme systems is low, but it is unclear whether this reflects lack of fitness or aging per se (6,27).

On the venous side of the circulation, most elderly subjects show some varicosities, with a corresponding increase in capacity of the peripheral reservoirs (9). At the same time, deterioration of the venous valves increases the pressure in the venous system.

## FUNCTIONAL CONSEQUENCES

Systemic Pressures. The more rigid arteries accept the cardiac stroke volume less readily than in a younger person. Thus, there is an increase in the resting pulse pressure and the resting systolic blood pressure. The situation during vigorous exercise depends upon the health of the myocardium and its ability to withstand increased after-loading. During maximum effort, most authors find a somewhat higher pressure than in a younger individual (2,16,22,23,37). Sidney and Shephard (unpublished observations) found average maxima of 217 mm Hg (29.9 kPa) in elderly men and 206 mm Hg (27.5 kPa) in elderly women, compared with 180 mm Hg (24.0 kPa) in young adults. On the other hand, some "post-coronary" patients had difficulty in sustaining systolic pressure as the work rate was increased (40); this is evidence of persistent myocardial ischaemia, and the patients concerned are particularly vulnerable to reinfarction.

Peripheral Resistance. The peripheral resistance may be increased by (i) atheromatous plaques in the vascular lumina, (ii) weakness of the skeletal muscles, causing individual muscle groups to contract at a high percentage of maximum force, and obstructing blood flow thereby (25), and (iii) failure of vasodilatation in response to exercise. The elderly person in consequence sustains a 20% higher systemic pressure in the face of perhaps a halving of maximum cardiac output. There is no ready method of deciding how far this increase of peripheral resistance is an inevitable consequence of aging, and how far it is environmentally determined. In the short term, regular physical activity can reduce the resting systemic pressure by about 5 mm Hg, but it has little

influence upon the terminal pressure in maximum effort. The
maximum cardiac output may show a small increase, and if this
is sustained at the same pressure, a proportional reduction of
peripheral resistance must be presumed. It is less clear
whether a life-time of physical activity would lead to more
dramatic preservation of a youthful peripheral resistance.
Studies of some primitive ethnic groups suggest this may be
the case (28), but there are many other factors contributing
to a low incidence of hypertension and cardiovascular disease
in such populations.

Only in pathological cases (exercise-induced angina,
intermittent claudication, gangrene) does the restriction of
flow come to the attention of the sedentary older person.
Nevertheless, electrocardiographic abnormalities such as ST-
segmental depression show a progressive increase with age,
and restriction of flow to skeletal muscles is indicated by
(i) a progressive increase in the discrepancy between treadmill and bicycle ergometer estimates of maximum oxygen intake,
and (ii) a progressive discrepancy between step test and bicycle ergometer predictions of maximum oxygen intake.

Flow Distribution. There has been little examination of
the peripheral distribution of blood flow in the elderly. Under resting conditions, skin flow may be quite poor, creating
a vulnerability to chilblains, ulcers, and pressure sores.
However, during exercise the flow to the skin is likely to be
greater than in a younger person, since (i) conduction of heat
to the surface is impeded by a thick layer of sub-cutaneous
fat, and (ii) sweating is induced less readily because of a
low level of physical fitness. As a result of thes factors
plus (i) reduced arterial oxygen saturation, (ii) reduced
haemoglobin, and (iii) reduced activity of tissue enzyme systems, the maximum arterio-venous oxygen difference is commonly reduced somewhat by aging.

## HEART

### STRUCTURE

Gross Anatomy. As in other tissues of the body, there is
a progressive degeneration of cardiac structures with advanced
age, including a wasting of the heart muscle, a loss of

elasticity (20), fibrotic changes in the valves of the heart
and infiltration with amyloid (33); it is less certain how far
these changes are an unavoidable consequence of aging and how
far they reflect chronic myocardial oxygen lack.

Certainly, heart volumes are fairly well maintained provided that subjects remain active (3,10,12,45). Kavanagh and
Shephard (24) found that in Master's athletes the radiographic
estimate of heart volume was 12.0±1.7 ml/kg at age 40-50,
12.4±1.7 ml/kg at age 50-60, 13.9±2.8 ml/kg at age 60-70, and
13.2±3.0 ml/kg in a small sample aged 70-90 years. At the age
of 45 years, Saltin and Grimby (35) observed a volume of 15.0
ml/kg in active orienteers, compared with 11.1 ml/kg in those
sportsmen who had become inactive. At the age of 65 years,
the figure for active subjects had diminished to 13.2 ml/kg.
Again, it is difficult to separate the inevitable loss of lean
tissue with aging from the consequences of slackening of
training and selective recruitment of subjects in different
age groups.

Cellular Changes. Cellular changes occur much as elsewhere in the body (4). The nucleus becomes larger and may
show invagination of its membrane. Nucleoli increase in size
and number. The chromatin shows clumping, shrinking, fragmentation or dissolution, and there is an increased likelihood of
finding chromosomal abnormalities. The mitochondria show alterations in size, shape, cristal pattern and matrix density
reducing their functional surface. The cytoplasm is marked by
fatty infiltration or degeneration, vacuole formation, and a
progressive accumulation of pigments such as lipofuscin. Lipofuscin is thought to arise by the peroxidation of lipid/pro-
tein mixtures, and in the myocardium increases at a rate of
about 0.3 percent per decade. Thus, at the age of 90, 6-7%
of the intracellular volume is occupied by the pigment (46).
There is no evidence that this material impairs either normal
function or the capacity for cardiac hypertrophy (47). Another compound that often accumulates is amyloid. Pomerance
(33) found amyloid in the hearts of 12% of men aged 80 years
and older. Again, minor lesions probably have little functional significance, but extensive amyloidosis could be one
cause of senile cardiac failure.

As the cell ages, the sodium pump becomes less effective,

and there is an increase of intracellular water (47) noted as
a "cloudly swelling" in histological preparations. There is
also a decrease in the activity of key enzymes such as ATPase
(13) and lactic dehydrogenase (36).

## FUNCTIONAL CONSEQUENCES

Heart Rate. The maximum heart rate shows a progressive
decline from the age of about 25 years, although it is now
recognized that the widely used formula of (220 - age in
years) underestimates the maximum for sedentary North Americans. At 65 years, a maximum of at least 170 beats/min can be
attained (38). Slowing does not seem a consequence of myocardial oxygen lack, since the values found in a young adult
cannot be restored by the administration of pure oxygen.
Greater stiffness of the ventricular wall is a second possibility. This might increase the time required for filling of
the ventricles, and modify the "feedback" of information of
venous filling to the cardio-regulatory centres. Lastly, the
sympathetic drive to the cardiac pacemaker may diminish with
age.

Stroke Volume. The strength of the ventricular muscle
is indicated by the ability to maintain stroke volume in the
face of increased pre- and after-loading. Elderly subjects
develop almost the same stroke volume as younger individuals
at light work loads, but the stroke output diminishes as effort is increased towards a maximum (5,16,17,18,31). The
stroke volume during exhausting work is thus 10 to 20 percent
smaller than in a young adult. However, the mechanism (poor
myocardial perfusion, lesser cardiac compliance, or poor contractility) remains uncertain.

Myocardial Contractility. The resting pre-ejection
period (P.E.P.) increases from about 80 msec at age 25 to 95-
100 msec in a 65 year old person (14,20,30), at least a half
of this difference persisting when the P.E.P. is "corrected"
for heart rate effects. Interpretation of the longer P.E.P.
is complex. It could reflect electrical changes associated
with a decrease of resting sympathetic tonus, but in an older
person it is more likely to reflect a diminution of myosin
ATPase activity with a mechanical slowing of tension development in the myocardial fibres (1) and/or a general loss of

coordination of the contractile process (43).

Cardiac Output. Under resting conditions, a normal heart rate and a reduced stroke volume lead to a low cardiac output in the elderly (7,15,16,26,42,45,48), this change being larger than would be anticipated from associated decreases of resting metabolism.

During light work, the cardiac output is much as in a younger person. However, the peak cardiac output is attained at a lower percentage of maximum oxygen intake and at age 65 is 20-30% lower than in a young adult (38).

Cardiac Failure. While a young person readily accepts a sustained increase of cardiac load, an equivalent stress in an older individual may give rise to cardiac failure. Adverse features include systemic hypertension, malfunction of the cardiac valves, and degeneration of the myocardium. Repeated minor infarctions may bring a person to the state where pro- longed rest is needed after even mild activity (8). Warning symptoms include excessive shortness of breath during exer- tion, anginal pain, persistent fatigue and peripheral cya- nosis. The heart rate may show a progressive rise over the normal working day, with a poor recovery during rest pauses. The blood pressure fails to rise during activity, and the stroke volume decreases rather than increases as the power output is raised. The oxygen debt is disproportionate to the required effort, and both ventilation and heart rate show a slow recovery on ceasing exercise. If an old person is showing this type of picture, care must be taken to hold exercise below an intensity and duration that would precipi- tate cardiac failure.

Electrical Activity. Coronary atherosclerosis is usually considered as a pathological rather than a normal consequence of aging. Nevertheless, many 65 year old subjects have mild to moderate coronary vascular changes, and the resultant electrocardiographic abnormalities are a frequent cause of concern to physicians and others concerned with the arrange- ment of practical exercise programmes for the elderly.

The resting electrocardiogram often has a lower voltage than in a young adult, particularly if the chest is emphyse- matous. The electrical axis tends to be horizontal, particu- larly if the subject is obese, and sinus arrhythmia is less

obvious than in a young person (29). The PR interval may be
increased (19), and local ischaemia of the atrio-ventricular
node can lead to various types of heart block. The amplitude
of the T wave is often small, reflecting poor physical fitness
and a small stroke volume (29,43) and an increased proportion
of subjects show a saddle-shaped rather than a flat and
"healthy" looking iso-electric segment.

The most obvious change during exercise is the appearance
of a horizontal or downward sloping depression of the ST segment of the electrocardiogram. The likelihood of detecting
such a sign increases progressively with age. In men, the
phenomenon is a warning of serious myocardial ischaemia, and
it carries an increased risk of myocardial infarction and sudden death. In elderly women, ST depression is at least as
common as in men, but for some reason that is poorly understood (39) there is often little or no evidence of associated
vascular disease in the female.

Exercise also increases the proportion of subjects
showing various types of conduction block and aberrant
rhythms. Considered independently, an exercise-induced dys-
rhythmia is a warning of myocardial ischaemia with some increase in the risk of suddent death (39). However, it is less
clearly established that this sign adds to the warning provided by a horizontal or down-sloping ST segment.

## PRACTICAL IMPLICATIONS

The detection of electrocardiographic abnormalities is an indication for caution when prescribing exercise. Nevertheless,
if all elderly people with unusual electrocardiograms were
prohibited from exercising, there would be relatively few
senior citizens attending exercise facilities. Unfortunately,
we have no categoric information on the risks involved. Even
in older adults, episodes are sufficiently rare that it is
difficult to collect precise statistics. The overall experience of a post-coronary programme is unlikely to be better
than that of the elderly exerciser. In the Toronto Rehabilitation Centre programme, Dr. Kavanagh and I have seen about
one cardiac emergency for every 110,000 hours of exercise, or
given a typical class of 50 patients meeting three times per
week, one episode in 15 class-years. Anyone working with the

elderly should certainly be prepared to undertake two or three resuscitations in the course of his or her career, but such events are not frequent enough to have a major influence upon the decision to exercise. Furthermore, it is uncertain that the exercise bout has worsened prognosis even if resuscitation is unsuccessful; the physical activity may merely have localized an impending heart attack to the gymnasium.

Specific precautions to minimize the risk of activity for the elderly have been widely discussed. Medical examination prior to a stress electrocardiogram makes a relatively small contribution to safety; different physicians exclude from 1 to 15% of those examined from stress-testing, yet the proportion of abnormal exercise e.c.g.s detected is almost independent of the number of exclusions (41). It is probably a wise precaution to obtain a vigorous exercise electrocardiogram on all elderly exercise candidates, defining the heart rate at which frequent premature ventricular contractions and major horizontal or downsloping ST depression develop. The intensity of prescribed exercise can then be held below this threshold. It is further useful to train subjects not only to count their pulse accurately, but also to recognise premature ventricular contractions and early angina. Finally, the oxygen demand upon the heart muscle can be held to a minimum by reducing the prescription if the blood pressure is increased by cold weather or any emotional disturbance, and avoiding activities that involve isometric muscle contractions.

## REFERENCES

1. Albert, N.R., H.H. Gale and N. Taylor. The effect of age on contractile protein ATPase activity and the velocity of shortening. In: Factors Influencing Myocardial Contractility, edited by R.D. Tanz, F. Kavaler and J. Roberts. New York: Academic Press, 1967.

2. Åstrand, I. Blood pressure during physical work in a group of 221 women and men 48-63 years old. Acta Med. Scand. 178:41-46, 1965.

3. Åstrand, P.O. Physical performance as a function of age. J. Amer. Med. Assoc. 205:729-733, 1968.

4. Bakerman, S. Aging Life Process. Springfield: C.C. Thomas, p. 10, 1969.

5. Becklake, M.R., H. Frank, G.R. Dagenais, G.L. Ostiguy and G.A. Guzman. Influence of age and sex on exercise cardiac output. J. Appl. Physiol. 20:938-947, 1965.

6. Björntorp, P., M. Fahlén, J. Holm, T. Scherstén and J. Stenberg. Changes in the activity of skeletal muscle succinic oxidase after training. In: Coronary Heart Disease and Physical Fitness, edited by O.A. Larsen and R.O. Malmborg. Copenhagen: Munksgaard, pp. 138-42, 1971.

7. Brandfonbrener, M., M. Landowne and N.W. Shock. Changes in cardiac output with age. Circulation 12:557-566, 1955.

8. Bruce, R.A. Evaluation of functional capacity in patients with cardiovascular disease. Geriatrics 12:317-328, 1957.

9. Carlsten, A. Influence of leg varicosities on the physical work performance. In: Environmental Effects on Work Performance, edited by G.R. Cumming, D. Snidal and A.W. Taylor. Ottawa: Canad. Assoc. Sports Sciences, pp. 207-214, 1972.

10. Davies, C.T.M. The oxygen transporting system in relation to age. Clin. Sci. 42:1-13, 1972.

11. Dotter, C.T. and I. Steinberg. The angiocardiographic measurement of the great vessels. Radiology 52:353-7, 1949.

12. Durusoy, F.P., E.J. Klaus, D. Clasing and W. Niemann. Herz-kreislauf-untersuchungen bei 68 über 60 jährigen Altersturnern in Ruhe. Sportarzt und Sportmedizin 19:443-446, 1968.

13. Edington, D.W. and V.R. Edgerton. The Biology of Physical Activity. Boston: Houghton Mifflin, 1976.

14. Gabbato, F. and A. Media. Analysis of the factors that may influence the duration of isotonic systole in normal conditions. Cardiologia 29:114-131, 1956.

15. Granath, A., B. Jonsson and T. Strandell. Studies on the central circulation. Studies by right heart catheterization at rest and during exercise in supine and sitting positions in older men. Acta Med. Scand. 169:125-126, 1961.

16. Granath, A., B. Johnson and T. Strandell. Circulation in healthy old men studied by right heart catheterization at rest and during exercise in supine and sitting position. Acta Med. Scand. 176:425-446, 1964.

17. Grimby, C., N.J. Nilsson and B. Saltin. Cardiac output during sub-maximal and maximal exercise in active middle-aged athletes. J. Appl. Physiol. 21:1150-1156, 1966.

18. Hanson, J.S., B.S. Tabakin and A.M. Levy. Comparative exercise cardiorespiratory performance of normal men in the third, fourth and fifth decades of life. Circulation 37:345-360, 1968.

19. Harlan, W.R., A. Graybiel, R.E. Mitchell, A. Oberman and R.K. Osborne. Serial electrocardiograms: Their reliability and prognostic validity during a 24-hour period. J. Chron. Dis. 20:853-867, 1967.

20. Harrison, T.R., K. Dixon, R.O. Russell, P.S. Bidwai and H.N. Coleman. The relation of age to the duration of contraction, ejection and relaxation of the normal human heart. Amer. Heart J. 67:189-199, 1964.

21. Hass, G.E. Elastic tissue. III. Relation between the structure of the aging aorta and the properties of the isolated aortic elastic tissue. Arch. Path. 35:29-45, 1943.

22. Julius, S., A. Amery, L.S. Whitlock and J. Conway. Influence of age on the hemodynamic response to exercise. Circulation 36:222-230, 1967.

23. Kasser, I.S. and R.A. Bruce. Comparative effects of aging and coronary heart disease on submaximal and maximal exercise. Circulation 39:759-774, 1969.

24. Kavanagh, T. and R.J. Shephard. The effects of continued training on the aging process. Ann. N. Y. Acad. Sci. 301:656-670, 1977.

25. Kay, C. and R.J. Shephard. On muscle strength and the threshold of anaerobic work. Int. Z. Angew. Physiol. 27:311-328, 1969.

26. Kilböm, A. Physical training in women. Scand. J. Clin. Lab. Invest. 28: Suppl. 119:1-34, 1971.

27. Kraus, H. Effects of training on skeletal muscle. In: Coronary Heart Disease and Physical Fitness, edited by O.A. Larsen and R.O Malmborg. Copenhagen: Munksgaard, pp. 134-137, 1971.

28. Mann, G.V., R.D. Shaffer, R.S. Anderson and H.H. Sandstead. Cardiovascular disease in the Masai. J. Atherosclerosis Res. 4:289-312, 1964.

29. Mazer, M. and J.A. Resinger. An electrocardiographic study of cardiac aging based on records at rest and after exercise. Ann. Int. Med. 21:645-652, 1944.

30. Montoye, H.J., P.W. Willis, G.E. Howard and J.B. Keller. Cardiac pre-ejection period: Age and sex comparisons. J. Gerontol. 26:208-216, 1971.

31. Niinimaa, V. and R.J. Shephard. Training and oxygen conductance in the elderly. I. The respiratory system. II. The cardiovascular system. J. Gerontol. 33(3):354-367, 1978.

32. Párizková, J., E. Eiselt, S. Sprynarova and M. Wachtlova. Body composition, aerobic capacity and density of muscle capillaries in young and old men. J. Appl. Physiol. 31:323-325, 1971.

33. Pomerance, A. Pathology of the heart with and without failure in the aged. Brit. Heart J. 27:697-710, 1965.

34. Roy, C.S. The elastic properties of the arterial wall. J. Physiol. 3:125-159, 1880.

35. Saltin, B. and G. Grimby. Physiological analysis of middle-aged and old former athletes. Comparison of still active athletes of the same ages. Circulation 38:1104-1115, 1968.

36. Schmukler, M. and C.H. Barrows. Age differences in lactic acid malic dehydrogenase in the rat. J. Gerontol. 21:109-111, 1966.

37. Sheffield, L.T. and D. Roitman. Systolic blood pressure, heart rate and treadmill work at anginal threshold. Chest 63:327-335, 1973.

38. Shephard, R.J. Human physiological work capacity. IBP human adaptability project, Synthesis, vol. 4. New York: Cambridge University Press, 1978.

39. Shephard, R.J. Physical Activity and Aging. Chicago: Year Book, 1978.

40. Shephard, R.J. Recurrence of myocardial infarction. Observations on patients participating in the Ontario Multicentre Exercise-Heart Trail. Brit. Heart J. 42(2):133-138, 1979.

41. Shephard, R.J. Current assessment of the Canadian Home-Fitness Test. S. Afr. J. Sports Sci. 2, 63-72, 1979.

42. Shock, N.W. An essay on aging. In: Aging of the Lung, edited by L. Cander and J.H. Moyer. New York: Grune and Stratton, pp. 1-12, 1964.

43. Silver, H.M. and M. Landowne. The relation of age to certain electrocardiographic responses of normal adults to a standardized exercise. Circulation 8:510-520, 1953.

44. Starr, I. An essay on the strength of the heart and on the effect of aging upon it. Amer. J. Cardiol. 14:771-783, 1964.

45. Strandell, T. Circulatory studies in healthy old men. Acta Med. Scand. Suppl. 141:1-44, 1964.

46. Strehler, B.L., D.D. Marks, A.S. Mildvan and M.V. Gee. Rate and magnitude of age pigment accumulation in the human myocardium. J. Gerontol. 14:430-439, 1959.

47. Timiras, P.S. Developmental Physiology and Aging. New York: MacMillan, ch. 28, 1972.

48. Toscani, A. Physiology of muscular work in the aged. In: Work and Aging. Second International Course in Social Gerontology, edited by J.A. Huet. Paris: International Centre of Social Gerontology, pp. 185-220, 1971.

49. Wilens, S.L. The post-mortem elasticity of the adult human aorta. Its relation to age and to the distribution of atheroma. Amer. J. Path. 13:811-834, 1937.

Dr. R.J. Shephard is presently Director of the School of Physical and Health Education and Professor of Applied Physiology within the Department of Preventive Medicine, Faculty of Medicine, University of Toronto. He also holds academic appointments as Professor in the Department of Physiology and the Institute of Medical Sciences, and is a consultant to the Toronto Rehabilitation Centre, the Gage Research Institute, the Defence Research Board, and the Département des Sciences de la Santé (University of Québec at Trois Rivières). Prior to coming to Toronto in 1964, he held appointments in the Department of Cardiology (Guy's Hospital, London), the R.A.F. Institute of Aviation Medicine, the Department of Preventive Medicine (University of Cincinnati) and the U.K. Chemical Defence Experimental Establishment (Porton Down, U.K.). He holds four scientific and medical degrees from London University (B.Sc., M.B.B.S., Ph.D. and M.D.) and is former president of the American College of Sports Medicine, an editor of "Human Biology" and a former editor of "Medicine and Science in Sports." He is the author of some 12 books on exercise physiology, fitness and ergonomics, and has published over 400 scientific papers on related topics.

## AGING AND SKELETAL MUSCLE
Robert H. Fitts

## INTRODUCTION

A review of the published reports on age and skeletal muscle unveils a considerable amount of conflict. The words of Rothstein (55) perhaps best summarize the present state of affairs: "In a few cases, the activity of the same enzyme is reported to go up, go down or stay the same depending upon the investigator, the animal or the tissue being studied." Part of the problem results from the difficulty in separating specific age-dependent muscle changes from other factors that influence muscle such as physical activity, disease, cardio-vascular, hormonal or neural influences. The results have been further complicated by the use of adult animals (e.g., 12-18 month rats) in aged groups, young animals (e.g., 1-3 month rats) as adult controls, and the sampling of hetero-geneous muscles composed of more than one fiber type.

It is not my intention to present a complete review, but rather discuss selective studies emphasizing the important functional effects of aging on skeletal muscle. After de-scribing the physical and structural changes, the major metabolic and physiological alterations in muscle with age will be discussed.

## STRUCTURAL ALTERATIONS WITH AGING

In many regards the ultrastructural (33,36,37) and electro-physiological (27,33) alterations in skeletal muscle with aging resemble those observed with denervation. The classic cross-innervation studies of Buller et al. (16) established

31

the importance of the trophic influence on skeletal muscle function, and demonstrated that the metabolic and physiologic profile of a muscle fiber (i.e., the fiber type) was primarily determined by the type of neural innervation (phasic or tonic firing pattern and other trophic factors) received. Adult skeletal muscle is composed of 3 distinct fiber types (14)-- type IIA (fast twitch, high oxidative fiber), type IIB (fast twitch, low oxidative fiber), and type I (slow twitch, high oxidative fiber). Based upon the histochemical demonstration of myofibrillar ATPase (18,36,37) and the mitochondrial enzyme succinic dehydrogenase (36), this heterogeneous fiber pattern is lost with aging and fibers become more homogeneous in respect to their physiological and metabolic profile. With extremely old animals (30 month old rats) grouping of fibers of one type occurs, a process associated with denervation and subsequent reinnervation (18). Although Gutmann et al. (33) found no evidence of disintegration of the terminal axons in senile muscle fibers, they did observe major changes in the N-M junction. These changes included: 1. An increase in the number and agglutination of presynaptic vesicles, 2. appearance of neurotubules and neurofilaments in the peripheral axons, 3. enlargement of primary synaptic clefts, 4. thickening of the basement membrane, and 5. increased branching of the junctional folds. Gutmann et al. (33) concluded that these changes produced a slow reduction of synaptic contact in senile muscle and resulted in a "functional denervation" that likely compromised the normal neurotrophic influence (32,33). In addition to ultrastructural changes, the N-M junction in senile muscle shows a reduced frequency of miniature end-plate potentials (m.e.p.p.s.) (33), and a reduced conduction velocity in the presynaptic axons (19). Despite the reduced frequency of m.e.p.p.s. there is no increase in the size of the end plate receptor area or a change in its sensitivity to Ach.

It is well known that decreases in muscle mass occur with old age (66), with the proximal muscles of the lower limb particularly affected (28,44,48). This decrease in muscle mass is more marked than body weight loss (37,56) and appears due to a decrease in both fiber number and diameter (18,19,32,37, 56). Considerable controversy exists regarding the age related changes in the number and size of motor units (18,19, 31). Gutmann and Hanzlikova (31) found no change in the number of motor neural fibers, but the size of the motor unit decreased due to the loss of muscle fibers. Both Campbell et al. (19) and Caccia et al. (18) report fewer motor nerves in senile muscle with either no change or an increase in the unit size. Although Tauchi et al. (63) reported the decrease in fiber number to primarily affect the red oxidative fiber, the preponderance of evidence based on enzyme histochemistry (18,42) and physiological properties (19,44) suggest a greater loss in the fast type II fiber. The decrease occurs in both type IIA and IIB fibers such that the type IIB/IIA fiber ratio is unaltered with increasing age (42). As a result of this selective loss of type II fibers the percentage of type I fibers in the quadriceps muscle of man increased from 40% in the 20-29 age group to 55% in the 60-65 age group. Besides atrophy and decrease in number of fibers, senile skeletal muscle exhibits a number of ultrastructural changes (33,37) to include: 1. Thickening and protrusion of the sarcolemma into the extracellular space, 2. an increase in collagenous material in the extracellular space, 3. disorganized and disrupted myofilaments at the cell perhiphery, 4. proliferation of the tubular T-system, the sarcoplasmic reticulum, and the terminal cisternae, 5. enlarged mitochondria with vacuolated matrix, short cristae and loss of dense granules, 6. accumulation of ribosomes and polysomes in subsarcolemmal region, and 7. an increase in lysosomal vesicles and pinocytic activity. The majority of these age related ultrastructural changes are located at the fiber surface where considerable cell debris associated with proteolytic activity can also be observed (33,37).

The decrease in senile muscle mass is associated with a decrease in total protein and nitrogen concentration (15,65) and an increase in connective tissue and fat (40). Intracellular water and potassium have been reported to be unaltered (45) or decreased (2,65), while muscle amino acid concentration increases (45) with aging. Extracellular water, sodium, and chloride are all higher in older adults (24,45).

The molecular mechanism of the age related muscle atrophy is not clearly understood, but the process is likely linked to the neural and neuromuscular changes reviewed earlier. The rate of total body protein synthesis decreases throughout life but when related to metabolic rate (protein synthesis per calorie) no differences are observed between young and elderly adults (67). The rate of myofibrillar and sarcoplasmic muscle protein synthesis is depressed with old age (49). The increase in lysosomal vacuoles (33), acid hydrolases (49), and cathepsin (8) are all suggestive of an increased rate of protein catabolism; however, studies measuring the rate of disappearance of radioactive metheonine indicate only a slight increase in protein catabolism in the elderly (8).

## BIOCHEMICAL ALTERATIONS WITH AGING

Respiratory Capacity. In man it is well known that aging, beyond the second decade of life, is associated with a progressive decline in physical work capacity (6). Maximal oxygen uptake (liters/minute $\dot{V}O_2$ maximum) shows a steady decline past age 20 in both males and females (6,23). The decline in maximal $\dot{V}O_2$ with age is related to cardiovascular (see Shephard this volume), respiratory (see Reddan this volume) and peripheral (skeletal muscle) changes.

Some controversy exists concerning alterations in muscle respiration with age. It is fairly well established that liver and kidney mitochondria undergo ultrastructural changes (60,65) and a decrease in number (9). Inamdar et al. (39) found no change in the number or size of mitochondria in 20 month old hamster skeletal muscle, although they did report a decreased mitochondrial yield (protein/g tissue) from old muscles which they (30) and others (64) have attributed to an increased fragility. More recently, Orlander et al. (46) found the mean mitochondrial volume to decrease with age primarily due to a decrease in mitochondrial size, although they did report a decrease in the apparent number of mitochondria in the subsarcolemma region.

The effect of age on the state 3 oxidation rate of heart and skeletal muscle mitochondria appears to be substrate dependent (20,39). Chen et al. (20) found the state 3 respiration rate in senile heart mitochondria to be depressed with glutamate-malate, glutamate-pyruvate, palmityl carnitine, and β-hydroxybutyrate while no change was observed using pyruvate-

malate, succinate, palmityl CoA-carnitine or ascorbate-cytochrome C. Senile skeletal muscle mitochondria showed a depressed state 3 respiration using glutamate-malate substrate,
but no change with succinate (20,39), ascorbate-cytochrome C,
palmityl carnitine, palmityl CoA-carnitine or pyruvate-malate
(39). The efficiency of energy conservation as determined by
the ADP:O ratio, and the rate of state 4 respiration is not
altered in senile heart or skeletal muscle mitochondria (20,
39). Chen et al. (20) conclude that the substrate dependency
of the age related change in state 3 respiration make it unlikely that the electron transport chain (ETC), a common pathway in substrate oxidation, is altered in senile muscle. They
suggest that pathways before the ETC such as specific dehydrogenases, and/or transport associated systems may be altered
in senile muscle. Before conclusions can be drawn, the whole
question of state 3 oxidation needs to be reevaluated uti-
lizing homogeneous samples representative of type I, IIA, and
IIB fibers. These studies should include an evaluation of
specific dehydrogenases or transport systems unique to the
oxidative pathway of any substrate that is affected by the
aging process.

Enzymes of Oxidate Metabolism. Succinate dehydrogenase
(SDH) is perhaps the most widely studied oxidative enzyme.
Inamdar et al. (39), and Howells and Goldspink (38) found SDH
activity to decrease with aging in hamster skeletal muscle; a
similar finding has been reported by others (25). Cytochrome
oxidase activity has also been observed to decrease with
aging (65), as has pyruvate and malate dehydrogenase (MDH)
(11,25). Bass et al. (11), in one of the few studies evaluating oxidative enzymes in a particular fiber type, observed
citrate synthase and MDH to decrease more with age in slow
(type I) than fast (type IIA and IIB) rat muscle. As mentioned earlier, senile skeletal muscle is characterized by a
reduced mass (28,44,56,58,65) and a more homogeneous fiber
pattern (11,18,36,37). These changes in part can be explained
by a selective loss of type II fibers (18,19,42,44). The
total decrease in a particular enzyme with aging is considerably greater than the activity change (expressed in IU/g
muscle) suggests due to the large loss in muscle mass. The
observation that fast muscle is less susceptible to an age-

dependent decrease in oxidative enzyme activity (11) might be
explained by a selective loss of the low oxidative type IIB
fiber. Orlander et al. (46) found no change in 3-hydroxyacyl-
CoA dehydrogenase, a fatty acid β-oxidation marker, citrate
synthase, a citric acid cycle marker or cytochrome oxidase, an
ETC marker, in biopsy samples taken from the mixed vastus
lateralis in subjects ranging in age from 22 to 76 years.
Since the enzyme activity was constant despite a drop in mitochondrial volume, Orlander et al. (45) concluded that the
amount of enzyme per unit mitochondrial volume actually increased with age.

    Enzymes of Glycolysis. The words of Rothstein quoted
previously are particularly appropriate for this group of
enzymes. The exception is lactate dehydrogenase, the activity
of which has consistently been reported to decrease with age
(11,25,56,57) in both slow and fast muscle (11). Aldolase,
perhaps the most widely studied glycolytic enzyme, has been
reported to undergo no change in specific activity per mg of
protein (25,30) or to decrease (59) with aging. Although
muscle aldolase activity did not decrease significantly with
aging (30), 1.4 times as much antiserum was needed to inactivate a given enzyme activity in old mice (30). This suggests
the presence of inactive or partially inactive molecules in
senescent mouse muscle (30). These data are contradicted by
Steinhagen-Thiessen and Hilz (59) who reported a 50 percent
decrease in human muscle aldolase specific activity per mg
soluble protein, and little change in the amount of antiserum
needed to inactivate a given enzyme activity. The discrepancy
may be due to species differences and/or to a different fiber
type population in the sample studied. Bertolini (12) reported hexokinase activity to decrease in mixed senile skeletal muscle. When fast and slow muscles were evaluated, the
hexokinase activity was unaltered in the fast extensor digitorum longus while it dropped 30 percent in the senile
soleus muscle (11). Despite conflicting reports on the effect
of age on glycolytic enzyme activity (11,12,25,30,59), age-
dependent changes in carbohydrate metabolism are indicated by:
1. A depressed muscle glycogen content (12,25), 2. a reduced
glucose tolerance, and 3. an impairment in glucokinase in-
duction following fasting (1). Besides glycogen, muscle high

energy phosphogens (ATP, CP) are reduced and creatine and ADP elevated in senile skeletal muscle. The specific activity of creatine kinase, the enzyme catalysing creatine phosphate restitution, has been reported to decrease (59) or remain the same (25) with age.

Although definitive conclusions are difficult to make, a decrease in the activity of both glycolytic and aerobic enzymes occurs with aging (11). In many cases the depressed activity and/or altered enzyme structure does not occur until very old age (e.g., 30 month old rats), and this fact partially explains some of the discrepancies reviewed here (11,25,30,39,45).

ATPase Enzymes. Rockstein and Brandt (53,54) precipitated the myofibrils from rat gastrocnemius muscle homogenate and measured the $Mg^{++}$ activated ATPase of the remaining supernatant. They reported the ATPase activity of this fraction to decrease with age (26 month rat). Because of the preparation used (crude supernatant containing both sarcoplasmic reticulum, the mitochondrial ATPase), and the heterogeneity of the muscles sampled, these results are not conclusive. Bertrand et al. (13) measured $Ca^{++}$ and $Mg^{++}$ ATPase activity of purified SR membranes. They reported the ATPase activity to decrease between 2 and 12 months of age and to increase from 12 to 28 months. They observed a similar increase in oxalate-stimulated $Ca^{++}$ transport activity from 12 to 28 months. These studies were performed on a heterogeneous fiber type sample and thus no conclusions can be made concerning age-related changes in a specific fiber type.

$Ca^{++}$ activated myofibril ATPase decreases in very old muscles (25,61), and this decrease was noted in both fast and slow skeletal muscle (61).

Rockstein and Brandt (53,54) found no age-related changes in actomyosin isolated from rat gastrocnemius. However the assay was run at an unphysiological pH (pH - 9.0), which may have disrupted the actomyosin, leading to the measurement of myosin rather than actomyosin ATPase. Kaldor and Min (41) have shown myosin to be unaffected by age between 12 and 29 months (rat hind limb), while $Mg^{++}$-activated actomyosin ATPase decreased. They suggested that the change may be due to an altered myosin structure. Others have found myosin ATPase to be unchanged at 24 months (61) but markedly reduced at 36 months in fast and elevated in slow rate muscle (11,34,61, 62). Type I fibers in the adult soleus muscle contain myosin light chains of the slow type only (29,62); however, after 30 months of age soleus muscle myosin contains light chains of the slow and fast type (62). This structural alteration in myosin may partially explain the increased myosin ATPase activity observed in soleus muscle in very old rats.

## PHYSIOLOGICAL ALTERATIONS WITH AGING

Muscle Membrane Properties. The resting membrane potential is unaltered in old rats (27,33) but decreases in very old age (27). This change may be due to a decrease in intracellular potassium (2,27,66). The amplitude of the action potential has been reported to be unaltered (33) or depressed (27) in senile rat skeletal muscle. There appears to be no difference in the rise time or duration of the action potential (33). Senile skeletal muscle is less excitable due to a higher threshold potential (27), and reduced end plate potential in response to a given stimulus (33). As a result in old age fewer fibers contract in response to a given stimulus strength. An increase in the relative and absolute refractory period decreases the senile muscles' capacity to respond to high frequency stimulation (27).

Muscle Contractile Properties. Studies as early as the beginning of the nineteenth century (50) and others (4,6,17) have shown muscle strength to decrease with increasing age in man. Recently, with the development of the isokinetic dynamometer, the effect of age on dynamic as well as isometric strength has been evaluated (43,44), and both increase up to the third decade, remain constant until the fifth decade, and then decrease with increasing age (43,44). Petrofsky and Lind (47) found no change in maximal isometric hand grip strength between 22 and 62 years of age. This result conflicts directly with earlier studies (4,6,17) in which grip strength was reported to decline with increasing age. The discrepancy might be due to the fact that the subjects in the Petrofsky and Lind study were a homogeneous group of machine workers involved in daily arm exercise. The reduced strength with increasing age is most likely due to a reduction in the

number and size of the fibers (particularly type II) within
senile skeletal muscle (18,19,42,44) as well as to a decrease
in the number of motor units recruited (27,33). This idea
gains support from the observation that the muscle fibers of
the proximal lower limb show the greatest atrophy and strength
loss with age.

The maximum knee extension velocity, MEV (isotonic shortening speed), undergoes a similar pattern of change with age
as isometric strength (44). However, the decrease observed
from 40 to 60 years in MEV was 7 percent compared to decreases
of 26-38 percent for the strength measurements (44). Beside
muscle strength and shortening velocity in vivo experiments
have shown motor coordination to deteriorate with age (3).

Endurance, when measured as the ability to continue prolonged heavy work, decreases with age beyond the third decade
(6,17,27). When endurance is measured at the same relative
load (e.g., same percentage of one's maximal strength) no age-
dependent decline is seen in either isometric (43,47) or
dynamic (43) strength.

Although the in vivo whole limb studies described above
supply valuable functional information, they cannot separate
muscle changes from neural or cardiovascular alterations.
Thus in vitro studies evaluating the isometric and isotonic
contractile properties and endurance capacity of specific
muscles are required. Unfortunately, a complete systemic
study of this kind evaluating both fast and slow muscle has
not yet been conducted. There is no information on the force-
velocity relationship in senile muscle and few studies on the
isometric contractile properties. The age-dependent changes
in the isometric contractile properties appear to be fiber
type specific. Based upon the known decrease in muscle mass
(28,44,58,66), and reduced size and number of fibers (18,19,
42,44) one would predict a decrease in peak tetanic tension
(Po) in senile skeletal muscle. Although Po has not to my
knowledge been measured, peak twitch tension (Pt) is depressed
in senile fast-twitch skeletal muscle (19,33,34,61). Fast
twitch muscle (composed of type IIA and IIB fibers) develops
a prolonged isometric twitch duration with age (19,33,34,61)
and this is due to an increase in both contraction time (CT)
and one-half relaxation time (1/2 RT). In contrast, the

senile slow soleus muscle has a decreased CT (34,36), and prolonged 1/2 RT (34). Gutmann and Syrovy (34) and Syrovy and
Gutmann (62) attribute the observed changes in the CT of
senile muscle to a depressed and elevated myosin ATPase in
fast (34) and slow (34,62) skeletal muscle, respectively.
However, there is an ever-growing body of evidence (22,26,48,
52) that the isometric CT, 1/2 RT, and twitch duration are
regulated by the amount and/or kinetic properties of the sarcoplasmic reticulum, and not by the myosin ATPase activity. The
rate of tension development (dp/dt), and fusion frequency (Hz
required for a fused tetanus) are also depressed in senile
fast muscle (33,36). The endurance capacity of isolated
senile skeletal muscle as reflected by metabolic and physiological measurements has not yet been determined.

## SUMMARY

During development distinct fiber types (IIA, IIB, I) emerge
from undifferentiated fibers following the establishment of
neural contact, and the metabolic and physiologic characteristics of each fiber are dependent on the type of innervation
received. With aging major structural and functional changes
develop in the N-M junction leading to a slow reduction in
synaptic contact and in the neurotrophic influence. As a
result of this "functional denervation" skeletal muscle de-
differentiates and develops a homogeneous fiber composition.
The absolute number and size of the fibers decrease with an
apparent selective loss in fast-twitch type II fibers. As
a result senile muscle mass is reduced approximately 50 percent compared to adult muscle.

Muscle state 3 respiration rate decreases with some but
not all substrates. This suggests that age-mediated changes
in oxidative metabolism affect specific dehydrogenases or
transport-associated systems rather than common pathways of
metabolism such as the electron transport chain. The specific
activity of oxidative and glycolytic enzymes are either
unaltered or depressed in senile muscle, while the total
amount of enzyme is reduced due to the loss of muscle mass.
Some evidence exists for an increased synthesis of partially
or completely inactive enzyme. These metabolic changes do
not manifest until very old age.

Functionally, advancing age is accompanied by a loss of strength, both isometric and dynamic, and to a lesser extent a reduced speed of movement. Endurance expressed as the ability to continue a specific task decreases, but the relative work capacity measured to 50 percent of one's maximum capacity is unaffected by age. The effects of aging on the physiological characteristics of specific fiber types has not been adequately studied. The available physiological evidence, however, supports the concept of dedifferentiation of muscle with aging. For example, fast muscles develop a prolonged CT and 1/2 RT, while slow muscles exhibit a somewhat shorter CT. Furthermore, the senile soleus develops myosin light chains that are peculiar to adult fast and embryonic fast and slow muscle, and this is suggestive of a reduced neural influence.

Definitive conclusions concerning the functional effects of aging on fast and slow skeletal muscle await a thorough evaluation of the isometric and isotonic contractile properties of fast and slow motor units. Furthermore, the physiological studies should be correlated with a detailed structural and functional investigation of the SR, myosin (as well as the other contractile proteins), mitochondria, and metabolic characteristics of senile skeletal muscle.

## REFERENCES

1. Adelman, R.C. An age-dependent modification of enzyme regulation. J. Biol. Chem. 245:1032-1035, 1970.
2. Allen, T.H., E.C. Anderson and W.H. Langham. Total body potassium and gross body composition in relation to age. J. Gerontology 15: 348-357, 1960.
3. Aniansson, A., G. Grimby, M. Hedberg, A. Rundgren and L. Sperling. Muscle function in old age. Scand. J. Rehab. Med. Suppl. 6:43-49, 1978.
4. Asmussen, E. and P. Mathiasen. Some physiologic functions in physical education students re-investigated after twenty-five years. Am. Geriat. Soc. J. 10:379-387, 1962.
5. Astrand, I. Aerobic work capacity in men and women with special reference to age. Acta Physiol. Scand. Suppl. 169:1-92, 1960.
6. Astrand, P.O. and K. Rodahl. Textbook of Work Physiology. St. Louis: McGraw-Hill, 1970.
7. Astrand, I., P.O. Astrand, I. Hallback and A. Kilborn. Reduction in maximal oxygen uptake with age. J. Appl. Physiol. 35:649-654, 1973.
8. Bakerman, S. Aging Life Processes. Springfield: C.C. Thomas Publisher, 1969.
9. Barrows, C.H., L.M. Roeder and J.A. Falzone. Effect of age on the activities of enzymes and the concentrations of nucleic acids in the tissues of female wild rats. J. Gerontol. 17:144-147, 1962.

10. Bartoc, R., S. Bruhis, R. Klein, E. Moldoveanu, I. Oeriu and S. Oeriu. Effect of age and -SH active groups on the activity of some enzymes involved in the carbohydrate metabolism. Exp. Geront. 10:161-164, 1975.

11. Bass, A., E. Gutmann and V. Hanzlikova. Biochemical and histochemical changes in energy supply-enzyme pattern of muscle of the rat during old age. Gerontologia 21:31-45, 1975.

12. Bertolini, A.M. In: Gerontologic Metabolism, edited by A.M. Bertolini. Springfield: C.C. Thomas Publisher, pp. 463-504, 1962.

13. Bertrand, H.A., B.P. Yu and E.J. Masoro. The effect of rat age on the composition and functional activities of skeletal muscle sarcoplasmic reticulum membrane preparations. Mech. Ageing Dev. 4:7-17, 1975.

14. Brooke, M.H. and K.K. Kaiser. Muscle fiber types: How many and what kind? Arch. Neurol. 23:369-379, 1970.

15. Brozek, J. Changes of body composition in man during maturity and their nutritional implications. Fed. Proc. 11:784-793, 1952.

16. Buller, A.J., J.C. Eccles and R.M. Eccles. Interaction between motoneurons and muscles in respect of the characteristic speeds of their responses. J. Physiol. 150:417-439, 1960.

17. Burke, W.E., W.W. Tuttle, C.W. Thompson, C.D. Janney and R.J. Weber. The relation of grip strength and grip-strength endurance to age. J. Appl. Physiol. 5:628-630, 1953.

18. Caccia, M.A., J.B. Harris and M.A. Johnson. Morphology and physiology of skeletal muscle in aging rodents. Muscle and Nerve 2:202-212, 1979.

19. Campbell, M.J., A.J. McComas and F. Petito. Physiological changes in ageing muscles. J. Neurol. Neurosurg. Psychiat. 36:174-182, 1973.

20. Chen, J.C., J.B. Warshaw and D.R. Sanadi. Regulation of mitochondrial respiration in senescence. J. Cell Physiol. 80:141-148, 1972.

21. Dehn, M.M. and R.A. Bruce. Longitudinal variations in maximal oxygen intake with age and activity. J. Appl. Physiol. 33:805-807, 1972.

22. Drachman, D.B. and D.M. Johnston. Development of a mammalian fast muscle: Dynamic and biochemical properties correlated. J. Physiol. 234:29-42, 1973.

23. Drinkwater, B.L., S.M. Horvath and C.L. Wells. Aerobic power of females ages 10 to 68. J. Gerontol. 30:385-394, 1975.

24. Dubois, J. Water and electrolyte content of human skeletal muscle. Variations with age. Eur. J. Clin. Biol. Res. 17:505-515, 1972.

25. Ermini, M. Ageing changes in mammalian skeletal muscle. Gerontology 22:301-316, 1976.

26. Fitts, R.H., W.W. Winder, M.H. Brooke, K.K. Kaiser and J.O. Holloszy. Contractile, biochemical, and histochemical properties of thyrotoxic rat soleus muscle. Am. J. Physiol. 238:C15-C20, 1980.

27. Frolkis, V.V., O.A. Martynenko and V.P. Zamostyan. Aging of the neuromuscular apparatus. Gerontology 22:244-279, 1976.

28. Fujisawa, K. Some observations on the skeletal musculature of aged rats. J. Neurol. Sci. 22:353-366, 1974.

29. Gauthier, G.F. and S. Lowey. Distribution of myosin isoenzymes among skeletal muscle fiber types. J. Cell Biol. 81:10-25, 1979.

30. Gershon, H. and D. Gershon. Altered enzymic molecules in senescent organisms: Mouse muscle aldolase. Mech. Ageing Dev. 2:33-41, 1973.

31. Gutmann, E. and V. Hanzlikova. Motor unit in old age. Nature 209-921-922, 1966.

32. Gutmann, E., V. Hanzlikova and B. Jakoubek. Changes in the neuromuscular system during old age. Exp. Geront. 3:141-146, 1968.

33. Gutmann, E., V. Hanzlikova and F. Vyskocil. Age changes in cross striated muscle of the rat. J. Physiol. 216:331-343, 1971.

34. Gutmann, E. and I. Syrový. Contraction properties and myosin-ATPase activity of fast and slow senile muscles of the rat. Gerontologia 20:239-244, 1974.

35. Gutmann, E. and V. Hanzlikova. Denervation, reinnervation and regeneration of senile muscle. Adv. Exp. Med. Biol. 53:431-440, 1975.

36. Gutmann, E. and V. Hanzlikova. Fast and slow motor units in ageing. Gerontology 22:280-300, 1976.

37. Hanzlikova, V. and E. Gutmann. Ultrastructural changes in senile muscle. Adv. Exp. Med. Biol. 53:421-429, 1975.

38. Howells, K.F. and G. Goldspink. The effect of age and exercise on the succinic dehydrogenase content of individual muscle fibers from fast, slow and mixed hamster muscles. Histochemistry 38:195-201, 1974.

39. Inamdar, A.R., R. Person, P. Kohnen, H. Duncan and B. Mackler. Effect of age on oxidative phosphorylation in tissues of hamsters. J. Gerontology 29:638-642, 1974.

40. Inokuchi, S., H. Ishikawa, S. Iwamoto and T. Kimura. Age related changes in the histological composition of the rectus abdominis muscle of the adult human. Human Biology 47:231-249, 1975.

41. Kaldor, G. and B.K. Min. Enzymatic studies on the skeletal myosin A and actomyosin of aging rats. Fed. Proc. 34:191-194, 1975.

42. Larsson, L., B. Sjödin and J. Karlsson. Histochemical and biochemical changes in human skeletal muscle with age in sedentary males, age 22-65 years. Acta Physiol. Scand. 103:31-39, 1978.

43. Larsson, L. and J. Karlsson. Isometric and dynamic endurance as a function of age and skeletal muscle characteristics. Acta Physiol. Scand. 104:128-136, 1978.

44. Larsson, L., G. Grimby and J. Karlsson. Muscle strength and speed of movement in relation to age and muscle morphology. J. Appl. Physiol: Respirat. Environ. Exercise Physiol. 46:451-456, 1979.

45. Möller, P., J. Bergström, S. Eriksson, P. Fürst and K. Hellström. Effect of aging on free amino acids and electrolytes in leg skeletal muscle. Clin. Sci. 56:427-432, 1979.

46. Orlander, J., K.H. Kiessling, L. Larsson, J. Karlsson. Skeletal muscle metabolism and ultrastructure in relation to age in sedentary men. Acta Physiol. Scand. 104:249-261, 1978.

47. Petrofsky, J. and A.R. Lind. Aging, isometric strength and endurance, and cardiovascular responses to static effort. J. Appl. Physiol. 38:91-95, 1975.

48. Pette, D., W. Muller, E. Leisner and G. Vrbova. Time dependent effects on contractile properties, fiber population, myosin light chains and enzymes of energy metabolism in intermittently and continuously stimulated fast twitch muscles of the rabbit. Pflugers Arch. 364:103-112, 1976.

49. Pelström, L., V. Vihko, E. Aström, and A.U. Arstila. Activity of acid hydrolases in skeletal muscle of untrained, trained and detrained mice of different ages. Acta Physiol. Scand. 104:217-224, 1978.

50. Quetelet, A. Sur l'Homme et le Development de ses Facultes. Brussels, Belgium: Hauman, 1836.

51. Ramirez, B.U. and D. Pette. Effects of long-term electrical stimulation on sarcoplasmic reticulum of fast rabbit muscle. FEBS Lett. 49:188-190, 1974.

52. Robinson, S., D.B. Dell, S.P. Tzankoff, J.A. Wagner and R.D. Robinson. Longitudinal studies of aging in 37 men. J. Appl. Physiol. 38:263-267, 1975.

53. Rockstein, M. and K.F. Brandt. Changes in phosphorus metabolism of the gastrocnemius muscle in aging white rats. Proc. Soc. Exp. Biol. Med. 107:377-380, 1961.

54. Rockstein, M. and K.F. Brandt. Muscle enzyme activity and changes in weight in ageing white rats. Nature 196:142-143, 1962.

55. Rothstein, M. Aging and the alteration of enzymes: A review. Mech. Ageing Dev. 4:325-338, 1975.

56. Rowe, R.W.D. The effect of senility on skeletal muscles in the mouse. Exp. Geront. 4:119-126, 1969.

57. Schmuklei, M. and C.H. Barrows. Age differences in lactic and malic dehydrogenases in the rat. J. Geront. 21:109-111, 1966.

58. Simonson, E. Physical fitness and work capacity of older men. Geriatrics 2:110-119, 1947.

59. Steinhagen-Thiessen, E. and H. Hilz. The age-dependent decrease in creatine kinase and aldolase activities in human striated muscle is not caused by an accumulation of faulty proteins. Mech. Ageing Dev. 5:447-457, 1947.

60. Strehler, B.L. Time, Cells and Aging. N.J.: Academic Press, 1962.

61. Syrový, I. and E. Gutmann. Changes in speed of contraction and ATPase activity in striated muscle during old age. Exp. Geront. 5:31-35, 1970.

62. Syrový, I. and E. Gutmann. Differentiation of myosin in soleus and extensor digitorum longus muscle in different animal species during development. Pflugers Arch. 369:85-89, 1977.

63. Tauchi, H., T. Yoshioka and H. Kobayashi. Age change in skeletal muscles of rats. Gerontologia 17:219-227, 1971.

64. Weinback, E.C. and J. Garbus. Oxidative phosphorylation in mito-chondria from aged rats. J. Biol. Chem. 234:412-417, 1959.

65. Wilson, P.D. and L.M. Franks. The effect of age on mitochondria ultrastructure and enzymes. Adv. Exp. Med. Biol. 53:171-183, 1975.

66. Yiengst, M.J., C.H. Barrows and N.W. Shock. Age changes in the chemical composition of muscle and liver in the rat. J. Gerontol. 14:400-404, 1959.

67. Young, V.R., W.P. Steffee, P.B. Pencharz, J.C. Winterer and N.S. Scrimshaw. Total human body protein synthesis in relation to protein requirements at various ages. Nature 253:192-193, 1973.

Robert H. Fitts was trained in general mammalian physiology in the Department of Physiology at Buffalo University where he received his M.A. degree in 1969. He received further training in muscle and exercise physiology, and biochemistry at the University of Wisconsin where he received his Ph.D. degree in Physiology in 1972. In January, 1973, Dr. Fitts joined the laboratory of Dr. John O. Holloszy at Washington Univer-stiy in St. Louis where he worked as a postdoctoral fellow studying the effects of exercise on the mechanical and metabolic properties of skeletal muscle. In 1976, Dr. Fitts joined the faculty of Marquette University as an Assistant Professor of Biology. During the past four years he has developed a laboratory of muscle research, and is presently involved in a number of projects studying the effects of use, disuse, disease, and aging on muscle function.

# FLEXIBILITY IN THE AGING ADULT
## Marlene J. Adrian

The primary anatomical structure which governs the flexibility
(mobility) of the human body is the joint. Allman (1) has
suggested that with age, the joints become less stable and
less mobile. Whether or not this is true may be determined
through an analysis of changes with age in the components of
the joint: the cartilage, ligaments, tendons, and synovial
fluid. These tissues and fluid act to connect the two bones
forming the joints and serve in maintaining the integrity of
the joint and its function. Although muscles also influence
mobility of joints, changes in muscle with age are reviewed
in another paper of this symposium and will not be described
here.

## CONNECTIVE TISSUE

Since cartilage, ligaments and tendons are forms of connective
tissue, a general description of the morphology of connective
tissue and age-related changes in connective tissue will be
reviewed prior to the description of age-related changes in
cartilage, ligaments, and tendons. Connective tissue always
consists of cells and extracellular fibers embedded in a
ground substance containing tissue fluid, in particular, the
fluid known as hyaluronic acid (3). The extracellular components related to mechanical support consist of elastic and
collagenous fibers. These fibers allow the tissue to yield
to externally applied forces, to return to its original shape
when the forces are removed, and also to provide resistance
to these forces. Connective tissue also functions as a

protection against infection.   Thus, this tissue is the cause
of the local inflammatory reaction noted when injury or infection occurs.   In addition, the cells (fibroblasts) readily respond to injury by proliferation and fibrogenesis.   An example
of this repair is the connective "scar tissue" following a
heart attack.

Connective tissue also acts as an exchanger of metabolites between blood and other tissue and as a storage of
energy reserves in adipose cells.   The vitreous material
(ground substance) is an important element in the metabolic
function of connective tissue.

Structural and functional changes take place within the
connective tissue from birth to death.   Some of these age-
related changes cited by Balazs (3) are as follows:

1.   increase in yellow color and fluorescence of elastin
2.   decrease in aldimines, which results in an increase
     in cross-links in the tissue matrix
3.   increased stability of collagen fibers
4.   thickening of the basement membrane--that membrane
     separating the connective tissue from other tissues:
     neural, muscle, epithelial, etc.
5.   increase, decrease, no change in hyaluronic acid

Each of these changes act to alter the metabolic activities
and to increase the resistance offered by the connective
tissue to the surrounding tissue.   Therefore, in general,
these changes in connective tissue result in a tissue which is
less responsive to mechanical stress, that is, a stiffer or
more rigid tissue (15) than prior to these changes.

The primary concern with mobility of the joint with
respect to connective tissue is the aging of the fibrous
proteins, elastin and collagen, since these proteins are a
part of the connective structure of tendons, muscles, cartilage and ligaments.   These proteins influence the response of
tissue to stress, the amount of deformation, the return to
original length after deformation, and the method of transmission of force within the tissue.

Two distinct altered or degraded states of collagen are
noted:   pseudoelastin and cellulose fibers.   These appear in
elderly tissue, but not in young tissue.   In addition a
greater number of deposits of lipids is seen in the elderly

tissue. The total implications of these changes are not known. Furthermore, it is difficult to distinguish between true aging changes in connective tissue and those changes related to pathological conditions (15).

## CARTILAGE

The three types of cartilage (hyalin, elastic and fibro), are unique in that none has nerves or blood vessels of its own. Each type of cartilage is nurtured via the surrounding tissues, such as bone and synovial fluid. Thus, changes in these latter two substances will affect cartilage function. Progressive age changes have been identified in the cartilage of animals and humans, in both weight-bearing and non-weight-bearing joints (7,9,19,27,30,37). Such changes were specified as occurring as early as 20-30 years of age (17). General morphological changes include the color change from a translucent blue to an opaque yellow before the age of 20 years. Surface changes consisting of cracking, fraying, and shredding were noted as occurring prior to age 30 years. Excess stress and trauma may further damage the cartilage, causing deep fissures (31).

In addition, progressive cell death occurs throughout adulthood and a reduction in the depth of the cartilage is noted with age (3).

The synovial membrane may become more fibrous with age and a decreased viscosity of the synovial fluid, however, appears to differ with respect to specific joint, species, and individual (3). For example, the hock joint of a cow has a rigidity 1/6 that of the synovial fluid of the carpal joint. No differences were noted with respect to age (16). Therefore, one might speculate that the difference is functional, not age-related, since the cow supports more weight on the forelimbs than the hind limbs. Some researchers (2,3) have speculated that changes in hyaluronic acid (and, therefore, synovial fluid viscosity) are due to misuse, by humans, of their joints. They further state that the joints which are not subjected to excess trauma would remain normal. Young persons with osteoarthritis show the same changes as "normal" old persons. In general, the histological changes attributed to aging are identical to those changes attributable to osteoarthritis, a disease.

## OSTEOARTHRITIS AND AGE-RELATED CHANGES IN CARTILAGE

The degenerative joint diseases, osteoarthritis and osteoarthrosis, occur in humans, as well as in a variety of
animals. Kellgren and Lawrence (18) report that over 80% of
men and women 55-64 years of age have signs of osteoarthrosis
in some joint of the body. The osteoarthrosic joint has a
greater resistance to movement of the bones forming the
joint. In more severe cases there is pain when movement is
initiated.

Males and blacks appear to be more susceptible to, or
exhibit greater severity to, the disease than do females or
whites (37). This is the opposite of what has been found with
osteoporosis. Heredity, hormonal, and nutritional factors
seem to affect the incidence of osteoarthritis. For example,
relatives of persons with multiple arthritic involvement more
frequently suffer from osteoarthritis than do others (2,3,18).
Anderson, et al. (2) suggest that osteoarthritis is related
to the amount of mechanical stress at the joint. Although
osteoarthritis does not differentiate between weight- and
non-weight-bearing joints, the more clearly defined degenerative changes occur in joints which bear greatest weight or
experience greatest shock. For example, the knee, hip, and
vertebral joints have a high incidence of osteoarthritis.

Wright (41) ranked the presence and tolerance of pain in
the arthrosic joint as being greatest in the hip, next
greatest in the knee and, in descending order, in the first
metatarsalphalangeal joint, hand, and wrist. Obesity appears
to aggravate the symptoms, but does not alter the arthrosic
condition. The existence of an age factor is likely since
the onset of hip osteoarthrosis coincides with the fifth,
sixth and seventh decades of life.

The spinal column serves as the structure for upright
posture. A complex system of forces and stresses are borne by
the column and the vertebral joints. The intervertebral cartilage shows a loss in water content with age (16). The
number of cells decreases and loss of matrix material results
and the cartilage becomes friable, that is, will crumble or be
easily pulverized. These degenerative changes, coupled with

bone changes, lead to atrophy and compression fractures of the spinal column (28).

Pathological conditions of the spinal column are common in human adults. Injuries from lifting or twisting while lifting heavy objects, injuries from sports, and the engagement of heavy physical work are related to "back problems." Since males and blacks more frequently engage in these activities than do females and whites this supports the Anderson et al. (2) theory that mechanical stress is a primary factor in the so-called "aging" of joints.

One of the results of the osteoarthritic or osteoarthrosic joint is a surgical replacement of the joint with a prosthetic device. During the past decade, total hip replacements have become a routine operation. The joint reaches a point of degeneration such that locomotion is painful, difficult or impossible. Several investigators (11,13,40) have studied the effects of artificial hip implants upon locomotion and other forms of physical functioning and found that many persons, including those 70 years and older, are able to lead normal lives and conduct routine activities of daily living without difficulty after implantation of an artificial hip. Improved mobility for older persons also is possible with surgical replacements of the knee and other joints.

The literature is not clear as to the separation of age-related changes in cartilage and synovial fluid and disease, or over-use-related changes. For example, damage to a knee because of an injury in a sports situation, and subsequent surgery to the joint predisposes the joint to degeneration. A controlled study of the effects of surgery upon the joints in dogs showed a direct relationship between the amount of degeneration and the amount of cartilage removed from the joint. Degenerative changes were half as severe when 1/4 of the meniscus was removed than when 1/2 of the meniscus was removed.

In an effort to isolate the age-related changes in articular cartilage from osteoarthrosic changes, Kempson et al. (19) conducted indentation tests to determine progressive softening of visibly normal cartilage. They concluded that degeneration occurring around and spreading posteriorly and inferiorly from the fovea may be attributed to aging, whereas changes occurring over the supero-medial aspect of the cartilage could be considered a result of osteoarthrosis. No research has been conducted to determine the incidences of these degeneration sites in the elderly population.

Silverberg et al. (29) showed that osteoarthritis of the sternoclavicular joint appeared about the third decade, increased until age 80 and then decreased dramatically. The reasons for this may be explained by the Differential Survivalship Principle: The diseased die and the healthy remain. Thus, these data suggest that persons need not acquire osteoarthritis or aging changes before the eighth decade of life.

Reduced enzyme activity, increased lipid accumulation within the cartilage cells, and decreases in such substances as glycosaminoglycan and hexuronic acid have been identified as occurring with age (37). These changes, however, may be normal changes necessitated by the decrease in growth activity of the body after maturity. Thus, the age-related changes in cartilage are influenced by heredity, nutrition, hormones, growth needs, trauma, excessive stress, disease, and changes in other systems of the body, in particular the circulatory system.

We know very little about restorative or injury repair properties of cartilage with respect to age, or the significance of the latent growth potential seen in cartilage.

### CHANGES IN MECHANICAL PROPERTIES OF CARTILAGE

Despite the documentation of histological and morphological changes in cartilage with age, there is a dearth of literature concerning the changes in mechanical properties of cartilage with age. Baseline data concerning tensile stress of articular cartilage from five different cadavers showed that the more normal joints had greater tensile strength and greater stiffness than those showing visible signs of degeneration (32). Although the older cadavers showed decrements in strength and stiffness, the sample size was too small to relate these results to age.

No age-correlated change in stiffness in articular cartilage was found by Sokoloff (30). Recovery of both costal and articular cartilage from load deformation also was non-age-dependent. Reduction in creep in middle age costal cartilage

did occur, however, compared with that of young costal cartilage. It is evident that costal cartilage does not necessarily age the same as articular cartilage (31). Since costal
cartilage is vascular in nature, its changes may be related
more directly to the changes in the cardiovascular system
than may be the articular cartilage. In articular cartilage,
the presence of normal synovial fluid is vital to prevent
frictional destruction of the joint, especially the cartilage.

## LIGAMENTS AND TENDONS

Tendons and ligaments are classified as collagenous tissues.
The tendon consists of thick, glistening white collagenous
bands running parallel to the length of the tendon. The collagen content is 30% wet weight and 70% dry weight (7). Since
tendons connect muscle to bone, they act as a transmitter of
tensile forces and show a gradual change in morphology from
tendon to fibrocartilage, to mineralized fibrocartilage, to
lamellar bone (7). There is no penetration of a blood supply
into the osteotendonous junction. There is a sparse blood
supply in mature tendon, with greater vascularity at the
muscle-tendonous junction. Viidik (38) suggests that the
mechanical stability of this proximal junction is dependent
upon the collagen tendon bundles projecting into the muscle
fasciculi.

The fiber bundles of ligaments not only are parallel but
also oblique and spiral in order to provide maximal restraint
of joint displacement. In addition, there are elastic and
reticular fibers between the collagen fibers. The cellular
progression in ligaments is similar to that of tendons:
fibrocyte, to chondrocyte, to osteocyte. Ligaments also have
greater blood supply at the proximal junction, but have both
an intrinsic and extrinsic blood supply. Thus the characteristic changes described with respect to connective tissue are
identical to those seen in ligaments and tendons.

Since ligaments and tendons are viscoelastic materials
their mechanical characteristics are time-dependent and the
measurement of these characteristics is complex. Strain
rate, force relaxation, creep, and hysteresis, ultimate
strength and failure, however, have been studied in both tendons and ligaments (4,19,21,22,32,33,34,35,36,42). In

general, decrements in these properties appear to occur with advancing age. Both increases and decreases in strength have been reported.

An excellent review of the mechanical properties and changes with age with respect to tendons and ligaments may be found in Butler et al. (7). There are difficulties in the interpretation of these data since most of the data have been collected from isolated animal tissues, and human donors. The animal data may reflect changes prior to maturation and developmental aspects of aging, not degeneration due to "old age." The donor data are cross-sectional data and are likely to be biased due to the small number of specimens, lack of randomization, and the life styles of the old and young cohorts. At present no longitudinal data on human tendon and ligament characteristics exist.

Noyes et al. (22) have shown three principal modes of failure in the bone-ligament system: ligamentous, bone avulsion, and cleavage at the ligament-bone interface. The testing of 28 femur--anterior-cruciate ligament--tibia specimens from donors 16-86 years of age showed age-related decreases in maximum stress, elastic modulus, and strain energy, with ages 16-48 but not with ages 48-86 (21). The failures for the older specimens however were of the bone avulsion type, whereas the younger specimens showed ligamentous failure. Thus the mechanical properties of the older ligaments actually were never tested. A comparison of one of the 60 year old specimens with that of young specimens showed comparable elastic characteristics.

Failure of ligaments and tendons may be due to age-related changes in macro- and micro-structure of these tissues, as well as changes produced by such factors as immobilization, sex, disease, and use. The extent of each of these for any individual is not known. Numerous studies (4,8,33,34,35,36,42) have been conducted to determine the role of physical activity and of immobilization upon ligaments and tendons. These results show an increase in ligament and tendon strength, and ligament elongation with training using rats and dogs as subjects. Detraining and cage restriction produce the opposite effects. Noyes et al. (22) has shown that immobilization of rhesus monkeys produces decreases in

stiffness, ultimate strength, and energy to failure in ligaments. Conversely, conditioning programs return the tissue
to pre-immobilization levels.

One other characteristic change in tendon was discussed
by Gutmann (14). Elongation of the achilles tendon and a loss
of the reflex has been reported in men between the ages of 70
and 90. Both characteristics may in fact be the result of
shortening of muscle and not be an age-related change in
tendon.

## EVALUATION OF THE JOINTS

The evaluation of a joint may be made with respect to evaluation of radiographs, range of motion, and resistance to
motion. Excluding the radiographs of clinical osteoarthritic
cases, there is only one set of radiographic data which identifies age-related changes in joints (24,25). Radiographs of
the left hands of 478 participants of the Baltimore Longitudinal Study were assessed qualitatively on a 0-4 point scale
with respect to visible signs of degeneration. Comparisons of
radiographs from two or more visits, with the mean interval
between visits being 2-9 years, showed a maximum rate of
degeneration of one point over 12-16 years in the distal
interphalangeal joints. These changes appeared to be age-
related. A much lower rate of change was noted in the proximal interphalangeal joints, and these changes were not age-
related. The reasons for these differences between joints
could not be explained by the investigators.

Brewer (6) investigated the aging of the rotator cuff
by means of radiographs, photomicrographs, and the scanning
electron microscope. Autopsy specimens were obtained from
each of one 20, 50 and 70 year old cadaver. With age there
was degeneration of the greater tuberosity of the femur,
deformity and fragmentation of the articular cartilage, and
loss in cellularity and disorganization of fibers in the
supraspinatus tendon. Whether or not the changes in tendon
were the characteristics of aging or the characteristics of
the pathology of degenerative tendonitis was not determined.

Range of motion at the joint is specific to each joint
and is dependent upon the anatomical structure of the joint
and the habitual use of each joint (10,20,26). For example,

children tend to be more flexible than adults; sports performers tend to increase flexibility in joints important to the sport; and habitual postures of laborers tend to decrease flexibility in selected joints. Thus research which relates range of motion to age may be relating a coincident factor rather than a primary factor to range of motion. Range of motion differences have been identified with respect to age in a Japanese population (39). There also is a relationship of prevalence of osteoarthritis with age in that same population (23). No attempt was made to relate the range of motion to age-related anatomical changes.

Differences in flexibility not only with respect to age, but also with respect to joint, were reported by Boone and Azen (5). A primarily Caucasian population of 109 males, ages 18 months to 54 years, were compared on 28 range of motion measurements taken by means of a goniometer. Although right and left joint measurements were comparable for all ages, some decrement with age was noted. The most noticeable was the decrease in hip rotation of 15-20 degrees during the first decades of life and 5 degrees per decade thereafter. Decreases with age in extension and lateral rotation at the shoulder also were greater than the other measurements. Thus the greatest differences were noted in movements not habitually performed. In fact, older persons tend to reduce their movement patterns, both in range and speed (unpublished observations). For example, rarely is more than half the range of motion at the knee utilized during activities of daily living, whereas in sports and exercise activities two thirds or greater movement is noted. The speed of extension at the elbow usually is less than 300 degrees per second during activities of daily living, but is greater than 800 degrees per second for older women during sports activities (unpublished observations).

The stiffness of a joint, that is, the passive resistance to motion, has been measured in osteoarthrosic joints and a reduced range of motion noted. Goddard et al. (12) attribute the increased stiffness and reduced range of motion to wear of surfaces, stiffening and thickening of joint capsule, presence of wear debris in joint, and growth of osteophytes. They also found that reduction in range of motion occurred in joints after a short rest or period of joint immobility. Although Goddard et al. (12) hypothesized that this might be due to articular gelling, their research showed no such thing. Since the normal range of motion was acquired easily after several trials, they concluded that the cause was elastic (muscles, tendons, or ligaments) and not viscous (synovial fluid).

In summary, histological and morphological changes in cartilage, ligament, and tendon do occur within the life cycle of animals and humans. These may be a result of biological aging processes. Decreased flexibility has been reported as occurring with advancing age. There is no evidence that biological aging processes cause this decrease in flexibility, since most research links degenerative diseases with loss of flexibility. Research is needed which controls the amount and type of use of the joints, in order to separate age-related changes and pathological changes of the tissues comprising the joints.

## REFERENCES

1. Allman, F.L. Conditioning for sports. In: Sports Medicine, edited by A.J. Ryan and F.L. Allman. New York: Academic Press, 1974.

2. Anderson, C.E., J. Ludowieg, H.A. Harper and E.P. Engleman. The composition of the organic component of human articular cartilage. J. Bone Jt. Surg. 46A:1176-1183, 1964.

3. Balazs, E.A. Intercellular matrix of connective tissue. In: Handbook of the Biology of Aging, edited by C. Finch and L. Hayflick. New York: Van Nostrand Reinhold, pp. 222-240, 1977.

4. Benedict, J.V., L.B. Walker and E.H. Harris. Stress-strain characteristics and tensile strength of unembalmed human tendon. J. Biom. 1:53-63, 1968.

5. Boone, D.C. and S.P. Azen. Normal range of motion of joints in male subjects. J. Bone Jt. Surg. 61A:756-759, 1979.

6. Brewer, B.J. Aging of the rotator cuff. Am. J. Sports Med. 7: 102-110, 1979.

7. Butler, D.L., E.S. Grood, F.R. Noyes and R.F. Zernicke. Biomechanics of ligaments and tendons. In: Exercise and Sport Sciences Reviews, edited by R. Hutton. Philadelphia: Franklin Press, pp. 125-282, 1979.

8. Cabaud, H.E., A. Chatty, V. Gildengorin and R.J. Feltman. Exercise effects on the strength of the rat anterior cruciate ligament. Am. J. Sports Med. 8:79-86, 1980.

9. Casscells, S.W. The torn or degenerated meniscus and its relationship to degeneration of the weight-bearing areas of the femur and tibia. Clin. Orthop. 132:196-200, 1978.

10. Clarke, H.H. Joint and body range of movement. Phys. Fit. Res. Digest, Series 5, 1975.

11. Collopy, M.C., M.P. Murray, G.M. Garnder, R.A. Diulio and D.R. Gore. Kinesiologic measurements of functional performance before and after geometric total knee replacement: One-year follow-up of twenty cases. Clin. Orthop. 126:196-202, 1977.

12. Goddard, R.D. Dowsan, M. Longfield and V. Wright. A study of articular gelling. In: Lubrication and Wear in Joints, edited by V. Wright. London: Sector Publishing Limited, pp. 134-139, 1969.

13. Gore, D.R., M.P. Murray, G.M. Gardner and S.B. Sepic. Roentgenographic measurements after Muller total hip replacement. Correlations among roentgenographic measurements and hip strength and mobility. J. Bone Joint Surg. 59:948-953, 1977.

14. Gutmann, E. Muscle. In: Handbook of the Biology of Aging, edited by C. Finch and L. Hayflick. New York: Van Nostrand Reinhold, pp. 445-469, 1977.

15. Hall, D.A. The Aging of Connective Tissue. London: Academic Press, 1976.

16. Hansen, H.J. Studies of the pathology of the lubosacral disc in female cattle. Acta Orthopaed Scand. 25:161-182, 1956.

17. Jeffery, M.R. The waning joint. Am. J. Med. Sci. 239:104-124, 1960.

18. Kellgren, J.H. and J.S. Lawrence. Radiological assessment of osteoarthrosis. Annals Rheum. Dis. 16:494-502, 1957.

19. Kempson, G., C. Spivey, M. Freeman and A. Swanson. Indentation and stiffness in articular cartilage in normal and osteoarthrosic femoral heads. In: Lubrication and Wear in Joints, edited by V. Wright. London: Sector Publishing Limited, pp. 62-70, 1969.

20. Leighton, J.R. A study of the effect of progressive weight training on flexibility. J. Assoc. Phys. Ment. Rehabil. 18:101-110, 1964.

21. Noyes, F.R. and E.S. Grood. The strength of the anterior cruciate ligament in humans and rhesus monkeys: Age-related and species-related changes. J. Bone Joint Surg. 58A:1074-1082, 1976.

22. Noyes, F.R., P.J. Torvik, W.B. Hyde and J.L. Delucas. Biomechanics of ligament failure. II. An analysis of immobilization, exercise, and reconditioning effects in primates. J. Bone Joint Surg. 56A:1406-1418, 1974.

23. Ota, H. Prevalence of osteoarthrosis of the hip and other joints in Japanese population. Nippon Seikeigeka Gakkai Zasshi 53: 165-180, 1979.

24. Plato, C.C. and A.H. Norris. Osteoarthritis of the hand: Age specific joint-digit prevalence rates. Am. J. Epidemiol. 109:169-180, 1979.

25. Plato, C.C. and A.H. Norris. Osteoarthritis of the hand: Longitudinal studies. Am. J. Epidemiol. 110:740-746, 1979.

26. Rasch, P.J. and R.K. Burke. Kinesiology and Applied Anatomy. Philadephia: Lea and Febiger, pp. 30-32, 1978.

27. Shephard, R.J. and K.H. Sidney. Exercise and aging. In: Exercise and Sport Sciences Reviews, edited by R. Hutton. Philadelphia: Franklin Press, pp. 1-57, 1979.

28. Silberberg, R. Changes in the vertebral column of aging mice. Gerontologia 17:236-252, 1972.

29. Silberberg, M., E.L. Frank, S.R. Jarrett and R. Silberberg. Aging and osteoarthritis of the human stenoclavicular joint. Am. J. Pathol. 35:851-865, 1959.

30. Sokoloff, L. Elasticity of aging cartilage. Fed. Proc. 25: 1089-1095, 1966.

31. Sokoloff, L. The Biology of Degenerative Joint Disease. Chicago: The University of Chicago Press, 1969.

32. Swanson, A., G. Kempson and M. Freeman. Tensile properties of articular cartilage. In: Lubrication and Wear in Joints, edited by V. Wright. London: Sector Publishing Limited, pp. 71-75, 1969.

33. Tipton, C.M., R.D. Matthes and R.K. Martin. Influence of age and sex on the strength of bone-ligament junctions in knee joints of rats. J. Bone Joint Surg. 60:230-234, 1978.

34.   Tipton, C.M., R.D. Matthes, J.A. Maynard and R.A. Carey.  The influence of physical activity on ligaments and tendons.  Med. Sci. Sports 7:165-175, 1975.

35.   Tipton, C.M., R.D. Matthes and D.S. Sandage.  In situ measurement of junction strength and ligament elongation in rats.  J. Appl. Physiol. 37:758-761, 1974.

36.   Tipton, C.M., R.J. Schild and R.J. Tomanek.  Influence of physical activity on the strength of knee ligaments in rats.  Am. J. Physiol. 212:783-787, 1967.

37.   Tonna, E.A.  Aging of skeletal-dental systems and supporting tissues.  In: Handbook of the Biology of Aging, edited by C. Finch and L. Hayflick.  New York:  Van Nostrand Reinhold, pp. 470-495, 1977.

38.   Viidik, A.  Functional properties of collagenous tissues.  Int. Rev. Conn. Tissue Res. 6:127-215, 1973.

39.   Watanabe, H., K. Ogata, T. Amano and T. Okabe.  The range of joint motions of the extremities in healthy Japanese people--the differences according to the age.  Nippon Seikeigeka Gakkai Zasshi 53: 275-361, 1979.

40.   Wilcock, G.K.  Benefits of total hip replacement to older patients and the community.  Br. Med. J. 2:37-39, 1978.

41.   Wright, V.  Tribology and arthritis.  In: Lubrication and Wear in Joints, edited by V. Wright.  London:  Sector Publishing Limited, pp. 15-19, 1969.

42.   Zuckerman, J. and G.A. Stull.  Effects of exercise on knee ligament separation force in rats.  Med. Sci. Sports 5:44-49, 1973.

Marlene J. Adrian received her Doctor of Physical Education at Springfield College, Massachusetts.  She is Professor of Physical Education and Research Professor in Veterinary Science at Washington State University.  She coordinates a Ph.D. program in Physical Education with a specialty in Biomechanics, is Director of the Biomechanics Laboratory, and member of the Unit on Aging Advisory Board at this institution.  She is a Fellow of the American College of Sports Medicine, member of the American and the International Societies of Biomechanics, the Alliance for Health, Physical Education, Recreation and Dance, and the International Society of Electro-Physiological Kinesiology.

BONE MASS AND STRENGTH DECLINE WITH AGE
Everett L. Smith, Christopher T. Sempos and Robert W. Purvis

Osteoporosis is a major bone mineral disorder in the older
adult. It has been estimated that at least six million persons in the United States have a significant degree of osteoporosis (62). This bone loss has been characterized by a
decreased bone mineral mass, an enlarged medullary cavity, a
normal mineral composition, and biochemical normalities in
plasma and urine (16,75,192). The rate of bone loss is about
0.75 to 1% per year for women starting at age 30 to 35 and for
men at age 50 to 55.
    Due to the decreased mass and an increased cell death,
osteoporotic bone is weaker than normal bone. Osteoporosis
is often defined by the presence of fractures which occur
spontaneously or as the result of only mild trauma (10). This
results in an increased probability of fracture and poses a
significant hazard to the aged (187,241,249). The fractures
most commonly associated with osteoporosis are fractures of
the radius, ulna, femoral neck and vertebral column (17).
Beals reported on the mortality of 607 aged patients treated
for hip fracture from 1956 until 1961 (26). He observed a
hospital mortality of 12.5% and a 50% mortality after one
year.
    In a strict sense, osteoporosis, or bone loss, is a sign
or clinical finding which occurs by itself or in association
with osteomalacia. This loss may be a manifestation of
several metabolic conditions (or their treatment) such as
hyperthyroidism, diabetes, hypogonadal states, lymphoma,
chronic renal disease, rheumatoid arthritis, adrenal or

59

pituitary tumors, etc. (11,19,52,67,142,165,175,181,186,222, 237). It can, however, also occur in hypodynamic states such as bed rest, disuse atrophy, or weightlessness (32,99,150,153, 251,267). Senile or idiopathic osteoporosis, for which no etiological factor has yet been assigned, is common in the elderly. The incidence of senile or idiopathic osteoporosis is higher in women than in men, and is higher in Caucasians than in Negroes (35,115,176). Recently proposed controversial etiological factors in the development of osteoporosis in the elderly have included: Hyperparathyroidism secondary to decreased renal function, decreased exogenous Vitamin D because of increased atmospheric ozone, stimulation of parathyroid activity by cigaret smoking, and calcium malabsorption and inactivity (27,28,40,69,187).

Qualitatively, osteoporotic bone exhibits a reduction in bone mass with a resulting decrease in bone strength. However, there is some evidence that alterations occur in the composition and structure of bone in the aged (33,270). Evans observed that the tensile strength of a bone in man is related to the size and number of osteons (72). He demonstrated that bone taken from young men (age 41.5) had a greater average tensile breaking load, ultimate tensile strength, and an increased density than bone from older men (age 71.0) (71). He found that bone from older men had smaller osteons and fragments and more cement lines than the younger men. Evans suggested this would account for some of the reduced bone strength of the older bone specimens (72). The remaining difference in the strength of the bone may have resulted from the geometric structure of the bone in its distribution per unit area as a response to environmental stress placed upon the bone. In elderly subjects, regions of devitalized tissue with osteocyte lacunae and Haversian canals containing amorphous mineral deposits have been described (142,253). Frost identified these regions as micropetrotic and noted an increase of frequency in the skeleton with age (77,78). Thus, it is clear that qualitative skeletal changes occur with aging (17).

In women, aged 40 to 54 years, Bauer (10,23) has reported a sevenfold increase in the annual incidence of fractures of the distal end of the radius. He speculated that this rise in fracture incidence in aging women may be associated with a decline in the mechanical quality of the bone as well as the quantity of bone.

## ETIOLOGY

Osteoporosis is clearly a multifactorial disorder which results in bone loss with advancing age (102,216,191). Despite this fact the development and clinical features of osteoporosis are fairly homogeneous. Some of the common features of osteoporosis are: (1) Universal age-associated bone loss in both men and women of all races; (2) the temporal association of that bone loss with menopause in women and declining testosterone production in men; (3) the increase in endostial bone resorption while bone formation remains normal; (4) all clinical tests are normal in osteoporosis except that some have high urinary hydroxyproline/creatinine ratios; and (5) back pain (119,191,84).

At the present time, most investigators believe that some bone loss is a universal concomitant of the aging process (3, 48,83,84,85,90,221,240,252). Most of these same investigators believe that fractures occur in those people who are on the low end of a continuous skeletal status distribution or spectrum. Other investigators, however, believe that although a certain amount of bone loss does accompany aging, the rapid loss of bone to an extent sufficient to produce "spontaneous" fractures is a definite abnormality. Some investigators believe that hypodynamic, circulatory, dietary, and endocrine factors play contributory roles in the development of senile osteoporosis, either singularly or additively.

The previously described association between hypogonadal states and osteoporosis led Albright and his followers to suggest that osteoporosis found in elderly women is secondary to the endocrine changes which produce the menopause (5,6,7,8,9, 63,169,170,207). That theory has been expanded by Heaney (100,101,102) into a model of bone loss which incorporates all of the factors involved in age related bone loss and osteoporosis. His model of a "unified concept of osteoporosis" stresses the role of bone in the maintenance of calcium homeostasis. The major feature of the model is that with aging there is a differential alteration of end-organ responsiveness to parathyroid hormone (PTH). The PTH-vitamin D system helps to maintain extracellular calcium concentration by (1) reducing calcium clearance in the kidney; (2) increasing phosphate clearance by the kidney; (3) increasing calcium absorption in the intestine through indirect stimulation of the active form of vitamin D $(1,25(OH)_2D_3)$ by PTH, and (4) increasing the activation of osteocytic resorption of bone to release calcium from bone. Estrogens, calcitonin and possibly androgens depress the effect of PTH and vitamin D on bone; so that with menopause bone becomes more sensitive to PTH while its effects on other end organs remain the same. The estrogen deficiency → increased calcium release from bone → decreased PTH secretion → decreased conversion of 25 OH(D) to $1,25(OH)_2D$ → decreased plasma levels of $1,25(OH)_2D$ → decreased calcium absorption (102,64,216).

In support of Heaney's theory it has been found that when osteoporotics are compared to age matched normals the osteoporotics have normal to below normal serum levels of PTH (36, 215), below normal serum levels of $1,25(OH)_2D$ (80,178,195) and decreased calcium absorption (46,80). As further support it has been shown that estrogen replacement, calcium supplementation and vitamin D therapy all result in decreased bone resorption, decreased rate of bone loss, increased calcium balance and a decrease in urinary hydroxyproline (105,106,136, 183,191,205). There is additional evidence that age related deficiencies of growth hormone (211) and calcitonin (175) may be important in the etiology of age related bone loss.

Nordin supports the concept that osteoporosis may result at least partially from prolonged dietary calcium insufficiency or malabsorption (190,192,193,245,246,255). Bullmore further substantiated this in later studies reporting on decreased intestinal calcium absorption in the aged (38). Lender in a recent study, using calcium ([47]Ca) reported slower calcium absorption in the old than in the young (133). Nordin et al. indicated that this malabsorption in the elderly was related to the active transport component of the absorption mechanism.

Data from animal studies have suggested that bone loss with aging and osteoporosis are the result of a calcium deficiency (26,119). This calcium deficiency would lead to a negative calcium balance and bone loss. The calcium deficiency may be the result of a diet which is low in calcium or the consequence of interactions between calcium and other dietary factors which would decrease the absorption, retention or utilization of calcium (163).

The recommended dietary allowance (RDA) for calcium is 800 mg/day (182). Cross-sectional dietary surveys have shown that the average level of calcium consumption in women 45 years of age or older is 600 mg/day (82,194). Many researchers feel that the RDA and calcium intake of perimenopausal women are too low (4,104,118,149,189). Heaney et al. (104,105,106) have reported the premenopausal and postmenopausal women consuming self-selected diets containing an average of 660 mg/day calcium were in negative calcium balance, losing an average of 20 mg/day and 43 mg/day calcium, respectively. Heaney et al. also estimated by regression analysis that a daily intake of 1.25 g/day calcium would be necessary to achieve calcium balance.

A negative calcium balance may be the result of interactions between calcium and other dietary factors. Of many dietary factors, only the effects of protein, phosphate and fiber seem at present to be significant.

Dr. Linkswiler et al. have noted that increased protein intake leads to negative calcium balance in young men (113, 140). In a thirty day metabolic study (145) it was shown that moderate levels of protein intake (50 gm or 110 gm) in a diet containing 713 mg calcium resulted in negative calcium balance in normal and osteoporotic postmenopausal women. Both groups of postmenopausal women were in negative calcium balance at both levels of protein intake. No significance in mean calcium balance was observed between the two groups. The mean calcium balances were -31 and -42 mg/day. Similar results have been reported by Heaney (101).

Further evidence for the possible role of diet in preventing osteoporosis is the report of Matkovic et al. (157). They compared the bone status, fracture rates and dietary habits of two districts in Yugoslavia. Results of this study show that the district with a high intake of calcium, phosphorus and protein had a greater cortical bone mass in middle life, and a much lower proximal femur fracture rate.

The importance of phosphorus to calcium and bone metabolism is controversial.  High phosphorus diets or diets with a low calcium to phosphorus ratio have been shown to cause bone loss in rats and dogs (66,122).  Human balance studies have shown that the level of phosphorus in the diet does not affect calcium balance (246), but in a clinical trial with human subjects with osteoporosis, a daily dose of 1 g phosphorus resulted in a decrease in the bone-forming surface and an increase in the bone resorbing surface (89).

A high fiber diet has been shown to decrease calcium balance (59,126).  This may be especially important to elderly individuals who are regular users of bulk stimulants.

Physical inactivity has also been proposed as a contributory factor in senile osteoporosis.  A more thorough discussion of physical activity and osteoporosis may be found later in the text.

## TREATMENT

### INTRODUCTORY COMMENTS

One of the confusing facts about osteoporosis is that although both men and women lose bone as they age, only few men and some women develop osteoporosis.  About 25-40% of all post-menopausal women develop osteoporosis (191).

The difficult problem in dealing with bone loss associated with aging is that specific treatment modalities for similar clinical features do not result in similar responses in all subjects (191).  The treatment modality for any case thus becomes that which best fits the specific patient.

It is possible that advanced osteoporosis may be irreversible.  Therefore the ability to prevent or retard the development of bone loss is of major importance.  The objective in treating a case with spontaneous fractures is to alleviate any pain and if possible prevent further deterioration.  This may require the use of treatment modalities which may result in increased risk to the patient due to side effects, but if left untreated those individuals will develop further fractures (120,91,191).

The general lack of definitive procedures for objective and precise evaluation of skeletal status is probably a factor

in the inconsistent and disappointing results obtained to date
with various treatment modalities. With the current improved
measurement techniques it is now possible to effectively
evaluate treatment modalities (5,25). This would be especially important to the women who experience a rapid rate
of bone loss after surgical menopause (127).

Other diagnostic features which may be used to locate
persons at greater risk of developing osteoporosis are: (1)
kyphosis or height loss; (2) a high urinary hydroxyproline to
creatinine ratio; (3) a Singh index of III or less; (4) low
serum values of $1,25(OH)_2D$ (< 20 Ng/ml); (5) low serum values
of 25(OH)D (< 8 pg/ml); and (6) calcium malabsorption (80,
120,191,216).


## CALCIUM SUPPLEMENTATION
Most women over the age of 35 are in negative calcium balance.
The simplest and safest measure to correct the negative balance would be to supplement an individual's diet with calcium
from either food sources such as milk and dairy products or
through the use of calcium supplements. This should be recommended as a general preventive measure which should be begun
early in life. Studies have shown that women with higher
bone mineral at middle life are less inclined to develop
osteoporosis in later life (157). Heaney (104) recommends
1.25 g/day as the minimum for maintenance of a positive calcium balance in adult females. This level of dietary calcium
may not prevent bone loss or protect all women from osteoporosis but it has been shown to maintain bone or slow bone
loss.

Many researchers (53,70,85,114) have reported that the
ingestion of oral dietary calcium supplement results in an
increased positive intestinal calcium absorption, thus aiding
in the maintenance of bone homeostasis. However, this positive response has been observed to decrease or show minimal
effects after four months to two years (53,93,114,143,228,
266). Schwartz et al. demonstrated decreased bone loss in
five osteoporotic men during a long-term combination radiocalcium, kinetic and metabolic study using an oral calcium
supplement of 4 g/day (228). Bernstein and Guri and Shapiro
et al. reported that dietary calcium does not seem to reverse

osteoporosis (30,229) while Nordin has indicated reduced spontaneous fractures in subjects treated with supplemental dietary calcium (188,190). Riggs et al. have found that when subjects were given 2 to 2.5 g of calcium and 400 IU vitamin D there was a decrease in bone resorbing surfaces, a decrease in iPTH, and a decrease in bone turnover (218).

In a double blind study recently completed in our laboratory the group receiving a calcium (750 mg/day)-vitamin D (400 IU/day) supplement over a 36 month period demonstrated a 3.5% increase in bone mineral divided by bone width while the control group declined by 2.6% (p < .01). In vivo bone mineral content and width were determined using photon absorptiometry (238). Similar results have been found by Horsman et al. (107) and Recker et al. (205).

Crilly et al. (57) reported that osteoporotic subjects who received 30 mmol of supplemental calcium as citrate a day showed an increased metacarpal cortical area, maintained a positive calcium balance and exhibited decreased urinary hydroxyproline excretion. In that experiment several other treatment modalities were compared to a control group (Ergocalciferol 10-50,000 IU/day; $1\alpha$-(OH)$D_3$ 1-2 µg/day; ethinyl oestradiol 25-50 µg daily) and only the treatment combination of oestradiol and $1$ -(OH)$D_3$ resulted in more positive results. The results from the literature reviewed and our three-year study give strong implication that the oral dietary calcium may be an important therapy modality in bone maintenance and prevention of osteoporosis.

## ESTROGEN

Albright's hypothesis provided a rational basis for treatment of postmenopausal osteoporosis with gonadal steroids. The effects of estrogen on bone loss have been studied prospectively (57,107,136,137,138,139,181,205) and retrospectively (93,94,108). These studies suggest convincingly that if estrogen therapy is started shortly after cessation of ovarian function bone loss and osteoporosis can be lessened or prevented.

In a ten year double blind prospective study with estrogen replacement therapy (ERT) (conjugated estrogens 2.5 mg/day plus progesterone, 10 mg daily for 7 days of each month) subjects were matched by age and diagnosis to a group of subjects receiving a placebo. It was found that ERT halted bone loss and determined that the length of time after menopause that therapy was initiated was of significant importance. Subjects who began ERT within 3 years of their last menstrual period (LMP) gained in bone mass while subjects who began therapy more than three years after LMP showed little or no bone loss (181).

Recker et al. (205) found that skeletal mass decreased 1.18% in the control group as compared to 0.15% (p < .05) in the ERT group (cycled conjugated equine estrogen, 0.625 mg daily and methyltestosterone 5 mg) as measured by radiogrammetry, and 2.88% in the control group and 0.73% in the ERT group when photon absorptiometry was used. The authors also reported that bone surface resorption in the ERT group was reduced by 50%, and that serum phosphorus levels were significantly (p < 0.05) reduced. Horsman et al. (107) reported similar results for women receiving estradiol ERT (25 or 50 µg daily for three weeks out of four).

Lindsey et al. (136,138) found a decrease in urinary hydroxyproline in ERT subjects. Crilly et al. (52) reported that osteoporotics receiving ERT demonstrated an increased cortical area, increased calcium balance and a decrease in urinary hydroxproline excretion. They also found that when $1\alpha-(OH)D_3$ (1 to 2 µg daily) was combined with ERT the positive effects were even more dramatic, leading the authors to recommend that $1\alpha-(OH)D_3$ or $1,25(OH)_2D_3$ be given in conjunction with ERT.

Two retrospective studies have shown that the risk of hip/radial fracture or osteoporosis is greatly reduced by ERT. In one study it was found that the "risk" of radial or hip fracture was almost 4 times greater for the group that had not received ERT (108). Hammond et al. (93) found that the "new occurrence" of osteoporosis was significantly (p < 0.001) lower for the ERT group.

The most controversial issue regarding long-term use of ERT is the possibility that it may cause endometrial cancer (2,91,127,132,199,250). It has been reported that the incidence rates of endometrial cancer are 8 to 12 times greater for persons who have received ERT (92,94,146,151,236,273).

Several review articles have outlined the clinical recommendations and contraindications for estrogen use (91,127,132, 199,202). But taking into account the very positive effects of ERT in preventing osteoporosis Quigley and Hammond stated:

> Although administration of estrogen is not without risk, its use should not be withheld from a woman with symptoms due to a lack of the hormone. Informed consent with particular reference to the probable increased incidence of endometrial carcinoma and to the fact that the symptoms for which estrogen is prescribed are not life threatening is vital. In our opinion, the benefits of post-menopausal estrogen therapy outweigh the risks in informed patients for whom estrogen is indicated, progestogen is added and any uterine bleeding is promptly investigated (202).

## FLUORIDE

Reports that the incidence of fracture and/or osteoporosis is higher in areas where the water supply has a low fluoride content than in areas with high fluoride content has encouraged the use of sodium fluoride to treat osteoporosis (24,29, 110,208,209,217,219,248). The results to date have been disappointing.

The established effects of fluoride treatment are: (1) primarily osteoblasts are affected (217); (2) fluoride may impair osteoid synthesis and bone mineralization (24,217) which can be offset or minimized by supplementing the diet with calcium and vitamin D (117,123,217); and (3) fluoride is the only substance to consistently show an increase in bone mass (120). But questions still remain about the safety of using fluoride. Riggs et al. (217) found that one half of the patients in their study suffered from either rheumatic or gastrointestinal side effects. Other symptoms found in these subjects, but not thought to be related to fluoride therapy, were dyspepsia, mild arthralgias, joint stiffness and hair loss. The antifracture efficacy is also called into question because of the fact that fluoride increases the crystallinity and elasticity which results in decreased bone strength (217). Until the safety and antifracture efficacy are soundly determined, fluoride should not be recommended for general use (23).

## PHYSICAL ACTIVITY

Physical activity has been proposed as a treatment modality for osteoporosis but has minimal research support at this time. Further explanation of physical activity as a treatment modality will be given later in the text.

## OTHERS

Vitamin D has been known to affect bone metabolism since 1946. In current work with the active form of Vitamin D, $1\alpha-(OH)D$ and $1,25(OH)_2D$ have been shown to increase intestinal calcium absorption and bone mineral content. However, this has been observed mainly in patients with low calcium absorption (46, 58,98,135). When the active form of Vitamin D is used with ERT the results have been more positive, but further research is required (58). A danger in the use of the active form of Vitamin D is that too high a dosage will promote hypercalcemia (64,216).

While osteoporosis is less frequent in males, it does occur and has been reported to be related to androgen deficiency in some cases. In a recent case study testosterone therapy increased bone formation and bone mineralization in two 30 year old osteoporotic males. These results suggest that hormonal replacement therapy may be appropriate for treatment of osteoporosis in males (21).

Preliminary experiments using thyrocalcitonin to promote long-term reversal of bone loss in animals have been disappointing because of the development of secondary or compensatory hyperparathyroidism (116,203,265). However, Milhaud and associates report long-term improvement in calcium balance in 16 patients treated with low doses of calcitonin (173).

Use of calcium infusions to suppress parathyroid activity and induce secondary hypercalcitoninism has resulted in positive calcium balances for osteoporotic patients studied for short periods of time, but long-term results have been disappointing in women with postmenopausal osteoporosis (121,134, 264). The use of this approach requires careful supervision of the patient because of the potential complications of induced hypercalcemia. Alternating phosphorus and calcium infusions have resulted in an increased calcium balance, relief of bone pain, increased cortical bone thickness and prevention of future fractures. But the clinical use of such a regimen is limited to selected patients because of its long duration and complexity (200).

Growth hormone in the treatment of osteoporosis has been considered for many years. However, many researchers question its use. Kuhlencordt and co-workers concluded that growth hormone was not useful in treatment of osteoporosis on the basis of bone biopsy and Ca-47 kinetic studies (131).

Arnstein and associates used disodium etidronate in an attempt to retard loss of bone in patients with spinal cord injuries (18). Thirteen patients received the drug and 13 patients received a placebo for 24 weeks in the double-blind study. The bone mineral contents of the radial metaphyses and fibular diaphyses showed no significant response to the drug. However, the mineral contents of the tibial diaphyses of the patients receiving the drug averaged 100.4% of the initial values at the end of 12 weeks. The corresponding value for the control or placebo treated patients was 96.8%. This difference is significant at the 5% level of confidence. Jowsey reported secondary stimulation of parathyroid activity with long term diphosphonate administration (117,124).

## MEASUREMENT TECHNIQUES

Currently, there are several practical methods for quantitative measurement of skeletal status which do not require bone biopsy. These methods are non-invasive techniques based on radiological assessment of skeletal status. They include measurement of x-rays, absorptiometry, neutron activation of calcium, computed tomography and dynamic measurement using vibratory properties of the bone.

Measurement of the small rates of bone loss which occur during aging or immobilization necessitates use of methods which are precise, accurate, and sensitive. These methods must also demonstrate long term reliability. Additionally, there are changes of soft tissue composition with aging which may affect bone measurements (76,130).

Diagnosis of disease and evaluation of the effectiveness of treatment are the goals of the clinician. Safety, cost, and convenience must also be considered in choosing a measurement technique.

Different measurement sites on the skeleton have been used in order to provide maximal advantage for the diagnosis and treatment of osteoporosis. Trabecular bone, in the vertebrae and in the ends of long bones, has been suggested to respond more rapidly to stress and therapy than compact bone (183). However, compact bone, forming the shafts of long bones, provides sites of measurement which are uniform in shape, reducing repositioning error. Whole body measurements provide information on change in calcium retention and excretion but provide minimal information on local distribution. Bone biopsy data have shown that there is a wide biological variation in the pattern of bone loss within and between individuals with advanced age (159). There is also structural variation at the microscopic level (259), which, combined with individual exposure to various degrees of stress, results in an overlap in many measurement values between normals and osteoporotics.

## RADIOGRAPHY

There are several methods based on measurement qualification and quantification of radiographs. Singh et al. (232,233) suggest that the trabeculae in the femoral head corresponds to the lines of maximal compression and tension in the bone. Erosion of these trabeculae, which can be detected radiographically, affects the strength of this bone. Singh's method has the advantage of simplicity, but lacks precision and accuracy in comparison to other techniques.

Thickness of cortical bone has been used as an indicator of bone disease (82,256). Measurement of radiographs have been correlated with bone mass, photon absorptiometric measurements and total body calcium (12,152). However, measurement errors and problems with intracortical porosity and endosteal erosion in bone disease limit the accuracy of assessment (172).

Absorption of radiation by bone mineral determines the exposure of radiographic film. The optical density of the radiographic bone image can be measured by a photodensitometer. The radiation from the conventional x-ray tube has a continuous energy spectrum, and absorption coefficients for such a beam cannot be well-defined. In addition, the heterogeneous beam changes in quality or hardens as lower energy radiation is preferentially absorbed during passage through soft tissues and bone. Further, an undetermined and variable amount of scattered radiation from the surrounding soft tissues affects the radiographic bone image. Variations in film, film development and film exposure conditions may contribute to large systematic errors. Refinements include (a) scanning of special reference wedges, (b) methods to decrease scatter, (c) refinement of the optical photodensitometers, and (d) interfacing the latter to computers (260). The advantage of visualization of the scan site is weighed against the limitations on accuracy.

## ABSORPTIOMETRY
### SINGLE PHOTON ABSORPTIOMETRY
Photon absorptiometry uses the attenuation of a highly collimated mono-energetic beam of low energy (20-100 KeV) photons as an indicator of bone mineral mass (45). The beam intensity is monitored with a collimated scintillation detector and pulse height analyzer as the source and detector are passed across a limb bone. Changes in beam intensity are proportional to the bone mass. The system can be interfaced with a computer for both control functions and data analysis and storage. This technique minimizes the effects of beam hardening, scattered radiation, and non-linear system response which make radiographic techniques error-prone (42).

The accuracy of the absorptiometric method has been demonstrated on ashed bone sections (160). Varying the thickness and composition (muscle vs. fat) of surrounding tissue cover has little effect on the measurement. Typical measurement precision is 1-2%, if care is taken with repositioning. The high precision and low dosage (10 mrem) make longitudinal studies possible.

The use of absorptiometry as a diagnostic tool is limited somewhat by the overlap of values of osteoporotics and age-matched controls (55,88,90,229). Persons classified as

osteoporotics lie about 15% below levels of age-matched controls and about 30% below levels of young adults. This is due
in part to natural variation and the realization that bone
mineral content is not completely related to bone fracture
which is one of the major clinical criteria for diagnosis of
osteopenia. Also, mineral content in peripheral bone such as
the radius may not reflect conditions in the axial skeleton,
where predominantly trabecular bone such as the vertebra may
lose bone mineral and strength more rapidly than the compact cortical bone in the shaft of the radius.

## DUAL PHOTON ABSORPTIOMETRY

Dual photon absorptiometry (269) employs photons at two different energy levels in order to eliminate the need for a
constant soft tissue thickness and in general is capable of
measuring the bone mineral mass of the spine and other areas
of the body. High precision (< 2%) and accuracy (3%) allow
measurements of bone mineral changes as the result of disease
or therapy. While this technique is limited presently to a
few research facilities, the modifications necessary to
existing equipment are relatively simple and would allow such
systems to be set up easily in most nuclear medicine depart-
ments.

## COMPUTED TOMOGRAPHY

Computed tomography (224) is similar in principle to photon
absorptiometry. It employs a highly collimated beam of gamma
rays which transverses the object with constant velocity at
the section of bone to be analyzed. After each linear scanning process, the gamma beam is rotated by a set number of
degrees until the section has been scanned through $180°$
($n\theta = 180°$). The data is analyzed to determine the geometric
distribution of the local absorption coefficients in the plane
of the scans, resulting in a matrix which is then used for
quantification of bone mineral distribution. By assigning
different gray levels to the matrix elements according to
their magnitude, the mineral distribution is visualized.
Quantitative analysis of the computed density values of each
picture element yields information concerning (1) the actual
outer contour of the bone section examined, (2) the

distribution of the compacta in its area and (3) the separate
mineral contents of the compacta and the spongiosa. This
technique has the potential for measuring trabecular bone
changes in the spine precisely and accurately (159).

## NEUTRON ACTIVATION ANALYSIS

While photon absorptiometry has been used for measuring
regional bone mass, total body neutron activation analysis has
been applied to the measurement of total body bone mineral.
Neutron activation measures the total body calcium providing
an index of total bone mass. This technique uniformly exposes
the subject to a beam of partially moderated fast neutrons
which induce the reaction $^{48}Ca$ $(n,\gamma)$ $^{49}Ca$. The quantity of
induced $^{49}Ca$ is measured by a whole body counter (12). The
high accuracy of neutron activation correlations ($r = 0.70$,
$p < .001$ (237); $r = 0.77$, $p < .01$ (152)) compares with the
photon absorptiometry. The disadvantage of neutron activation
use with volunteers may be one of ethics as well as cost
(about $300.00 per scan). Each measurement results in a
whole-body dosage of 200 millirades (152). Manzke indicated
that repeated neutron activation measurements were not done
after a short time interval because of patient radiation
dosage. The radiation dosage of neutron activation is about
20 times the photon absorptiometry dosage which is isolated to
the limbs rather than the total body. While neutron activation gives good total calcium readings, there is still some
question of its sensitivity. Manzke et al. (152) noted that
the 8 cm. site reflects a more rapid mineral loss with age
than does the entire skeleton measured by neutron activation.

## DYNAMIC METHODS

Measurement of bone vibratory properties provides a method of
skeletal evaluation which determines the functional characteristics of bone rather than its mineral mass. Several investigators have related the breaking strength of bone to its
mineral content, density, elasticity, size and shape as well
as the age and sex of the donor (27,28,60,155,156,261). Since
the speed of sound in bone is related to its elasticity and
density (128), several laboratories have studied acoustical or
vibratory methods of skeletal evaluation. Rich and associates

exploited the difference between the speed of sound propagation in bone and in soft tissue to build a scanner for measurement of bone quantity (210). It worked reasonably well for compact bone, but the attenuation of ultrasound in bone is limited, especially if any cancellous portions are present, so that their technique was impractical. Smith and Keiper measured the elasticity of excised bone segments by a vibratory technique (242). Abendschein and Hyatt obtained the speed of sound in excised bone segments by ultrasound propagation and related this measurement to the density and elasticity of the bone sample (1). It is generally recognized that bone is somewhat inhomogeneous with respect to strength and elasticity, but an average or effective value may be measured (13, 72,263).

## REFERENCES

1. Abendschein, W. and G. Hyatt. Ultrasonics and selected physical properties of bone. Clin. Orthop. 69:294-301, 1970.
2. Adlin, E.V. Postmenopausal estrogen therapy. Ann. Int. Med. 91:488, 1979.
3. Albanese, A., A. Edelson, E. Lorenze and E. Wein. Quantitative radiographic survey technique for detection of bone loss. J. Amer. Geriat. Soc. 17:142-154, 1969.
4. Albanese, A., A. Edelson, E. Lorenze, M. Woodhull and E. Wein. Problems of bone health in elderly. N.Y. State J. Med. Feb.:326-333, 1975.
5. Albright, F. Osteoporosis. Ann. Intern. Med. 27:861-882, 1947.
6. Albright, F., E. Bloomberg and P. Smith. Post-menopausal osteoporosis. Trans. Assn. Amer. Physicians 55:298-305, 1940.
7. Albright, F., C. Burnett, O. Cope and W. Parson. Acute atrophy of bone (osteoporosis) simulating hyperparathyroidism. J. Clin. Endocr. 1:711-716, 1941.
8. Albright, F. and E. Reifenstein. Parathyroid Glands and Metabolic Bone Disease. Baltimore: Williams and Wilkins Company, 1948.
9. Albright, F., P. Smith and A. Richardson. Post-menopausal osteoporosis: Its clinical features. J. Amer. Med. Assn. 116:2465-2474, 1941.
10. Alffram, P. and G. Bauer. Epidemiology of fractures of the forearm. J. Bone Jt. Surg. 44A:105-114, 1962.
11. Alhava, E. Diseases contributing to fragility of bone in patients with hip fractures. Ann. Clin. Res. 6:246-252, 1974.
12. Aloia, J.F., A. Vaswani, H. Atkins, I. Zanzi, K. Ellis and S.H. Cohn. Radiographic morphometry and osteopenia in spinal osteoporosis. J. Nucl. Med. 18:425-431, 1977.
13. Amtmann, E. The distribution of breaking strength in the human femur shaft. J. Biomech. 1:271-277, 1968.
14. Anderson, J., J. Shimmins and D. Smith. A new technique for measurement of metacarpal density. Brit. J. Radiol. 39:443-450, 1966.
15. Arnold, J. Quantitation of mineralization of bone as an organ and tissue in osteoporosis. Clin. Orthop. 17:167-175, 1960.
16. Arnold, J. and P. Gitta. Vertebral fractures in aging and disease. The Gerontologist 8(3):17, 1968.

17. Arnold, J., M. Bartley, S. Tont and D. Jenkins. Skeletal changes in aging and disease. Clin. Orthop. 49:17-38, 1966.

18. Arstein, A., F. Blumenthal, J. Bevan, S. Michaels and D. McCann. The effects of diphosphonate therapy on the bone loss of immobilization. In: International Conference on Bone Mineral Measurement, edited by R.B. Mazess. Washington, D.C.: DHEW Publ. No. NIH 75-683, 1973.

19. Atkinson, M., B. Nordin and S. Sherlock. Malabsorption and bone disease in prolonged obstructive jaundice. Quart. J. Med. 25: 299-312, 1956.

20. Baker, P., H. Schraer and R. Yalman. The accuracy of human bone composition determined from roentgenograms. Photogram. Engr. 25: 455-460, 1959.

21. Baran, D., M. Bergfeld, S. Teitelbaum and L. Avioli. Effect of testosterone therapy on bone formation in an osteoporotic hypogonadal male. Calc. Tiss. Res. 26:103-106, 1978.

22. Bauer, G. Epidemiology of fracture in aged persons. Clin. Orthop. 17:219-225, 1960.

23. Baylink, D.J. Sodium fluoride for osteoporosis--some unanswered questions. J. Am. Med. Assn. 243:463-464, 1980.

24. Baylink, D. and D. Bernstein. The effects of fluoride therapy on metabolic bone disease. Clin. Orthop. 55:51-85, 1967.

25. Beals, R. Survival following hip fracture. Long follow-up of 607 patients. J. Chron. Dis. 25:235-244, 1972.

26. Bell, G.H., D. Cuthbertson and J. Orr. The strength and size of bone in relation to calcium intake. J. Physiol. 100:299-317, 1941.

27. Berlyne, G., J. Ben-Ari, D. Galinsky, M. Hirsch, A. Kushellevsky and R. Shainkin. The etiology of osteoporosis. J. Amer. Med. Assn. 229:1904-1905, 1974.

28. Berlyne, G., J. Ben-Ari, A. Kushellevsky, A. Idelman, D. Galinsky, M. Hirsch, R. Shainkin, R. Yagil and M. Zlotnik. The etiology of senile osteoporosis: Secondary hyperparathyroidism due to renal failure. Quart. J. Med. 44:505-521, 1975.

29. Bernstein, D. and P. Cohen. Use of sodium fluoride in the treatment of osteoporosis. J. Clin. Endocr. 27:197-210, 1967.

30. Bernstein, D. and C. Guri. Osteoporosis: Etiology and therapy. Postgrad. Med. 34:407-409, 1963.

31. Bernstein, D., N. Sadowsky, D. Hegsted, C. Guri and F. Stare. Prevalence of osteoporosis in high- and low-fluoride areas in North Dakota. J. Amer. Med. Assn. 198:499-504, 1966.

32. Berry, C. Preliminary clinical report of the medical aspects of Apollos VII and VIII. Aerospace Med. 40:245-254, 1969.

33. Birkenhaeger, J. and D. Birkenhaeger-Frenkel. On the clinical significance of the chemical composition of bone. Folia Medica Neerlandica 11:155-161, 1968.

34. Bjelle, A. and B. Nilsson. Osteoporosis in rheumatoid arthritis. Calc. Tiss. Res. 5:327-332, 1970.

35. Bollet, A., G. Engh and W. Parson. Epidemiology of osteoporosis. Arch. Int. Med. 166:191-194, 1965.

36. Bouillon, R., P. Geusens, J. Dequeker and P. DeMoor. Parathyroid function in primary osteoporosis. Clin. Sci. 57:167-171, 1979.

37. Boyd, R., E. Cameron, H. McIntosh and V. Walker. Measurement of bone mineral content in vivo using photon absorptiometry. Canad. Med. Assoc. J. 111:1201-1205, 1974.

38. Browse, N. The Physiology and Pathology of Bed Rest. Springfield: C.C. Thomas, 1965.

39. Bullmore, J., J. Gallagher, B. Nordin and D. Marshall. Effect of age on calcium absorption. Lancet II:535-537, 1970.

40. Burton, J., F. Ensell, J. Leach and K. Hall. Atmospheric ozone and femoral fractures. Lancet I:795-796, 1975.

41. Cameron, J. Summary of data on the bone mineral of the radius in normals. AEC Contractor Report COO-1422-41, 1969.

42. Cameron, J., R. Mazess and J. Sorenson. Precision and accuracy of bone mineral determination by direct photon absorptiometry. Inv. Radiol. 3:141-150, 1968.

43. Cameron, J. and J. Sorenson. A reliable measurement of bone mineral content in vivo. In: Proceedings of the Fifth European Symposium on Calcified Tissues, edited by G. Milhaud, M. Owen and H. Backwood. Paris: Société d'edition d'enseignement Supérieur, 1969.

44. Cameron, J. and J. Sorenson. Longitudinal studies of bone-mineral content by the photon absorption technique. AEC Contractor Report COO-1422-3, 1965.

45. Cameron, J. and J. Sorenson. Measurement of bone mineral in vivo. Science 142:230-232, 1963.

46. Caniggia, A. and A. Vattimo. Effects of 1,25-dihydroxy-cholecalciferol on $^{47}$calcium absorption in post-menopausal osteoporosis. Clin. Endocrinol. (Oxf.) 11:99-103, 1979.

47. Cann, C., H. Genant and D. Young. Comparison of vertebral and peripheral mineral losses in disuse osteoporosis in monkeys. Radiol. 134:525-529, 1980.

48. Casuccio, C. Concerning osteoporosis. J. Bone Jt. Surg. 44B: 453-463, 1962.

49. Catto, G., A. MacDonald, J. McIntosh and M. MacLeod. Hameodialysis therapy and changes in skeletal calcium. Lancet 1: 1150-1153, 1973.

50. Catto, G., J. McIntosh and M. MacLeod. Partial body neutron activation analysis in vivo: A new approach to the investigation of metabolic bone disease. Phys. Med. Biol. 1:508-517, 1973.

51. Chamberlain, M., J. Fremlin, I. Holloway and D. Peters. Use of the cyclotron for whole body neutron activation analysis: Theoretical and practical considerations. Int. J. Appl. Radiat. Isot. 21:725-734, 1970.

52. Child, J. and I. Smith. Lymphoma presenting as "idiopathic" juvenile osteoporosis. Brit. Med. J. 1:720-721, 1975.

53. Clark, A. Factors in fracture of the female femur. Geront. Clin. 10:258-270, 1968.

54. Cohn, S.H., C. Combrowski and R. Fairchild. In vivo neutron activation analysis of calcium in man. Int. J. Appl. Radiat. Isot. 21: 127-137, 1970.

55. Cohn, S., K. Ellis, S. Wallach, I. Zanzi, H. Atkins and J. Aloia. Absolute and relative deficity in total-skeletal calcium and radial bone mineral in osteoporosis. J. Nucl. Med. 15:428-435, 1974.

56. Cohn, S., K. Shukla, C. Dombrowski and R. Fairchild. Design and calibration of a "broad-beam" 238-Pu, Be neutron source for total body neutron activation analysis. J. Nucl. Med. 13:487-492, 1972.

57. Colbert, C., J. Spuit and L. Davila. Biophysical properties of bone: Determining mineral concentration from the x-ray image. Trans. N.Y. Acad. Sci. Series II 30:271-290, 1967.

58. Crilly, R., A. Horsmann, D. Marshall and B. Nordin. Prevalence, pathogenesis and treatment of post-menopausal osteoporosis. Aust. N.Z. J. Med. 9:24-30, 1979.

59. Cummings, J.H., M. Hill, T. Jivraj, H. Huston, W. Branch and D. Jenkins. The effect of meat protein and dietary fiber on colonic functional metabolism. 1. Changes in bowel habit, bile acid excretion, and calcium absorption. Am. J. Clin. Nutr. 32:2086-2093, 1979.

60. Currey, J. The mechanical consequences of variation in the mineral content of bone. J. Biomech. 2:1-11, 1969.

61. Daniell, H. Increase in fracture of the femur in the elderly. Lancet 2:130, 1975.

62. Davis, M., L. Lanzl and A. Cox. The detection, prevention and retardation of menopausal osteoporosis. In: Osteoporosis, edited by U.S. Barzel. New York: Grune and Stratton, 1970.

63. Davis, M., N. Strandjord and L. Lanzl. Estrogens and the aging process. J. Amer. Med. Assn. 196:219-224, 1966.

64. Deluca, H. The vitamin D system in the regulation of calcium and phosphorus metabolism. Nutr. Rev. 37:161, 1979.

65. Dent, C., H. Engelbrecht and R. Godfrey. Osteoporosis of lumbar vertebrae and calcification of abdominal aorta in women living in Durban. Brit. Med. J. 4:76-79, 1968.

66. Draper, HH., T. Sie and J. Bergen. Osteoporosis in aging rats induced by high phosphorus diets. J. Nutr. 102:1133-1142, 1972.

67. Duncan, H. Osteoporosis in rheumatoid arthritis and corticosteroid induced osteoporosis. Orthop. Clin. N. Amer. 3:571-583, 1972.

68. Duncan, J., H. Frost, A. Villaneuva and J. Sigler. The osteoporosis of rheumatoid arthritis. Arth. Rheum. 8:943-954, 1965.

69. Eddy, T. Atmospheric ozone and femoral fractures. Lancet 1: 1388-1389, 1975.

70. Eisenberg, E. and G. Gordon. Skeletal dynamics in man measured by non-radioactive strontium. J. Clin. Invest. 40:1809-1825, 1961.

71. Evans, F. Mechanical properties and histology of cortical bone from younger and older men. Anat. Res. 185:1-12, 1976.

72. Evans, F. and M. Lebow. Regional differences in some of the physical properties of the human femur. J. Appl. Physiol. 3:563-572, 1951.

73. Exner, G., A. Prader, U. Elsasser and M. Anliker. Bone densitometry using computed tomography. Part II. Increased trabecular bone density in children with chronic renal failure. Brit. J. Radiol. 52: 24-28, 1979.

74. Exner, G., A. Prader, U. Elsasser, P. Ruegsegger and M. Anliker. Bone densitometry using computed tomography. Part I. Selective determination of trabecular bone density and other bone mineral parameters. Normal values in children and adults. Brit. J. Radiol. 52:14-23, 1979.

75. Felts, W.J.L. In vivo bone implantation as a technique in skeletal biology. Internat. Rev. Cyto. 12:243-302, 1961.

76. Forbes, G. Changes in body water and electrolyte during growth and development. In: Body Composition in Animals and Man. Washington, D.C.: Nat. Acad. Sci., 1968.

77. Fraser, R. The problem of osteoporosis. J. Bone Jt. Surg. 42A:138-143, 1960.

79. Frost, H. Micropetrosis. J. Bone Jt. Surg. 42A:144-150, 1960.

80. Gallagher, J.C., B. Riggs, J. Eisman, A. Hamstra, S. Arnaud and H. DeLuca. Intestinal calcium absorption and serum vitamin D metabolites in normal subjects and osteoporotic patients. J. Clin. Invest. 64:729-736, 1979.

81. Garn, S. An annotated bibliography on bone densitometry. Amer. J. Clin. Nutr. 10:59-67, 1962.

82. Garn, S. The Earlier Gain and the Later Loss of Cortical Bone in Nutritional Perspective. Springfield: C.C. Thomas, 1970.

83. Garn, S., C. Rohmann, E. Pao and E. Hull. Normal "osteoporotic" bone loss. In Progress in Development of Methods in Bone Densitometry, edited by G. Wedon, W. Neumann and D. Jenkins. Washington, D.C.: NASA SP-64, 1966.

84. Garn, S., C. Rohmann and B. Wagner. Bone loss as a general phenomenon in man. Fed. Proc. 26:1729-1736, 1967.

85. Garn, S., C. Rohmann, B. Wagner, G. Davillia and W. Ascoli. Population similarities in the onset and rate of adult endosteal bone loss. Clin. Orthop. 65:51-60, 1969.

86. Geiser, M. and J. Trueta. Muscle action, bone rarefaction and bone formation. J. Bone Jt. Surg. 40B:282-311, 1958.

87. Genant, K. and D. Boyd. Quantitative bone mineral analysis using dual energy computed tomography. Invest. Radiol. 12:545-551, 1977.

88. Goldsmith, N., J. Johnston, G. Picetti and C. Garcia. Bone mineral in the radius and vertebral osteoporosis in an insured population. J. Bone Jt. Surg. 55A:1276, 1973.

89. Goldsmith, R.S., J. Jowsey, W. Dube, B. Riggs, C. Arnaud and P. Kelly. Effects of phosphorous supplementation on serum parathyroid hormone and bone morphology in osteoporosis. J. Clin. Endocrin. Metab. 43:523-532, 1976.

90. Goldsmith, N., J. Johnston, J. Ury, G. Vose and C. Colbert. Bone-mineral estimation in normal and osteoporotic women. J. Bone Jt. Surg. 53A:83-100, 1971.

91. Gordon, G. and C. Vaughn. Osteoporosis: Early detection, prevention and treatment. Consultant 20:64-81, 1980.

92. Gray, L., W. Christopherson and R. Hoover. Estrogens and endometrial carcinoma. Obstet. Gynecol. 49:385-389, 1977.

93. Hammond, C., F. Jeovsek, K. Lee, W. Creasman and R. Parker. Effects of long-term estrogen replacement therapy. I. Metabolic effects. Am. J. Obstet. Gynecol. 133:525-536, 1979.

94. Hammond, C., F. Jelovsek, K. Lee, W. Creasman and R. Parker. Effects of long-term estrogen replacement therapy. II. Neoplasm. Am. J. Obstet. Gynecol. 133:537-547, 1979.

95. Harrison, J., K. MacNeill, A. Hitchman and B. Britt. Bone mineral measurements of the central skeleton by in vivo neutron activation analysis for routine investigation of osteopenia. Invest. Radiol. 14:27-34, 1979.

96. Harrison, J., W. Williams, J. Watts and K. McNeill. A bone calcium index based on partial-body calcium measurements by in vivo activation analysis. J. Nucl. Med. 16:116-122, 1975.

97. Harrison, M., R. Fraser and B. Mullen. Calcium metabolism in osteoporosis. Lancet 1:1015, 1961.

98. Hass, H., M. Dambacher, J. Guncaga, T. Lauffenburger, B. Lammle and J. Olah. $1,25(OH)_2$ Vitamin $D_3$ in osteoporosis--A pilot study. Horm. Metab. Res. 11:168-171, 1979.

99. Hattner, R. and D. McMillan. Influence of weightlessness upon the skeleton. A review. Aerospace Med. 39:849-855, 1968.

100. Heaney, R.P. A unified concept of osteoporosis. Am. J. Med. 39:877, 1965.

101. Heaney, R.P. Calcium metabolic changes at menopause: Their possible relationship to post-menopausal osteoporosis. In: Osteoporosis II, edited by U.S. Barzel. New York: Gruen and Stratton, pp. 101-109, 1978.

102. Heaney, R.P. Pathophysiology of osteoporosis: Implications for treatment. Texas Med. 70:37-45, 1974.

103. Heaney, R.P. Radiocalcium metabolism in disuse osteoporosis in man. Amer. J. Med. 33:188-200, 1962.

104. Heaney, R.P., R. Recker and P. Saville. Calcium balance and calcium requirements in middle-aged women. Am. J. Clin. Nutr. 30:1603-1611, 1977.

105. Heaney, R., R. Recker and P. Saville. Menopausal changes in bone remodeling. J. Lab. Clin. Med. 92:964-970, 1978.

106. Heaney, R.P., R. Recker and P. Saville. Menopausal changes in calcium balance performance. J. Lab. Clin. Med. 92:953-963, 1978.

107. Horsman, A., J. Gallagher, M. Simpson and B. Nordin. Post-menopausal trial of oestrogen and calcium in postmenopausal women. Brit. Med. J. 2:789-792, 1977.

108. Hutinson, T., S. Polansky and A. Feinstein. Post menopausal oestrogens protect against fractures of hip and distal radius. A case control study. Lancet 2(9145):705-709, 1979.

109. Isherwood, I., R. Rutherford, B. Pullan and P. Adams. Bone-mineral estimation by computer-assisted transverse axial tomography. Lancet 2:712-715, 1976.

110. Iskrant, A. The etiology of fractured hips in females. Amer. J. Publ. Health 58:485-490, 1968.

111. Iskrant, A. and R. Smith, Osteoporosis in women 45 years and over related to subsequent fractures. Publ. Hlth. Repts. 84:33-38, 1969.

112. Jaworski, Z. Proceedings of the First Workshop on Bone Morphometry. Ottawa, Canada: University of Ottawa Press, 1976.

113. Johnson, N.E., E. Alcantara and H. Linkswilere. Calcium retention in the adult human male as affected by protein intake. J. Nutr. 100:1425-1430, 1970.

114. Johnson, R.W. A physiological study of the blood supply of the diaphysis. J. Bone Jt. Surg. 9:153-184, 1927.

115. Johnston, C., D. Smith, P. Yu and W. Deiss. In vivo measurement of bone mass in the radius. Metabolism 17:1140-1153, 1968.

116. Jowsey, J. An attempt to prevent dietary osteoporosis in cats with administration of porcine calcitonin. In: Osteoporosis, edited by U.S. Barzel. New York: Grune and Stratton, 1970.

117. Jowsey, J. Osteoporosis: Etiology, diagnosis and treatment. Contemp. Surg. 6:13-16, 1975.

118. Jowsey, J. Why is mineral nutrition important in osteoporosis? Geriatrics 33:39-48, 1978.

119. Jowsey, J. and J. Gershon-Cohen. Effect of dietary calcium levels in production and reversal of experimental osteoporosis in cats. Proc. Exptl. Biol. Med. 116:437-441, 1964.

120. Jowsey, J. and G. Grodan. Bone turnover and osteoporosis. In: The Biochemistry and Pathophysiology of Bone Volume III, second edition, edited by G.H. Bourne. New York: Academic Press, pp. 201-237, 1971.

121. Jowsey, J., R. Hoye, C. Pak and F. Bartter. The treatment of osteoporosis with calcium infusions. Amer. J. Med. 47:17-22, 1969.

122. Jowsey, J., E. Reiss and J. Canterbury. Long-term effects of high phosphate intake on parathyroid hormone levels and bone metabolism. Acta Orthop. Scand. 45:801-808, 1974.

123. Jowsey, J., B. Riggs, P. Kelly and D. Hoffman. Effect of combined therapy with sodium fluoride, vitamin D and calcium in osteoporosis. Amer. J. Med. 53:43-49, 1972.

124. Jowsey, J., B. Riggs, P. Kelly, D. Hoffman and P. Bordier. The treatment of osteoporosis with disodium ethane-1-hydroxy-1, 1-diphosphonate. J. Lab. Clin. Med. 78:574-584, 1971.

125. Jurist, J. and C. Hickey. Effects of sodium fluoride on ulnar resonant frequency in elderly women. AEC Contractor Report COO-1422-109, 1971.

126. Kelsay, J.L., K. Behall and E. Prather. Effect of fiber from fruits and vegetables on metabolic responses of human subjects. II. Calcium, magnesium, iron and silicon balances. Am. J. Clin. Nutr. 32:1876-1880, 1979.

127. Kemmann, E. and J. Jones. The female climacteric. Am. Fam. Pract. 20:140-151, 1979.

128. Kinsler, L. and A. Frey. Fundamentals of Acoustics. New York: John Wiley and Sons, 1950.

129. Kraner, H., J. Patterson and J. Smith. Combined cortical thickness and bone density determination by photon absorptiometry. Phys. Med. Biol. 23:1101-1114, 1978.

130. Krzwicki, H. and C. Consolazio. Body-composition methodology in military nutrition surveys. In: Body Composition in Animals and Man. Washington, D.C.: Nat. Acad. Sci., 1968.

131. Kuhlencordt, F., C. Lozano-Tonkin, H. Kruse, C. Schneider and E. Sommer. Uber die Anwendung von Wachstumshormon bei Osteoporose. Klin. Wschr. 52:1130-1131, 1974.

132. Landau, R. What you should know about estrogens or the periols of Pauline. J. Am. Med. Assn. 241:47-51, 1979.

133. Lender, M., E. Verner, H. Stankiewicz and J. Menczel. Intestinal malabsorption of $^{47}CA$ in elderly patients with osteoporosis, Paget's disease and osteomalacia. Effects of calcitonin, oestrogen, and vitamin $D_2$. Gerontology 23:31-36, 1977.

134. Lifschitz, M., C. Pak, D. Henneman, J. Jowsey, Y. Pilch and F. Bartter. Treatment of osteoporosis with calcium infusions. Trans. Assn. Amer. Phys. 83:254-265, 1970.

135. Lindholm, T., J. Savastigkoglou and U. Lindgren. Interim report on treatment of osteoporotic patients with 1 alpha-hydroxy-vitamin $D_3$ and calcium. Clin. Orthop. 135:232-240, 1978.

136. Lindsay, R., D. Hart, D. Purdie, M. Ferguson, A. Clark and A. Kraszewski. Comparative effects of oestrogen and a progestogen on bone loss in postmenopausal women. Clin. Sci. Mol. Med. 54:193-195, 1978.

137. Lindsay, R. and D. Hart. Oestrogens and post-menopausal bone loss. Scot. Med. J. 23:13-18, 1978.

138. Lindsay, R., D. Hart, J. Aitken and D. Purdie. The effect of ovarian sex steroids on bone mineral status in the oophorectomized rat and in the human. Post Med. J. 54 (Suppl. 2):50-58, 1978.

139. Lindsay, R., A. MacLean, A. Kraszewski, D. Hart, A. Clark and J. Garwood. Bone response to termination of oestrogen treatment. Lancet 1(8078):1325-1327, 1978.

140. Linkswiler, H.M., C. Joyce and C. Anand. Calcium retention of young adult males as affected by level of protein and of calcium intake. Trans. N.Y. Acad. Sci. 36:333-340, 1974.

141. Little, K. Bone resorption and osteoporosis. Lancet 2: 752-756, 1963.

142. Little, K. Some mechanisms involved in the osteoporotic process. Gerontologia 14:109-125, 1968.

143. Lutwak, L. High dietary calcium and osteoporosis. In: Dynamic Studies of Metabolic Bone Disease, edited by O.H. Pearson and G.F. Joplin. Philadelphia: Davis Company, pp. 87-99, 1964.

144. Lutwak, L. Nutritional aspects of osteoporosis. J. Amer. Geriat. Soc. 17:115-119, 1969.

145. Lutz, J. Effect of the level of protein intake on calcium metabolism and renal acid excretion of postmenopausal and osteoporotic women. Doctoral dissertation, University of Wisconsin-Madison, 1979.

146. MacDonald, T., J. Annegers, W. O'Fallon, M. Dockerty, G. Malkasian and L. Kurland. Exogenous estrogen and endometrial carcinoma: Case-control and incidence study. Am. J. Obstet. Gynecol. 127:572, 1977.

147. Mack, P., W. Brown and H. Trapp. Qauntitative evaluation of bone density. Amer. J. Roent. 61:808-825, 1949.

148. Mack, P., R. Hoffman and A. Al-Shawi. Physiologic and metabolic changes in Macaca nemestrina on two types of diets during restraint and non-restraint. II. Bone density changes. Aerospace Med. 39:698-704, 1968.

149. Mack, P. and P. LaChance. Effects of recumbency and space flight on bone density. Amer. J. Clin. Nutr. 20:1194-1205, 1967.

150. Mack, P., P. LaChance, G. Vose and F. Vogt. Review of medical findings of Gemini VII and related missions--bone demineralization. In: A Review of Medical Results of Gemini VII and Related Flights. Washington, D.C.: NASA Space Medicine Directorate, 1966.

151. Mack, T., M. Pike, B. Henderson, R. Gerkins, M. Arthur and S. Brown. Estrogen and endometrial cancer in a retirement community. N. Engl. J. Med. 294:1262-1267, 1976.

152. Manzke, E., C. Chestnut, J. Wegedal, D. Baylink and W. Nelp. Relationship between local and total bone mass in osteoporosis. Metabolism 24:605-615, 1975.

153. Marshall, C., A. Viau, L. Berkovitz, W. Davis, D. Chu and N. Naftchi. Changes in bone mineralization in hemiplegia. In: International Conference on Bone Mineral Measurement, edited by R. Mazess. Washington, D.C.: DHEW Publ. No. NIH 75-683, 1973.

154. Mason, R. and G. Ruthven. Bone density measurements in vivo: Improvement of x-ray densitometry. Science 150:221-222, 1965.

155. Mather, B. Comparison of two formulae for in vivo prediction of strength of the femur. Aerospace Med. 38:1270-1272, 1967.

156. Mather, B. The effect of variation in specific gravity and ash content on the mechanical properties of human compact bone. J. Biomech. 1:207-210, 1968.

157. Matkovic, V., K. Kostial, I. Simonovic, R. Buzina, N. Brodarec and B. Nordin. Bone status and fracture rates in two regions of Yugoslavia. Am. J. Clin. Nutr. 32:540-549, 1979.

158. Mayer, E., H. Trostle, E. Ackerman, H. Schraer and O. Sittler. A scintillation counter technique for the x-ray determination of bone mineral content. Rad. Res. 13:156-167, 1960.

159. Mazess, R. Measurement of skeletal status by noninvasive methods. Calc. Tiss. Intern. 28:89-92, 1979.

160. Mazess, R., J. Cameron, R. O'Connor and D. Knutzen. Accuracy of bone mineral measurement. Science 145:388-389, 1964.

161. Mazess, R., J. Jurist and C. Hickey. Bone mineral in elderly women treated with fluorides: A preliminary report. AEC Contractor Report COO-1422-101, 1971.

162. Maziere, B., D. Kuntz, D. Comar and A. Ryckewaert. In vivo analysis of bone calcium by local neutron activation of the hand: Results in normal and osteoporotic subjects. J. Nucl. Med. 20:85-91, 1979.

163. McBean, L. and E. Speckmann. A recognition of the interrelationships of calcium with various dietary components. Am. J. Clin. Nutr. 27:603-609, 1974.

164. McConkey, B., G. Fraser and A. Bligh. Osteoporosis and purpura in rheumatoid disease: Prevalence and relation to treatment with corticosteroids. Quart. J. Med. 31:419-427, 1962.

165. McConkey, B., G. Fraser and A. Bligh. Transparent skin and osteoporosis. Ann. Rheum. Dis. 24:219-223, 1965.

166. McFarland, W. Evaluation of bone density from roentgenograms. Science 119:810-811, 1954.

167. McNeill, K., H. Kostalas and J. Harrison. Effects of body thickness on in vivo neutron activation analysis. Int. J. Appl. Radiat. Isot. 25:347-353, 1974.

168. McNeill, K., B. Thomas, W. Sturtridge and J. Harrison. In vivo neutron activation analysis for calcium in man. J. Nucl. Med. 14: 502-506, 1973.

169. Meema, H. Menopausal and aging changes in muscle mass and bone mineral content. J. Bone Jt. Surg. 48A:1138-1144, 1966.

170. Meema, H., M. Bunker and S. Meema. Loss of compact bone due to menopause. Obstet. Gynec. 26:33-343, 1965.

171. Meema, H., J. Harrison, K. McNeill and D. Oreopoulos. Correlations between peripheral and central skeletal mineral content in chronic renal failure patients and in osteoporotics. Skel. Radiol. 1: 169-172, 1977.

172. Meema, H. and S. Meema. Cortical bone mineral density versus cortical thickness in the diagnosis of osteoporosis: A roentgenologic-densitometric study. J. Am. Geriat. Soc. 17:120-141, 1969.

173. Milhaud, G., J. Talbot and G. Coutris. Calcitonin treatment of post-menopausal osteoporosis. Biomedicine 23:223-232, 1975.

174. Milhaud, G., M. Benezech-Lefevre and M. Moukhtar. Deficiency of calcitonin in age related osteoporosis. Biomedicine 29:272-276, 1978.

175. Moldawer, M. Osteoporosis. In: Restorative Medicine in Geriatrics, edited by M. Dasco. Springfield: C.C. Thomas, 1963.

176. Moldawer, M., S. Zimmerman and L. Collins. Incidence of osteoporosis in elderly whites and elderly Negroes. J. Amer. Med. Assn. 194: 859-862, 1965.

177. Morgan, D., F. Spiers, C. Pulvertaft and P. Fourman. The amount of bone in the metacarpal and the phalanx according to age and sex. Clin. Radiol. 18:101-198, 1967.

178. Morita, R., I. Yamamoto, M. Fukunaga, S. Dokoh, J. Konishi, T. Kousaka, K. Nakajima, K. Torizuka, T. Aso and T. Motohashi. Changes in sex hormones and calcium regulating hormones with reference to bone mass associated with aging. Endocrinol. (Jpn.) 26 (Suppl.):15-22, 1979.

179. Mueller, M. and J. Jurist. Skeletal status in rheumatoid arthritis: A preliminary report. Arth. Rheum. 16:66-70, 1973.

180. Mundy, G., L. Raisz, R. Cooper, G. Schechter and S. Salmon. Evidence for the secretion of an osteoclast stimulating factor in myeloma. N. Engl. J. Med. 291:1041-1046, 1974.

181. Nachtigall, L., R. Nachtigall, R. Nachtigall and E. Beckman. Estrogen replacement therapy I: A 10-year prospective study in the relationship to osteoporosis. Obstet. Gynecol. 53:277-281, 1979.

182. National Research Council, Food and Nutrition Board. Recommended Dietary Allowances, 9th revised ed. Washington, D.C.: Nat. Acad. Sci., 1980.

183. Newton-John, H. and D. Morgan. The loss of bone with age, osteoporosis, and fractures. Clin. Orthop. 71:229-252, 1970.

184. Nicholas, J. and P. Wilson. Osteoporosis of the aged spine. Clin. Orthop. 26:19-33, 1963.

185. Nicholas, J., P. Saville and F. Bronner. Osteoporosis, osteomalacia, and the skeletal system. J. Bone Jt. Surg. 45A:391-405, 1963.

186. Nimann, K. and H. Mankin. Fractures about the hip in the elderly indigent patient. I. Epidemiology. Geriatrics 23:150-158, 1968.

187. Nordin, B. Calcium absorption in the elderly. Calcif. Tiss. Res. 21:442-451, 1976.

188. Nordin, B. Calcium balance and calcium requirement in spinal osteoporosis. Amer. J. Clin. Nutr. 10:384-390, 1962.

189. Nordin, B. Metabolic Bone and Stone Diseases. Baltimore: The Williams and Watkins Company, 1971.

190. Nordin, B. Osteoporosis and calcium deficiency. In: Bone as a Tissue, edited by K. Rodahl, J. Nicholson and E. Brown. New York: McGraw-Hill Book Co., 1960.

191. Nordin, B. Treatment of postmenopausal osteoporosis. Drugs 18:484-492, 1979.

192. Nordin, B., J. MacGregor and D. Smith. The incidence of osteoporosis in normal women: Its relation to age and the menopause. Quart. J. Med. 35:25-38, 1966.

193. Nordin., B., D. Smith, J. MacGregor and J. Anderson. The application of measurements of bone volume and spinal density. In: Progress in Development of Methods in Bone Densitometry. Washington, D.C.: NASA SP-64, 1966.

194. O'Hanlon, P. and M. Kohrs. Dietary studies of older Americans. Am. J. Clin. Nutr. 31:1257, 1978.

195. Okano, K., R. Nakai and M. Harasawa. Endocrine factors in senile osteoporosis. Endocrinol. (Jpn.) 26:23-30, 1979.

196. Omnell, K. Quantitative roentgenologic studies on changes in mineral content of bone in vivo. Acta. Radiol. Suppl. 148:1-86, 1957.

197. Parsons, L. and S. Sommers. Gynecology, second edition. W.B. Saunders Co., pp. 1470-1493, 1978.

198. Palmer, H. Feasibility of determining total-body calcium in animals and humans by measuring 37-Ar in expired air after neutron irradiation. J. Nucl. Med. 14:522-527, 1973.

199. Palmer, H., W. Nelp, R. Murano and C. Rich. The feasibility of in vivo neutron activation analysis of total body calcium and other elements of body composition. Phys. Med. Biol. 13:269-279, 1968.

200. Popovtzer, M., M. Stjernholm and W. Huffer. Effects of alternating phosphorus and calcium infusions on osteoporosis. Am. J. Med. 61:478-484, 1976.

201. Posner, I. and H. Griffiths. Comparison of CT scanning with photon absorptiometric measurement of bone mineral content in the appendicular skeleton. Invest. Radiol. 12:542-544, 1977.

202. Quigley, M. and C. Hammond. Estrogen replacement therapy-- help or hazard. N. Engl. J. Med. 301:646-648, 1979.

203. Rao, J. and T. Bullard. The effect of calcitonin on disuse osteoporosis in young rats. Ind. J. Med. Res. 62:1906-1909, 1974.

204. Rasmussen, H. and P. Bodier. Vitamin D and bone. Metab. Bone Dis. and Rel. Res. 1:7-13, 1978.

205. Recker, R., P. Saville and R. Heaney. Effects of estrogens and calcium carbonate on bone loss in postmenopausal women. Ann. Int. Med. 87:649-655, 1977.

206. Reich, N., R. Seidelmann, R. Tubbs, W. MacIntyre, T. Meaney, R. Alfidi and R. Pepe. Determination of bone mineral content using CT scanning. Am. J. Roentgenol. 127:593-594, 1976.

207. Reifenstein, E. Relationship of steroid hormones to the development and management of osteoporosis in aging people. Clin. Orthop. 10:206-253, 1957.

208. Rich, C. and J. Ensinck. Effect of sodium fluoride on calcium metabolism of human beings. Nature 191:184-185, 1961.

209. Rich, C. and P. Ivanovich. Response to sodium fluoride in severe primary osteoporosis. Ann. Int. Med. 63:1069-1074, 1965.

210. Rich, C., E. Klink, R. Smith, B. Graham and P. Ivanovich. Sonic measurement of bone mass. In: Progress in Development of Methods in Bone Densitometry. Washington, D.C.: NASA SP-64, 1966.

211. Rico, H., A. Del Rio, T. Vila, R. Patino, F. Carrera and D. Espinos. The role of growth hormone in the pathogenesis of post-menopausal osteoporosis. Acta Intern. Med. 139:1263-1265, 1979.

212. Riggins, R., R. Rucker, M. Chan, F. Zeman and J. Beljan. The effect of sodium fluoride on bone strength: An experimental study with clinical implications. J. Bone Jt. Surg. 57A:575, 1975.

214. Riggs, B.L. Hormonal factors in the pathogenesis of post-menopausal osteoporosis. In: Osteoporosis II, edited by U.S. Barzel. New York: Grune and Stratton, pp. 111-122, 1978.

215. Riggs, B., C. Arnaud, J. Jowsey, R. Goldsmith and P. Kelly. Parathyroid function in primary osteoporosis. J. Clin. Invest. 52: 181-184, 1973.

216. Riggs, B., J. Gallagher and H. DeLuca. Osteoporosis and age-related osteopenia: Evaluation of possible role of vitamin D endocrine system in pathogenesis of impaired calcium absorption. In: Vitamin D Basic Research and Its Clinical Application, edited by A. Norman, K. Schaefer, D.V. Harrath, H.-G. Grigdeit, I.W. Coburn, H.F. DeLuca, E. Mower and T. Suda. New York: Walter de Gruyter Press, pp. 1-7, 1979.

217. Riggs, B.L., S. Hodgson, D. Hoffman, P. Kelly, K. Johnson and D. Taves. Treatment of primary osteoporosis with fluoride and calcium. J. Am. Med. Assn. 243:446-449, 1980.

218. Riggs, B., J. Jowsey, P. Kelly, D. Hoffman and C. Arnaud. Effects of oral therapy with calcium and vitamin D in primary osteoporosis. J. Clin. Endocrin. and Met. 42:1139-1144, 1976.

219. Romanus, B. Physical properties and chemical content of canine femoral cortical bone in nutritional osteopenia. Acta Orthop. Scand. Supp. 155:1-101, 1974.

220. Rose, G. A study of the treatment of osteoporosis with fluoride therapy and high calcium intake. Proc. Royal Soc. Med. 58: 436-440, 1965.

221. Rose, G. The irreversibility of osteoporosis. In: Osteoporosis, edited by U.S. Barzel. New York: Grune and Stratton, 1970.

222. Ruder, H., L. Loriaux and M. Lipsett. Severe osteopenia in young adults associated with Cushing's syndrome due to micronodular adrenal disease. J. Clin. Endocr. Metab. 39:1138-1147, 1974.

223. Ruegsegger, P., U. Elsasser, M. Anliker, H. Gnehm, H. Kind and A. Prader. Quantification of bone mineralization using computed tomography. Radiol. 121:93-97, 1976.

224. Ruegsegger, P., P. Niederer and M. Anliker. An extension of classical bone mineral measurements. Ann. Biomed. Eng. 2:194-205, 1974.

225. Saville, P. Osteoporosis: Disease or senescence? Lancet 1: 535, 1968.

226. Schneider, R. and J. Kaye. Insufficiency and stress fractures of the long bones occurring in patients with rheumatoid arthritis. Diag. Radiol. 116:595-600, 1975.

227. Schraer, H., R. Schraer, H. Trostle and A. D"Alfonso. The validity of measuring bone density from roentgenograms by means of a bone density computing apparatus. Arch. Biochem. Biophys. 83:486-500, 1959.

228. Schwartz, E., V. Panarielco and J. Saeli. Radioactive calcium kinetics during high calcium intake in osteoporosis. J. Clin. Invest. 44:1547, 1965.

229. Shapiro, J., W. Moore, H. Jorgensen, J. Reid, C. Epps and D. Whedon. Osteoporosis: Evaluation of diagnosis and therapy. Arch. Int. Med. 135:563-567, 1975.

230. Sherman, M. Estrogens and bone formation in the human female. J. Bone Jt. Surg. 30A:915-930, 1948.

231. Sherman, M. and W. Selakovich. Bone changes in chronic circulatory insufficiency. J. Bone Jt. Surg. 39A:892-901, 1957.

232. Singh, M., A. Nagrath, and P. Maini. Changes in trabecular pattern of the upper end of the femur as an index of osteoporosis. J. Bone Jt. Surg. 52A:457-467, 1970.

233. Singh, M., B. Riggs, J. Beabout and J. Jowsey. Femoral trabecular pattern index for evaluation of spinal osteoporosis. Ann. Int. Med. 77:63-67, 1972.

234. Sissons, H. Osteoporosis of Cushing's syndrome. J. Bone Jt. Surg. 38B:418-433, 1956.

235. Sissons, H. Osteoporosis of Cushing's syndrome. In: Bone as a Tissue, edited by K. Rodahl, J. Nicholson and E. Brown. New York: McGraw-Hill Book Co., 1960.

236. Smith, D., R. Prentice, D. Thompson and W. Herrmann. Association of exogenous estrogen and endometrial carcinoma. N. Engl. J. Med. 293:1164-1166, 1975.

237. Smith, E. The effect of physical activity on bone. Master's thesis, University of Minnesota, 1964.

238. Smith, E., W. Reddan and P. Smith. Physical activity and calcium modalities for bone mineral increase in aged women. In press.

239. Smith, E., S. Babcock and J. Cameron. Early recognition of osteoporosis in the aged female. In preparation.

240. Smith, R. Dietary and hormonal factors in bone loss. Fed. Proc. 26:1737-1746, 1967.

241. Smith, R., W. Eyler and R. Mellinger. On the incidence of senile osteoporosis. Ann. Int. Med. 52:773-781, 1960.

242. Smith, R. and D. Keiper. Dynamic measurement of visco-elastic properties of bone. Amer. J. Med. Elect. 4:156-160, 1965.

243. Solomon, L. Osteoporosis and fracture of the femoral neck in the South African Bantu. J. Bone Jt. Surg. 50B:2-13, 1968.

244. Sorenson, J. and J. Cameron. A reliable in vivo measurement of bone mineral content. J. Bone Jt. Surg. 49A:481-497, 1967.

245. Spencer, H., J. Menczel and I. Lewin. Metabolic and radio-isotope studies in osteoporosis. Clin. Orthop. 35:202-219, 1964.

246. Spencer, H., L. Kramer, D. Osis and C. Norris. Effect of phosphorus on the absorption of calcium and on the calcium balance in man. J. Nutr. 108:447-457, 1978.

247. Spencer, H., J. Menczel, I. Lewin and J. Samachson. Absorption of calcium in osteoporosis. Amer. J. Med. 37:223-234, 1964.

248. Spencer, H., I. Lewin, J. Fowler and J. Samachson. Effect of sodium fluoride on calcium absorption and balances in man. Amer. J. Clin. Nutr. 22:381-390, 1969.

249. Stevens, J., P. Freeman, B. Nordin and E. Barnett. The incidence of osteoporosis in patients with femoral neck fracture. J. Bone Jt. Surg. 44B:520-527, 1962.

250. Taylor, W.H. Postmenopausal oestrogen therapy. Lancet 2(8136): 248, 1979.

251. Trudel, J., V. DeWolfe, J. Young and F. LeFevre. Disuse phenomenon of lower extremity. J. Amer. Med. Assn. 185:1129-1131, 1963.

252. Urist, M. Osteoporosis. Ann. Rev. Med. 13:273-286, 1962.

253. Urist, M., N. MacDonald, M. Moss and M. Skoog. Rarefying disease of the skeleton: Observations dealing with aged and dead bone in patients with osteoporosis. In: Mechanisms of Hard Tissue Destruction. Washington, D.C.: Amer. Assn. Adv. Sci., 1963.

254. Van Huss, W., W. Heusner, J. Weber, D. Lamb and R. Carrow. The effects of pre-pubertal forced exercise upon post-puberty physical activity, food consumption and selected physiological and anatomical parameters. In: First International Congress of Psychology of Sport. Rome, 1965.

255. Vintner-Paulson, N. Calcium and phosphorus intake in senile osteoporosis. Geriatrics 8:76-79, 1953.

256. Virtama, P. and T. Helela. Radiographic measurements of cortical bone. Acta Orthop. Scand. Suppl. 293, 1969.

257. Vogel, J. Bone mineral changes in the Apollo astronauts. In: International Conference on Bone Mineral Measurement, edited by R. Mazess. Washington, D.C.: DHEW Publ. No. NIH 75-683, 1973.

258. Vogel, J. Changes in bone mineral content of the os calcis induced by prolonged bedrest. Fed. Proc. 28:374, 1969.

259. Vose, G. The relation of microscopic mineralization to intrinsic bone strength. Anat. Rec. 144:31-35, 1962.

260. Vose, G., S. Hoerster and P. Mack. New techniques for radiographic assessment of vertebral density. Amer. J. Med. Elect. 3:181-188, 1964.

261. Vose, G. and L. Hurxthal. X-ray density changes in the human heel during bed rest. Amer. J. Roent. 106:486-490, 1969.

262. Vose, G. and A. Kubala. Bone strength--its relationship to x-ray determined ash content. Hum. Biol. 31:262-270, 1959.

263. Walmsley, R. and J. Smith. Variations in bone structure and the value of Young's modulus. J. Anat. 91:693, 1957.

264. Walton, J., M. Dominguez and F. Bartter. Effects of calcium infusions in patients with postmenopausal osteoporosis. Metabolism 24:849-854, 1975.

265. Wase, A. Effects of parental thyrocalcitonin on the aged rat. The Gerontologist 8(3):15, 1968.

266. Wedon, G.D. Effects of high calcium intakes on bones, blood, and soft tissue; relationship of calcium intake to balance in osteoporosis. Fed. Proc. 18:1112-1118, 1959.

267. Whedon, G. Osteoporosis: Atrophy of disuse. In: Bone as a Tissue, edited by K. Rodahl, J. Nicholson and E. Brown. New York: McGraw-Hill Book Co., 1960.

268. Williams, E., K. Boddy, I. Harvey and J. Haywood. Calibration and evaluation of a system for total body in vivo activation analysis using 14 MeV neutrons. Phys. Med. Biol. 23:405-415, 1978.

269. Wilson, C. and M. Madsen. Dichromatic absorptiometry of vertebral bone mineral content. Invest. Radiol. 12:180-184, 1977.

270. Wray, J., E. Sugerman and A. Schneider. Bone composition in senile osteoporosis. J. Amer. Med. Assn. 183:118-120, 1963.

271. Wright, V., R. Catterall and J. Cook. Bone and joint changes in paraplegic men. Ann. Rheum. Dis. 24:419-431, 1965.

272. Yu, W., C. Siu, S. Shim, H. Hawthorne and J. Dunbar. Mechanical properties and mineral content of avascular and revascularizing cortical bone. J. Bone Jt. Surg. 57A:692-695, 1975.

273. Ziel, H. and W. Finkle. Increased incidence of endometrial carcinoma among users of conjugated estrogens. N. Engl. J. Med. 293: 1167-1170, 1975.

Christopher T. Sempos received his M.S. in Nutritional Sciences from the University of Wisconsin in 1979. He is working on a Ph.D. in Nutritional Sciences with the topic of diet and bone loss associated with aging. He is also completing a Master's of Epidemiology.

Robert W. Purvis received a B.S. in mathematics at the University of Wisconsin and is a Ph.D. candidate in Physical Education. He is a member of the American College of Sports Medicine and on the Board of Directors of the Wisconsin United Athletic Club.

# RESPIRATORY SYSTEM AND AGING
## William G. Reddan

The airways and gas exchange units of the lung are in intimate
contact with and highly sensitive to noxious substances contained within the environment. As a result, it is difficult
to separate the possible effects of the environment from age
related morphological or functional changes that are associated with time from those associated with disease. In addition, the lung normally enjoys a large reserve capacity and an
ability to repair injury; thus past injury may be suggestive
of degenerative or aged changes (36).

The focus of this review will be on gas exchange and
acid-base regulation which are the principal regulatory functions of the lung:thorax system. The metabolic, immunologic
and temperature regulatory functions of the lung will not be
discussed. The effects of age on lung clearance mechanisms
or specific hormonal or cellular immunity patterns are not
completely understood. However, clinical observations suggest a vulnerability to infection in the very young and very
old, and age variations in the major immunologic fractions
suggest a reduction in immunal surveillance that may accel-
erate the effects of degenerative diseases (75). A more complete review of the integrated cardio-respiratory changes with
age is covered by Shephard (59).

In young healthy individuals the pulmonary control systems ensure adequate gas exchange at a minimum of physiologic
cost during steady-state rhythmic exercise under a variety of
physiologic states and environmental conditions (15). However, known morphological and functional alterations

associated with aging reduce the potential reserve capacity of the lung and offer a greater challenge to the maintenance of arterial homeostasis under conditions of unusual stress, e.g. prolonged heavy exercise, exposure to low environmental oxygen tension (altitude) and marked acid-base disturbances.

After the age of 30 there is a progressive linear loss of pulmonary function which has been demonstrated in cross-sectional studies. Longitudinal studies, though few in number, indicate a gradual decline until the sixth decade followed by an accelerated loss (5, 12). However, generalizations are difficult to make because there are marked variations in the rate of change with age in the basic gas exchange areas of the lung (36,50), and the structural changes are not always associated with loss of function (59). Where significant loss of function does occur, it may be the result of a change in activity habitus or life style.

## MORPHOLOGICAL CHANGES

Aging is associated with a general disintegration of the supporting fibrous network so that the lungs appear smaller, lighter, and fluffier (Fig. 1) (20,36,50,77). The basic processes include a degeneration or atrophy of the alveolar-septal membrane (50,20,36), enlargement of the alveoli and alveolar ducts (77,58), and a general reduction of the substance of the lung (20) (Table 1). These processes may occur in only one area of a single terminal respiratory unit, and, although the resulting parenchymal pattern resembles that seen in mild panicar "emphysema" (20), it is more uniformly distributed throughout the lung, does not result in air-trapping (20,50), and is not seen in the chest radiograph (20). This pattern has been most commonly described as a degenerative process attributed to aging and is primarily seen in individuals over 60 years of age.

In advanced age there is a loss of functioning alveoli and associated capillary network which results in a decrease in the surface area available for alveolar-capillary gas exchange. The total alveolar surface area of a normal adult at age 20 is about 80 $M^2$, of which 85-95% is covered with pulmonary capillaries (77), presenting an alveolar capillary interface of approximately 70 $M^2$. A steady decline of 0.27 $M^2$/year

TABLE 1

MORPHOLOGICAL CHANGES IN THE THORAX AND LUNG WITH AGE

| MORPHOLOGICAL CHANGE | FUNCTIONAL SIGNIFICANCE | REFERENCE |
|---|---|---|
| **THORAX:** | | |
| Calcification of bronchial and costal cartilage | ↑ resistance to deformation of chest wall (↑ elastic work) | 36,55,64 |
| ↑ stiffness in costo-vertebral joints | ↑ use of diaphragm in ventilation | 67,20 |
| ↑ rigidity of chest wall | | 40 |
| ↑ anterior-posterior diameter (kyphosis) | ↓ tidal volume response to exercise hyperpnea | 48,20 |
| Wasting of respiratory muscles | ↓ maximal voluntary ventilation | 59 |
| **LUNG:** | | |
| Enlarged alveolar ducts | ↓ surface area for gas exchange | 77,58 |
| ↓ supporting duct framework, enlarged alveoli | ↓ pulmonary diffusing capacity | 78,20,51 |
| Thinning, separation of alveolar membrane | ↑ physiological dead space | 36,50,52 |
| ↑ mucous gland | | 29 |
| ↓ number, thickness of elastic fibers (?) | ↓ lung elastic recoil<br>↓ VC, RV/TLC%<br>↓ ventilatory flow rate<br>↓ ventilation distribution<br>↑ resistance to flow in small airways | 78 |
| ↓ tissue extensibility (alveolar wall) | | |
| ↓ pulmonary capillary network | | 66 |
| ↑ fibrosis of pulmonary capillary intima | ↓ ventilation: blood flow equality | 50,52 |
| ↑ fibrosis of pulmonary capillary intima | | 73,36 |

has been estimated, which is consistent with an age related decline in pulmonary diffusing capacity (51).

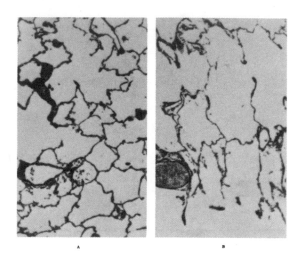

Figure 1.   Photomicrograph of alveolar regions:   (A) Male, aged 19; (B)  Female, aged 79; showing an increase in alveolar size (X120) (20).  Reprinted with permission of the publishers.

## FUNCTIONAL CHANGES

Perhaps the most significant functional changes in the respiratory system with age are the decline in the static elastic recoil force of the lung and the resistance to deformation of the chest wall (which includes the diaphragm and abdomen as well as the rib cage).  The opposing forces exerted by the tendency of the lung to recoil inward and the chest wall to expand outward are balanced at the end of a normal expiration or at functional residual capacity (FRC).  As the lung expands during inspiration, the elastic recoil pressure or force exerted by lung tissue increases and assists in expiration. The loss of recoil force of the lung with age means that less pressure or force by the chest wall is needed to affect a change in volume of the lung (an increase in lung compliance). Figure 2 summarizes the change with age in the static elastic recoil pressure of the lung at 60% of the total lung capacity (TLC).  The recoil pressure increases until cessation of somatic growth and then declines gradually.  The recoil force

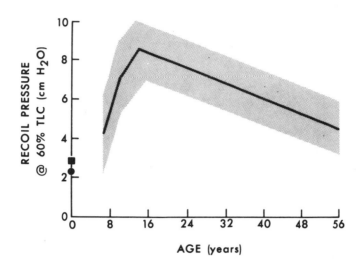

Figure 2. Static elastic recoil at 60 percent total lung
capacity (TLC) as a function of age. Shaded area
represents $\pm$ 1 standard deviation of mean values.
Mean values in newborn period (42). Reprinted
with permission of the publishers.

of the lung is derived from: (1) surface active material
lining the terminal respiratory units, and (2) tissue forces,
the elastin and collagen proteins. There is no evidence that
the surface active forces alter their basic mechanical behavior with age (42). Although connective tissue elements
account for 30% of the retractile force in an air-filled
lung, their role is not clear (72,42,9,66). The alveolar
septa and both large and small airways contain elastin, which
elongates or thins during inspiration, and collagen, which
'uncoils,' apparently serving as a check to prevent an over-
stretch (72). Although there is no apparent change with age
in protein content (48,9), a uniform reduction in both the
number and thickness of elastic fibers, particularly in
alveoli and alveolar ducts(78), loss of alveolar wall exten-
sibility (66), and an increase in co-polymerization of these

fibrous proteins with age (9), would all contribute to a reduction in the elastic properties of the lung. The functional
consequences of an increased lung compliance with age include
an alteration in lung volume and a decrease in both expiratory
flow rate and ventilation distribution in conjunction with
early closure of small airways at low lung volumes.

Contrary to the increase in lung compliance, chest wall
compliance shows a progressive reduction from 24-78 years
(40). The reduction in compliance or "stiffness" of the chest
wall is related to structural changes within the rib cage and
its articulations and to an altered thoracic diameter (kyphosis) (Table 1). Therefore, in the region of spontaneous
breathing, the compliance of the lungs increases with age
while that of the chest wall decreases (72,40). The reduction
in chest wall compliance is somewhat greater than the increase
in lung compliance, so that the compliance of the total lung:
thorax system is actually less in a 60 year old (72,40).
This change in compliance requires the older individual to
perform 20% more work to overcome elastic resistance than a
20 year old, and, at a given level of ventilation, he would
expend 70% of his total elastic work on the chest wall compared to only 40% in the 20 year old (72).

## LUNG VOLUME - VENTILATORY FLOW RATES

Both static and dynamic lung volumes are significantly affected by smoking and activity habitus (59); and, although
most regressions show a gradual decline in these functions
with age, many studies indicate a non-linear phenomenon, with
a more pronounced decline after age 50-60 (5,64). Static
lung volumes are determined by the elastic properties of the
lung and chest wall and the strength of the respiratory
muscles. Quantitative changes are outlined in Table 2.
Total lung capacity (TLC) is essentially unchanged with age
indicating sufficient inspiratory muscle force to overcome
the inward forces of the lung and chest wall. However, with
the loss of sufficient distending force applied to the lung
parenchyma, due to a compression of small airways at low
lung volumes (an increase in airway resistance) (56), the
residual volume (RV) increases from approximately 20% to 50%
of the TLC from age 25 to 60 (31).

As a consequence of the increasing RV, vital capacity (VC) also decreases; and the combined effect of altered chest wall and lung recoil forces results in a slight increase in end-expiratory or relaxation volume of the respiratory system (FRC) with age (41). At high lung volumes (at or near TLC), maximal expiratory flow is determined by subject effort and respiratory muscle force, in addition to the recoil force of the lung and the magnitude and distribution of airway resistance. Maximal flow at or near mid lung volume (60% VC) is independent of driving force or subject effort once a threshold is reached, and dependent upon recoil force and way resistance (56,47). Both maximal expiratory flow rate ($FEV_{1.0}$ and % VC) and flow rate in the effort independent range of the forced vital capacity ($\dot{V}_{max}$ 50) are significantly reduced with age (Table 2). In addition, the ability to sustain a maximal voluntary level of ventilation (MVV) is also reduced with age (41,65), presumably due to the loss of respiratory muscle force. The inability to sustain a high level of ventilation at rest is directly related to the maximal level of ventilation that may be achieved during exercise (55).

The reduction in pulmonary elastic recoil with age may also result in a non-uniformity of the mixing of inspiratory air in dependent portions of the lung where either airway closure or areas of no flow (the 'closing volume' - CV) exist (34,42,45,11). In older individuals (over 60 years), the closing volume, expressed as a percent of vital capacity, may actually exceed FRC. If this occurs, the terminal units of the closed airways will not be continuously ventilated during normal tidal breathing ($V_T$) (35). However, breathing maneuvers which involve a greater portion of the VC may improve the uniformity of ventilation because the $V_T$ and FRC combined would exceed the closing volume (19). Therefore, although early closure may be present at rest, the increase in mean lung volume that is reached during moderate to heavy exercise may prevent airway closure in the dependent portions of the lung and improve uniformity of gas distribution (59).

ALVEOLAR-ARTERIAL GAS EXCHANGE

The rapid rise in arterial oxygen tension ($PaO_2$) from birth to cessation of somatic growth and the subsequent decline with

TABLE 2

ALTERATIONS IN LUNG VOLUME AND VENTILATORY FLOW RATE WITH
AGE:   REPRESENTATIVE VALUES FOR (A) 20 AND (B) 60 YEAR OLD
INDIVIDUALS STANDARDIZED FOR HEIGHT AND WEIGHT

| FUNCTION | A | | B | | REFERENCE |
|---|---|---|---|---|---|
| | MEN | WOMEN | MEN | WOMEN | |
| Total lung capacity ($\ell$) | 7.20 | 5.10 | 6.90 | 4.70 | 72,43 |
| Vital Capacity ($\ell$) | 5.20 | 4.17 | 4.00 | 3.29 | 41,43 |
| Functional Residual Capacity ($\ell$) | 2.20 | 2.40 | 3.50 | 2.50 | 43,42 |
| Residual Volume % TLC | 25% | 28% | 40% | 40% | 42,43,45, 31 |
| Forced Expiratory Volume (One-second) | | | | | |
| a) $\ell$/BTPS | 4.45 | 3.26 | 3.17 | 2.26 | 41 |
| b) % VC | 81% | 80% | 71% | 70% | |
| Max. Vol. Vent. ($\ell$/min) | 150 | 110 | 99 | 77 | 41 |
| $\dot{V}_{max}$ 50 ($\ell$/sec) | 5.00 | 4.40 | 3.80 | 2.70 | 11 |
| Closing Volume (% VC) | 8% | 8% | 25% | 25% | 45,33,11,8 |
| Recoil Pressure of Lung at 60% TLC (cm $H_2O$) | 7.8 | Same | 4.4 | Same | 72,40 |
| Recoil Pressure of Chest Wall at 60% TLC (cm $H_2O$) | -6.0 | Same | -4.0 | Same | 72,40 |

age, parallels the reduction in lung elastic recoil over the same period (44,37,69,63) (Figure 2). Although the relationship is similar, a considerable variation exists in measures of $PaO_2$ with age due to subject selection (hospitalized patients without pulmonary disease) and sampling posture (44, 14). The loss of elastic recoil and subsequent closure of the dependent airways decreases ventilation to the distal gas exchange units, and, to a lesser extent, may also affect perfusion (26). As a result, a ventilation:perfusion ($\dot{V}_A/\dot{Q}$) imbalance is created and may be the primary reason for the reduction of $PaO_2$ with age (39,27,42). Under resting conditions, regardless of age, there is considerable inhomogeneity in the $\dot{V}_A/\dot{Q}$ of gas exchange units in different regions of the lung (74,22). In older individuals, the normal uneven distribution of air:blood is exaggerated so that there is a broader distribution of $\dot{V}_A/\dot{Q}$ units, particularly with the blood flow distribution skewed toward units with low ventilation (74,16). Although this unequal distribution has been shown with inert gas techniques, radioactive techniques show no topographical or interregional differences in $\dot{V}_A/\dot{Q}$ with age (26,10,34), presumably because of overlapping of normal and abnormal units within any lung region.

There is some evidence that the alveolar-arterial $PO_2$ difference increases with age (69) and the adequacy with which perfused alveoli are ventilated ($\dot{V}_A/\dot{Q}$) is the primary determinant of this difference. The normal A-a $PO_2$ difference of 10 mm Hg that is found in young adults, has been attributed to a $\dot{V}_A/\dot{Q}$ inhomogeneity of 6 mm Hg and to anatomically shunted blood of 4 mm Hg (22). The observed increase in the A-a $PO_2$ difference with age may be due to a greater proportional increase in the anatomical shunt (32). The increased shunt may be attributed to a reduction in mixed venous oxygen content as a consequence of an age-related decrease in cardiac output (42). Although the pulmonary diffusing capacity declines approximately 33% from age 20 to 60 (1,2,51), it is not considered a significant factor in the A-a $PO_2$ difference at rest as the entire difference may be attributed to $\dot{V}_A/\dot{Q}$ inequality and anatomical shunt when no diffusion disequilibrium is assumed (84,22).

Unlike arterial oxygen tension, once arterial $PCO_2$ and pH reach adult values of 40 mm Hg and 7.40 shortly after birth, they remain relatively constant throughout life. However, a two-fold recovery time to restore arterial pH after oral administration of ammonium chloride (60) suggests a reduction in the ability to restore equilibrium following a marked disturbance in acid-base balance. A significant reduction in ventilatory response to both hypoxia ($PO_2$) and hypercapnia ($PCO_2$) has also been shown in older subjects (64-73 years) (33). The diminished ventilatory drive was accompanied by a significant bradycardia. Alteration in peripheral chemoreceptor function may be only one of several possible reasons for this attenuated response, however, it indicates that the onset of hypoxia, for example, may not be signalled by respiratory distress or tachycardia.

## RESPIRATORY ADAPTATION TO EXERCISE

In young adults the respiratory system contributes to the maintenance of oxygen transport even during maximal exercise by means of a near optimal response of alveolar ventilation, lung and chest wall mechanics, and alveolar-arterial gas exchange. However, in the older individual, alterations in lung and chest wall compliance and $\dot{V}_A/\dot{Q}$ inequality that have been outlined at rest may increase the cost of assuring adequate alveolar ventilation or impose limitations on oxygen transport during increased metabolic demands.

The maximal oxygen intake (max $\dot{V}O_2$) declines with age, beginning at about 20 years in men, perhaps a little later in women, so that by age 65 it has declined approximately 35% (59). The rate of decline may be attenuated by the health history and activity habitus of the population studied but there is fairly good agreement between cross-sectional and longitudinal studies (49,5,59,62). The maximal ventilation ($\dot{V}_E$) achieved during maximal volitional effort is reduced, but appears to be coupled to, rather than limiting, the max $\dot{V}O_2$ (24,25,59).

## VENTILATION

Resting ventilation and its components breathing frequency ($\dot{f}$) and tidal volume ($V_T$) are directly related to the resting metabolic rate which tends to decrease slightly with age.

The respiratory minute volume ($\dot{V}_E$) responds to the increasing
metabolic demands of exercise in a similar manner in both
young and older individuals (59) (Figure 3). However, the
older individual has a higher ventilatory response at a given
submaximal metabolic demand ($\dot{V}_E/\dot{V}O_2$) (59,54,5,17,6), an
earlier onset of anaerobic metabolism, hence an earlier hyperventilation (70,71,76,59) and a reduction in maximal $\dot{V}_E$ (62,
59,6,7,54,17). In addition, both the time required to reach a
steady state level of $\dot{V}_E$ at the onset of exercise (54,70,71),
and the time to return to resting levels following a period
of moderate to severe exercise (54,60,61,70,71) increase with
age.

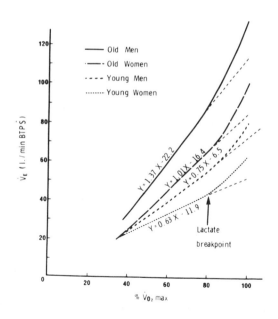

<u>Figure 3</u>.    Relationships between expired ventilation ($\dot{V}_E$) and
            percentage of aerobic power (% max $\dot{V}O_2$) during pro-
            gressive (5 minute/grade) treadmill walking in
            elderly persons. Comparison with young adults
            (59). Reprinted with permission of the publisher.

The mechanical work performed by the lung and chest wall is maintained within their maximal capacities by an appropriate choice of breathing frequency and tidal volume so that both elastic ($\uparrow V_T$) and flow resistive work ($\uparrow f$) are minimized (24,25). However, with age, the loss of elastic recoil and $\uparrow$FRC may inhibit the "effective" range of $V_T$ and early airway 'closure' ($\uparrow$CV % VC) may inhibit expiratory flow. deVries (17) has described a ventilatory response to progressive exercise in older men (69 years) in which the $V_T$ increases to near maximal levels at low levels of $\dot{V}_E$ and then plateaus to maximal volitional effort. The increase in $V_T$ would increase inspiratory flow and elastic work. On the other hand, the increase in $V_T$ would increase flow while the lung is displaced toward the upper portion of the pressure-volume curve where flow resistance is less and there is greater elastic recoil pressure to enhance expiratory flow (24). However, if the maximal $V_T$ exceeds 55-60% of the VC during exercise, dyspnea or shortness of breath ensues (13). The loss of VC that occurs with senescence would reduce the potential $V_T$ that may be reached during maximal exercise and, indeed, both the $V_T$ and VC are reduced with age (30,17).

Regardless of age, the dependence upon breathing frequency in moderate to heavy exercise indicates an increase in flow-resistive work. During expiration, airflow increases with an increase in pleural pressure and, at a given lung volume, there is a maximal pressure beyond which airflow does not increase further because of dynamic compression of the airways (47). If pleural pressure exceeds that level, ventilation may be "inefficient" in that there will be an increased work of breathing (to create more pressure) without an increase in air flow (47). At rest, only a minor fraction of the potential lung volume and flow changes are used and even during maximum exercise the maximal inspiratory and expiratory flow rates and volumes are not usually reached in sedentary young men (24,25). However, with increasing age, the maximum flow-volume curve becomes more curvilinear (38), so that, during moderate to heavy exercise the expiratory flow achieved during a tidal breath may be limited (24,25).

The ability to sustain a high $\dot{V}_E$ for any period of time is also dependent to a certain extent upon the strength and endurance of the respiratory muscles. For example, the maximum $\dot{V}_E$ that can be sustained during exercise has been estimated to be approximately 60% of the maximal voluntary ventilation (MVV) achieved at rest (56,55,57). A predicted MVV for a 60 year old man is approximately 130 l/min (65), which would suggest that he could sustain a ventilation of at least 78 l/min for a period of 15 minutes (56,55). This value exceeds the reported maximum $\dot{V}_E$ attained by men (63 l/min) in their 60's (59,54), suggesting that, although the maximum $\dot{V}_E$ is decreased with age, some 'reserve' remains to provide an adequate level of alveolar ventilation. Regardless of age, dyspnea may be associated with respiratory muscle fatigue resulting from a high sustained ventilatory activity or an increase in muscle weakness (57). Although the diaphragm is the predominant force at rest, during increasing exercise, contributions by the rib cage and abdomen reduce the diaphragmmatic load and, during active expiration the abdominal muscles assist the diaphragm to operate on a more favorable portion of its force-length characteristic (24,25). Because of increased stiffness in the rib cage with age, an altered rib cage-abdominal pattern may result and an increased proportion of ventilation would be undertaken by the diaphragm (53). More information is needed on whether the diaphragm or accessory muscles become fatigued or their coordination fails during sustained ventilatory activity. However, exertional dyspnea has often been reported as the reason for terminating a max $\dot{V}O_2$ test in older individuals (25,29).

## ALVEOLAR-CAPILLARY GAS EXCHANGE

The alveolar ventilation ($\dot{V}_A$) attained at rest and during exercise is a smaller fraction of the total ventilation in the aged due to an increase in dead space ventilation (69,13,59). The pulmonary diffusing capacity ($D_L$) is also reduced somewhat with age as a result of poorer ventilation distribution and loss of overall gas exchange surface (18,1,46). However, the higher $\dot{V}_E$ at a given level of $VO_2$ (mentioned previously) would assure an adequate diffusion gradient (alveolar to mean capillary $PO_2$). As with the young healthy individual, $D_L$ has been shown to rise linearly with increasing $\dot{V}O_2$ with no

evidence of leveling off up to a moderate exercise load (46).
An increase in the slope of $D_L$ from rest to exercise suggests
the $\dot{V}_A/\dot{Q}$ inhomogeneity responsible for the reduced $PaO_2$ described at rest (74) is proportionately less during exercise
and that adequate gas exchange is not significantly compromised in the healthy older adult (45).

The alveolar-arterial $PO_2$ difference widens with exercise
in middle-aged men similar to that in younger adults (28).
Evidence against the widening of the A-a $PO_2$ difference with
age includes a more uniform topographical distribution of
$\dot{V}_A/\dot{Q}$ with mild exercise (16), secondary to an increase in pulmonary artery pressure (68,21) and an increase in peak inspiratory flow to produce more uniform ventilation distribution (24,25). Although an improved overall $\dot{V}_A/\dot{Q}$ response is
similar to that reported in young subjects (22,26,74,16)
more information on older populations is needed. For example,
although overall $\dot{V}_A/\dot{Q}$ improves with exercise, low $\dot{V}_A/\dot{Q}$ units
within specific lung regions are sufficient to account for approximately one-half of the total A-a $PO_2$ difference during
exercise in young healthy subjects (22) and the contribution
of this intraregional inhomogeneity may be increased with age
due to an increased a-v $O_2$ difference and hence lower mixed
venous $PO_2$.

## SUMMARY

Although structural and functional changes associated with age
result in a decline in respiratory function, the degree and
rate of loss is variable and dependent upon the overall health
status of the individual and may be altered somewhat by the
individual's activity habitus. Healthy individuals of advanced age with the ability to sustain sufficient exercise intensity may increase their aerobic capacity with physical
training, which is accompanied rather than determined by an
increase in ventilatory capacity (45,17). Regardless of age,
adaptations of lung volume, ventilatory flow rate and alveolar-capillary gas exchange have not been consistently demonstrated with physical training (59,46) which supports the
contention that the lung:thorax system (with few exceptions)
has a near optimum response to steady-state exercise and that
oxygen transport is more critically dependent upon

cardiovascular function.

However, the tendency with age toward early airway closure and subsequent abnormalities in both ventilation distribution and lung perfusion present a challenge to gas exchange. This is especially true in the old-old individual (over 75 years) where this condition may be exacerbated due to a very low level of daily activity (estimated max $\dot{V}O_2$ = 9.0 ml/kg). Much more information is needed on the integrated cardio-respiratory function in this age group.

Regardless of age, more information is needed on the mechanisms that underlie the coupling of ventilation to exercise intensity. The integrated role of the diaphragm, chest wall and abdominal muscles in producing an adequate alveolar ventilation at minimal cost with a loss of lung compliance and an increase in rigidity of the rib cage needs to be elucidated. In addition, the integrated role of the rib cage and abdomen and subsequent choice of breathing frequency and tidal volume in "exertional dyspnea" need to be studied not only as a function of age but in the general population.

Finally, the available information suggests that the 'pulmonary reserve' capabilities in a healthy older adult are reduced and that there is less room for error in their control systems. Examples include the reduction in ventilatory responsiveness to both hypoxia and hypercapnia, prolonged recovery from exercise and other acid-base disturbances, reduction in immunological surveillance and possible susceptibility to certain lung diseases, and prolonged recovery from the anesthesia of surgery.

## REFERENCES

1. Anderson, T.W. and R.J. Shephard. Physical training and exercise diffusing capacity. Int. Z. angew. Physiol. 25:189-209, 1968.

2. Anderson, T.W. and R.J. Shephard. The effects of hyperventilation and exercise upon the pulmonary diffusing capacity. Respiration 25:465-484, 1968.

3. Anthonisen, N.R., J. Danson, P.C. Robertson and W.R.D. Ross. Airway closure as a function of age. Resp. Physiol. 8:58-65, 1969.

4. Anthonisen, N.R., M.B. Dolovich and D.V. Bates. Steady-state measurement of regional ventilation to perfusion ratios in normal man. J. Clin. Invest. 45:1349-1356, 1966.

5. Assmussen, E., K. Fruensgaard and S. Norgaard. A followup longitudinal study of selected physiologic functions in former physical education students after forty years. J. Am. Ger. Soc. 23:442-450, 1975.

6. Astrand, I. Aerobic work capacity in men and women with special reference to age. Acta Physiol. Scand. 49, Suppl. 169:1-92, 1960.

7. Astrand, I., P.O. Astrand, I. Hallbäck and A. Kilböm. Reduction in maximal oxygen uptake with age. J. Appl. Physiol. 35:649-654, 1973.

8. Begin, R., A.D. Renzetti, A. Bigler and S. Watanabe. Flow and age dependence of airway closure and dynamic compliance. J. Appl. Physiol. 38:199-207, 1975.

9. Boucek, R.J., N.L. Noble and A. Marcks. Age and the fibrous proteins of the human lung. Gerontologia 5:150-157, 1961.

10. Bristow, G.K. and B.W. Kirk. Venous admixture and lung water in healthy subjects over 50 years of age. J. Appl. Physiol. 30:552-557, 1971.

11. Buist, A.S. and B.B. Ross. Predicted values for closing volumes using a modified single breath nitrogen test. Am. Rev. Resp. Dis. 107: 744-752, 1973.

12. Cole, T.J. The influence of height on the decline in ventilatory function. Int. J. Epidem. 3:145-152, 1974.

13. Cotes, J.E. Lung Function. Asessment and Application in Medicine. Oxford: Blackwell Scientific, 1965.

14. Craig, D.B., W. Wahba, H. Don, J. Couture and M. Becklake. "Closing volume" and its relationship to gas exchange in seated and supine positions. J. Appl. Physiol. 31:717-721, 1971.

15. Dempsey, J.A., E. Vidruk and S. Mastenbrook. Pulmonary control systems in exercise. Fed. Proc. 39:29-37, 1980.

16. Derks, C.M. Ventilation-perfusion distribution and young and old volunteers during mild exercise. Bull. Europ. Physiopath. Resp. 16: 143-154, 1980.

17. deVries, H.A. and G.M. Adams. Comparison of exercise responses in old and young men. II. Ventilatory mechanics. J. Gerontol. 27: 349-352, 1972.

18. Donevan, R.E., W.H. Palmer, C.J. Varvis and D.V. Bates. Influence of age on pulmonary diffusing capacity. J. Appl. Physiol. 14: 783-792, 1955.

19. Edelman, N.H., C. Mittman, A.H. Norris and N.W. Shock. Effects of respiratory pattern on age differences in ventilation uniformity. J. Appl. Physiol. 24:59-63, 1968.

20. Edge, J.R., F.J.C. Millard, L. Reid and G. Simon. The radiographic appearance of the chest in persons of advanced age. Brit. J. Radiol. 37:769-774, 1964.

21. Emirgil, C., B.J. Sobol, S. Campodonico, W.H. Herbert and R. Mechtaki. Pulmonary circulation in the aged. J. Appl. Physiol. 23: 631-640, 1967.

22. Gledhill, N., A. Froese and J. Dempsey. Ventilation to perfusion distribution during exercise in health. In: Muscular Exercise and the Lung, edited by J. Dempsey and C. Reed. Madison: University of Wisconsin Press, pp. 325-344, 1977.

23. Goldman, M., G. Grimby and J. Mead. Mechanical work of breathing derived from rib cage and abdominal V-P partitioning. J. Appl. Physiol. 41:764-775, 1976.

24. Grimby, G. Pulmonary mechanics: The load. In: Muscular Exercise and the Lung, edited by J.A. Dempsey and C. Reed. Madison: University of Wisconsin Press, pp. 17-24, 1976.

25. Grimby, G. and J. Stiksa. Flow-volume curves and breathing patterns during exercise in patients with obstructive lung disease. Scand. J. Clin. Lab. Invest. 24:303-313, 1970.

26. Harf, A. and J.M.B. Hughes. Topographical distribution of $\dot{V}_A/\dot{Q}$ in elderly subjects using Krypton-81 m. Resp. Physiol. 34:319-327, 1978.

27. Harris, E.A., E. Seelye and R.M. Whitlock. The normal alveolar-arterial oxygen-tension gradient in man. Clin. Sci. Mol. Med. 46:89-104, 1974.

28. Hartley, L.H., G. Grimby, A. Kilböm, N.J. Nilsson, I. Astrand, J. Bjure, B. Ekblom and B. Saltin. Physical training in sedentary middle-aged and older men. III. Cardiac output and gas exchange at submaximal and maximal exercise. Scand. J. Clin. Lab. Invest. 24:335-344, 1969.

29. Hernandez, J.A., A. Anderson, W. Holmes, N. Morrone and A. Foraker. The bronchial glands in aging. J. Am. Ger. Soc. 13:799-804, 1965.

30. Jammes, Y., Y. Auran, J. Gouvernet, S. Delpierre and C. Grimaud. The ventilatory pattern of conscious man according to age and morphology. Bull. Europ. Physiopath. Resp. 15:527-540, 1979.

31. Jones, R.L., T. Overton, D. Hammerlindel and B.J. Sproule. Effects of age in regional residual volume. J. Appl. Physiol.: Respirat. Environ. Exer. Physiol. 44:195-199, 1978.

32. Kanber, G.J., F. King, Y. Eschar and J.T. Sharp. The alveolar-arterial oxygen gradient in young and elderly men during air and oxygen breathing. Am. Rev. Resp. Dis. 97:376-381, 1968.

33. Kronenberg, R.S. and C.W. Drage. Attenuation of the ventilatory and heartrate responses to hypoxia and hypercapnia with aging in normal men. J. Clin. Invest. 52:1812-1819, 1973.

34. Kronenberg, R.S., P. L'Heureux, R.A. Ponto, C.W. Drage and M.K. Loken. The effect of aging on lung perfusion. Ann. Int. Med. 76:413-421, 1972.

35. LeBlanc, P., F. Ruff and J. Milic-Emili. Effects of age and body position on 'airway closure' in man. J. Appl. Physiol. 28:448-451, 1970.

36. Liebow, A.A. Biochemical and structural changes in the aging lung. Summary. In: Aging of the Lung, edited by L. Cander and J.H. Moyer. New York: Grune and Stratton, pp. 97-104, 1964.

37. Mansell, A., C. Bryan and H. Levison. Airway closure in children. J. Appl. Physiol. 33:711-714, 1922.

38. Mead, J., J. Turner, P. Macklem and J. Little. Significance of the relationship between lung recoil and maximum expiratory flow. J. Appl. Physiol. 22:95-108, 1967.

39. Mellemgaard, K. The alveolar-arterial oxygen difference: Its size and components in normal man. Acta Physiol. Scand. 67:10-20, 1966.

40. Mittman, C., N.H. Edelman, A.H. Norris and N.W. Shock. Relationship between chest wall and pulmonary compliance and age. J. Appl. Physiol. 20:1211-1216, 1965.

41. Morris, J.F., A. Koski and L.C. Johnson. Spirometric standards for healthy non-smoking adults. Am. Rev. Resp. Dis. 103:57-67, 1971.

42. Murray, J.F. The Normal Lung. Philadelphia: W.B. Saunders Co., p. 334, 1976.

43. Needham, C.D., M.C. Rogan and I. McDonald. Normal standards for lung volumes, intra-pulmonary gas mixing and maximum breathing capacity. Thorax 9:313-325, 1954.

44. Neufeld, O., J. Smith and S. Goldman. Arterial oxygen tension in relation to age in hospital subjects. J. Am. Ger. Soc. 21:4-9, 1973.

45. Niinimaa, V. and R.J. Shephard. Training and oxygen conductance in the elderly. I. The respiratory system. J. Gerontol. 33:354-361, 1978.

46. Niinimaa, V. and R.J. Shephard. Training and oxygen conductance in the elderly. II. The cardiovascular system. J. Gerontol. 33:362-367, 1978.

47. Olafsson, S. and R. Hyatt. Ventilatory mechanics and expiratory flow limitation during exercise in normal subjects. J. Clin. Invest. 48: 564-573, 1969.

48. Pierce, J.A. and R.V. Ebert. Fibrous network of the lungs and its change with age. Thorax 20:469-476, 1965.

49. Plowman, S., B. Drinkwater and S. Horvath. Age and aerobic power in women: A longitudinal study. J. Gerontol. 34:512-520, 1979.

50. Pump, K.K. The aged lung. Chest 60:571-577, 1971.

51. Rankin, J., J.B.L. Gee and L.W. Chosy. The influence of age and smoking on pulmonary diffusing capacity in healthy subjects. Med. Thorac. 22:366-374, 1965.

52. Reid, L. The aged lung. In: The Pathology of Emphysema. London: Lloyd-Luke, 1967.

53. Rizzato, G. and L. Marrazini. Thoracoabdominal mechanics in elderly men. J. Appl. Physiol. 28:457-460, 1970.

54. Robinson, S. Experimental studies of physical fitness in relation to age. Arbeitsphysiol. 4:251-323, 1938.

55. Rochester, D.F. and N.T. Braun. The respiratory muscles. In: Basics of Respiratory Disease, Vol. 6. New York: American Thoracic Society, pp. 1-6, 1976.

56. Rodarte, J. and R.E. Hyatt. Respiratory mechanics. In: Basics of Respiratory Disease, Vol. 4. New York: American Thoracic Society, pp. 1-6, 1976.

57. Roussos, C.S. and D.T. Macklem. Diaphragmatic fatigue in man. J. Appl. Physiol. 43:189-197, 1977.

58. Ryan, S.F., T.N. Vincent, R.S. Mitchell, G.F. Filey and G. Dart. Ductectasia: An asymptomatic pulmonary change related to age. Med. Thorac. 22:181-187, 1965.

59. Shephard, R.J. Physical Activity and Aging. London: Croom Helm Ltd., 1978.

60. Shock, N.W. Physiological aspects of aging in man. Ann. Rev. Physiol. 23:97-166, 1961.

61. Shock, N.W. An essay on aging. In: Aging of the Lung, edited by L. Cander and J.H. Moyer. New York: Grune and Stratton, pp. 1-12, 1964.

62. Sidney, K.H. and R.J. Shephard. Maximum and submaximum exercise tests in men and women in the seventh, eighth and ninth decades of life. J. Appl. Physiol. 43:280-287, 1977.

63. Sorbini, C.A., V. Brassi, E. Solinas and G. Muiesan. Arterial oxygen tension in relation to age in healthy subjects. Resp. 25:3-13, 1968.

64. Stanescu, S. Investigations into changes of pulmonary function in the aged. Bull. Europ. Physiopath. Resp. 15:171-181, 1979.

65. Storstein, O. and A. Voll. New prediction formulas of ventilatory measurements: A study of normal individuals in the age group 20-59 years. Scand. J. Clin. Lab. Invest. 14:633-640, 1962.

66. Sugihara, T., C.J. Martin and J. Hildebrandt. Length-tension properties of alveolar wall in man. J. Appl. Physiol. 30:874-878, 1971.

67. Takahashi, E. and H. Atsumi. Age difference in thoracic forms as indicated by thoracic index. Human Biol. 27:65-74, 1955.

68. Tartulier, M., M. Bourret and F. Devrieux. Les pressions arterielles pulmonaires chez l'homme normal: effets de l'age et de l'exercice musculaire. Bull. Physio-Pathol. Respir. 8:1295-1321, 1975.

69. Tenney, S.M. and R.M. Miller. Dead space ventilation in old age. J. Appl. Physiol. 9:321-327, 1956.

70. Tlusty, L. Physical fitness in old age. I. Aerobic capacity and other parameters of physical fitness followed by means of exercise in ergometric examination of elderly individuals. Resp. 26:161-181, 1969.

71. Tlusty, L. Physical fitness in old age. II. Anaerobic capacity, anaerobic work in graded exercise, recovery after maximum work performance in elderly individuals. Resp. 26:287-299, 1969.

72. Turner, J.M., J. Mead and M.E. Wohl. Elasticity of human lungs in relation to age. J. Appl. Physiol. 35:664-671, 1968.

73. Wagenvoort, C.A. and N. Wagenvoort. Age changes in muscular pulmonary arteries. Arch. Path. 79:524-528, 1965.

74. Wagner, P., R. Laravuso, R. Uhl and J.B. West. Continuous contributions of ventilation-perfusion ratios in normal subjects breathing air and 100% $O_2$. J. Clin. Invest. 54:54-68, 1974.

75. Waldorf, D.S., R.F. Willkins and J.L. Decker. Impaired delayed hypersensitivity in an aging population. J. Am. Med. Assoc. 203:831-834, 1968.

76. Wasserman, K., B.J. Whipp, S.N. Koyal and W.L. Beaver. Anaerobic threshold and respiratory gas exchange during exercise. J. Appl. Physiol. 35:326-343, 1973.

77. Weibel, E.R. Morphometrics of the lung. In: Handbook of Physiology, edited by W.O. Fenn and H. Rahn. Washington, D.C.: American Physiological Society, pp. 238-306, 1964.

78. Wright, R.R. Elastic tissue of normal and emphysematous lungs. A tridimensional histologic study. Am. J. Pathol. 39:355-367, 1961.

# PHYSICAL ACTIVITY PROGRAMMING FOR THE AGED
Charles E. Morse and Everett L. Smith

Physical activity programming for the older adult requires
more care and thought than for any other age group. This is
necessary in part because of the dire medical consequences of
incorrect or thoughtless programming. The wide spectrum of
physical abilities displayed by older adults also indicates
the need for special program considerations. In particular,
it is necessary to distinguish between the "young" old (those
persons who seem little affected by their age and who continue with lifelong activity habits) and the "old" old (those
persons who are hindered by a variety of age-related disorders
which mentally or physically limit their physical capacity).
While many older individuals are limited in their ability to
pursue regular physical activity, the need for a minimum level
of daily exercise to prevent the problems associated with
hypokinesia has been established (7,20). In developing a program of exercise for an older individual or group, therefore,
it is necessary to carefully balance the risks of physical activity with the risks of a sedentary lifestyle.

## TESTING
The importance of stress testing each older adult before he or
she begins an exercise program has been emphasized (see Shephard, this text). The purpose of such a test is to identify
those individuals who are at high risk during moderately
strenuous exercise and to establish an appropriate level of
intensity at which exercise is to be pursued.
    The methods for testing the older adult are as varied as

the methods for testing the younger adult; treadmill, bicycle
and step tests have been used successfully with elderly subjects. Obvious differences in the older population, including
a greatly reduced aerobic capacity, limited ambulatory ability
and reduced neuromuscular function, suggest the need for a
modified testing method. Given the enhanced dangers associated with maximal exercise testing of sedentary elderly persons, stress testing has generally been limited to efforts up
to 75-85% of predicted maximum heart rate. Such a method of
testing is problematical, however, in that the prediction of
maximal $\dot{V}O_2$ is especially error prone in this population due
to variation in maximum heart rate (22). It has also been
shown that learning and habituation can result in substantial
changes in cardiovascular performance between two tests (19).
For this reason it is advised that two sessions be devoted to
testing if reliable measurements are sought for the purpose of
comparing pre- and post-training performance.

## TREADMILL TESTING

The Bruce Test has been used extensively in studies on ECG
changes with age and exercise (12,13,18,21). Although the
mean maximum subject age in these studies was 71 years, the
casual use of this test with older subjects is not advised.
This consideration is based on the prediction that the second
work load (2.5 mph, 12% grade) represents a maximal effort
(25 ml/Kg·min) for the average 70 year old male in the community.

Other studies involving elderly subjects have employed
protocols designed especially for an adult population. Stamford (25) screened candidates for a training study by having
the subjects walk at a constant speed (2.5 mph) and increasing
the grade 1% every 2 minutes, until the subject reached 80%
of his/her predicted maximum heart rate. Such a protocol,
though safe, is overly long for many older persons, lasting
up to 30 minutes. The same is true of the modified Balke
protocol which has been used with elderly women (6). A com-
promise between these methods is a protocol employed by Sidney
and Shephard (22,23). They walked elderly subjects at between
2.5 and 3.5 mph, adjusting the slope every 3 minutes. The
test was devised so that 75-85% of the maximum heart rate was

reached during the 9th minute of exercise. This method of treadmill testing is advisable because enough time is allowed for the subjects to stabilize at each work load and the length of the test is standard.

Many older people are limited by musculoskeletal disorders and/or display a reduction in neuromuscular coordination which present potential hazards in a treadmill test. However, some of these limitations may be overcome by test modifications. At the University of Wisconsin Biogerontology Laboratory we reduced the treadmill speed to 1.4 mph when measuring performance of nursing home residents. Even at these speeds, however, extensive orientation and warm-up was required before the subject achieved a semblance of a "natural gait." Many older adults required the assistance of a handrail, thus reducing the accuracy of metabolic cost predictions. Others were forced to terminate the test early because of pain in weightbearing joints. Still others suffered psychological and coincident physiological distress during the initial attempts to perform on the device.

## BICYCLE TESTING

For the reasons just mentioned many researchers have preferred to use the bicycle ergometer as the device for testing older subjects. The bicycle ergometer has the advantage of being weight supporting and allows the subject to maintain balance by holding onto handlebars. The subject also has the security of knowing that he or she may terminate the test at will and not have to worry about getting off a revolving belt. Other advantages are that the bicycle is less expensive than the treadmill, it is easy to transport and it does not always rely on the availability of electric power.

For the purpose of screening older individuals for abnormal responses to exercise, a continuous test is suggested that would involve 6 to 9 minutes of cycling. The subject should work up to 75-85% of his or her maximum predicted heart rate. Heart rate and ECG response as well as blood pressure may be measured relatively easily during exercise. It should be noted, however, that the bicycle may be unsuitable for subjects who suffer from leg pain or quadricep weakness, or those persons demonstrating poor coordination, resulting in lower mechanical efficiency.

## STEP TESTING

A stepping device is particularly useful for cardiovascular stress testing because of the common nature of the activity and the ease with which the subject can be oriented. The step test may also be adapted to test individuals of very low aerobic capacity and is a method that is unimposing and unthreatening. This method requires little calibration and is, by far, the least expensive. Problems with this method of testing, however, do exist. It is difficult to measure the blood pressure of the stepping subjects, and in the absence of ECG monitoring the pulse rate must be taken post-exercise, indicating the need for a discontinuous protocol. At high work loads, using a standard step height, the high frequency of stepping may result in some loss of efficiency.

A gradational step test involving increases in step height (15) or tests involving a single standard step height with progressive increases in cadence have been used to test elderly subjects. At our laboratory the latter method (using a step height of 4 to 12 inches, depending on individual ability) was able to provoke a heart rate response of 75-85% of the predicted maximum heart rate (at 24-30 steps/min). Also, the use of a handhold may be used to give support and provide security for the subject.

## PHYSICAL ACTIVITY PROGRAMMING

The optimum frequency, intensity, duration and mode of exercise for older adults depend to a large degree on the individual. Many older persons with cardiovascular disorders are limited to low exercise intensity and need to increase the frequency and/or duration of exercise to achieve the desired training benefits. Other older persons with musculoskeletal problems may be limited to modes of exercise such as swimming, walking or stationary bicycling.

The existence of a threshold level of intensity for training of older adults has been the subject of several articles (5,10). The determination of this level is important because exercise pursued at this intensity would insure cardiovascular improvement and at the same time minimize the risk

of injury due to over-exertion. The 60% level of intensity
(% of maximal $\dot{V}O_2$) has been shown to be effective in a number
of studies in which such training intensity was employed (1,
3,4,23,25). A training intensity of 50% proved effective in
a program involving chronically institutionalized geriatric
mental patients (25).

In general, there are three groups that must be considered when determining exercise intensity: 1) The "old" old,
those individuals (generally 75+ years) who need the support
environment of a nursing home, 2) the "young" old, persons
in the community (60-75 years) who still live in their own
home, and 3) the athletic old, the rare individuals who have
maintained a high degree of physical fitness and still participate in competitive sports events. Upon testing these individuals clear physiological groupings develop (Table 1).
The nursing home population averages from 2 to 4 METS on a
volitional maximal $\dot{V}O_2$ test, while the community population
averages 6 to 7 METS. The athletic old average 10+ METS.

TABLE 1

Maximal Volitional Treadmill Exercise Test in the Older Adult

| GROUPS | N | AGE | | $\dot{V}O_2$ (ml/kg·min) | | HEART RATE | |
|---|---|---|---|---|---|---|---|
| | | Mean | S.D. | Mean | S.D. | Mean | S.D. |
| Young Old | | | | | | | |
| Male | 13 | 72.15 | 4.26 | 20.12 | 2.82 | 130.69 | 8.69 |
| Female | 42 | 70.23 | 5.71 | 18.90 | 3.88 | 135.17 | 12.38 |
| Old Old | 24 | 84.54 | 6.15 | 9.51 | 2.52 | 114.79 | 13.20 |

Unpublished data collected at the University of Wisconsin-
Madison Biogerontology Laboratory, 1978-1980.

The frequency and duration of exercise are key elements
of the exercise prescription that have received little investigation within the older population. With younger subjects
it has been shown that the amount of improvement in maximal
$\dot{V}O_2$ is minimal when frequency is increased above 3 days per
week (8,16,17), with little change seen in persons exercising
less than two days per week (16). Although it appears that
older persons may also require at least two days of exercise

per week to show improvement (23), the tendency to exercise at lower intensity and shorter duration suggests that a frequency greater than 3 days per week might be in order.

Only one study, to date, has attempted to compare the effects of various exercise regimens on the cardiovascular fitness of older adults. Sidney and Shephard (23) analyzed improvement in subjects enrolled in a pre-retirement exercise program on the basis of the frequency of attendance and the intensity of effort (duration of exercise held constant). The results of the study indicated that intensity of effort was more highly correlated with improvement in physical work capacity over the first seven weeks of the program. After 14 weeks, however, improvement in physical capacity was similar for a low intensity/high frequency group and a high frequency/low intensity group. As was expected, the high frequency/high intensity group (greater than 3 times per week attendance and 70-80% intensity of maximum capacity) showed the greatest improvement. Those persons exercising about 1 time per week at 60% of the maximum predicted heart rate showed no improvement.

The mode of activity suggested for maintaining fitness in healthy adults by the American College of Sports Medicine is "any activity that uses large muscle groups, that can be maintained continuously and is rhythmical and aerobic in nature, e.g., running, jogging, walking-hiking, swimming, skating, bicycling, rowing, cross-country skiing, rope skipping and various endurance game activities" (2). There is reason to suggest that the mode of activity should be adapted for the older adult in view of the limitations mentioned. Because of the greater risk of injury in the older population, activities such as running-jogging, skating and cross country skiing are questionable. Rather, walking-hiking, swimming, various aerobic games and dancing would provide more appropriate modes of exercise.

A primary concern in developing an appropriate aerobic activity is that the participants enjoy the activity. Several factors should be considered when choosing an appropriate activity. First, in order to minimize risk of injury, age and ability level should dictate the mode of exercise for the individual or group. Second, one must consider the interests of the participants. Third, goals should be defined at the beginning of the program to point up the positive changes that result from the program. Fourth, the program leader should consider the social and psychological needs of the participants, developing a program that will maximize positive social contact and minimize negative competitive feelings and personality differences. This is not to say that all competition should be avoided among old people; many games such as shuffleboard and lawn bowling are highly popular, very likely because they include that element of sport that is dramatic and vital.

The importance of such games as shuffleboard and lawn bowling might be questioned as to their relevance to the physical fitness training of older adults. Although such activities involve only a small metabolic cost, the diminished aerobic capacity of these individuals is so low that the relative cost may have significance. These games may also be important in maintaining neuromuscular coordination (including balance and kinesthesis) and may aid in the prevention of muscle wasting (atrophy). Furthermore, if these activities are pursued for a long period of time they can amount to a significant total energy expenditure. It should be noted that for those persons suffering various cardiovascular disorders, such activities may be the only ones allowed by the personal physician.

In this light the importance of "chair" exercises is emphasized for those persons unable to engage in traditional aerobic activities. A number of books have been written on this subject whose authors develop programs designed around the chair, the floor or some other supporting medium or surface (see resource section of Serfass article, this text). Many of these exercises are devoted to maintenance of flexibility, strength, balance, kinesthetic sense and relaxation, elements of physical fitness that are equally as important as maintenance of aerobic capacity, especially in the older population.

## FITNESS TRAIL FOR OLDER ADULTS

In order to develop a program that satisfied the criteria for physical fitness training of adults set by the American College of Sports Medicine (2), and at the same time remain sensitive to the particular needs of the older population a strategy was developed by the recreational coordinator in Waukesha, Wisconsin in conjunction with researchers at the University of Wisconsin (9). With the knowledge that traditional aerobic training programs involve a high rate of attrition, and that among older people this attrition rate has been shown to be due to loss of interest as well as the recurrence of previous medical problems (4), the program leader attempted to create a program that was stimulating and challenging, but at the same time reduced the risk of injury to a minimum level.

The program convened in a county park, literally a minute's walk from the residence of many of the participants. The choice of the park setting was, in part, based on the knowledge that nearness to the exercise setting has a significant effect on attendance and attrition (26). Spouses and close friends were urged to attend with the knowledge that the positive attitude of the spouse towards exercise has a negative effect on attrition (11). The park setting also provided an esthetically pleasing environment in which to exercise. Shaded by a variety of trees and containing many winding paths, the park was bordered by a river and was decorated by colorful flower gardens. For the most part the terrain was level.

Noting the problems associated with hyperthermia in the elderly (14), the program convened early in the morning to avoid the hot midday hours. Subjects were also urged to dress lightly and to hydrate adequately during warm days.

Given the wide spectrum of physical abilities represented by the participants, small groups were formed (4-5 persons) representing different levels of fitness. Different trails were developed and marked for each group with the intent of having all groups finish the exercise session at the same time. The formation of groups required that individuals work together in recording their elapsed time and counting heart rates, and also fostered positive social interaction. Furthermore, each individual member felt a responsibility to the group to attend regularly and report promptly.

Some disadvantages were also noted with this method. These disadvantages related to the different personalities and motivational levels of individuals in the group, resulted in some disharmony and occasionally in a group's disintegration. Other groups were then formed.

## SAFETY
To insure that the individuals would face minimal risk as a result of participation in the program, a number of steps were taken. First, all persons were asked to be examined by their personal physicians prior to entry into the program. Second, a twelve lead ECG and a progressive submaximal treadmill test were given to each potential participant, the prescribed level of exercise being based on the safe attainment of that level during the stress test. Third, during the program blood pressures at rest were measured weekly, and pulse rates during exercise were monitored daily. Finally, there was constant supervision and observation by persons trained in CPR (with back-up emergency personnel and equipment on alert only minutes away).

## FITNESS TRAIL TRAINING
Training was conducted three days per week for 12 weeks, each session lasting approximately one hour. Each session began with a 10 to 15 minute warm-up (chair exercises, stretching), "briefing" on trail conditions, and general announcements of interest to the group. The participants then formed into their sub-groups and set off on the trail.

The trail itself was subdivided into quarter mile lengths with exercise stations located at these intervals. At the stations various tasks were performed, aimed at increasing strength and flexibility. Thus, walking was initially pursued at intervals with an exercise station located at the end of each interval. Many of the participants claimed that they required such "breaks" to "catch their breath." Later in the program, however, as walking distances were increased, continuous walking was pursued after 1 or 2 miles of interval work.

The first week of training was devoted to familiarization of the participants with the trail, the equipment at the exercise stations, and the recording procedures (each participant was required to keep a record of distance covered, elapsed

time and heart rates achieved). During the first week the
subjects walked an average of 1 mile. This distance was increased to 2 miles during the 4th week and to 3 miles in the
8th week. At the same time elapsed times and heart rates remained generally unchanged, suggesting the presence of a
training effect.

## PROBLEMS

Although the program ran smoothly with a very low attrition
rate (7%), several problems arose which bear mentioning. One
of the most irritating problems was the appearance of hordes
of mosquitoes incubated by the hot weather. This problem was
overcome, in part, by generous application of mosquito repel-
lant and also by faster, more continuous walking. Several
persons complained of persistent foot and knee soreness and
leg pain. One woman was forced to drop out of the program as
a result of persistent leg cramps. Others had to limit distances covered as a result of arthritic conditions. Some of
the male subjects were difficult to motivate, with one of
them admitting that he could see no purpose in all this
walking around.

## RESULTS AND CONCLUSIONS

Of the 30 subjects who began the program, 28 were able to
complete 12 weeks of exercise with no apparent ill effects.
One subject dropped out because of lack of interest. The
second could not continue because of a pre-existing vascular
disorder which resulted in severe leg pain after walking short
distances.

Post testing of the subjects revealed significant increases in both $O_2$ uptake at a heart rate of 130 and in predicted maximal $\dot{V}O_2$. At the same time blood pressure declined
significantly, at rest and at all workloads. The average
weight of the subjects was slightly reduced. Coincident with
these physiological changes, the subjects reported increased
vigor during and less fatigue following the second exercise
test.

The enthusiasm of the participants for the exercise program was made apparent by the hope expressed by many that the
program could somehow continue throughout the winter. The

summer program is now in its third year, with many of the original participants still walking.

It was concluded that the fitness trail is a safe, effective, inexpensive method for improving the aerobic fitness of elderly adults. The use of exercise stations also provided the opportunity for maintaining and improving upper body strength, flexibility and balance. Noting that several persons were plagued by musculoskeletal problems, the need for alternative programs involving weight-supporting modes of exercise (e.g., swimming, chair exercises) is apparent. Although the aerobic benefits of such alternative programs have not been determined, the reported benefits of improved mechanical functioning and enhanced body image are reason enough for further implementation and exploration of such programs with the elderly population.

## REFERENCES

1. Adams, G.M. and H.A. deVries. Physiological effects of an exercise training regimen upon women aged 52 to 79. J. Geront. 28:50-55, 1973.

2. American College of Sports Medicine. The recommended quantity and quality of exercise for developing and maintaining fitness in healthy adults. Sports Med. Bull. 13(3):1ff, 1978.

3. Barry, A.J., J.W. Daly, E.D.R. Pruett, J.R. Steinmetz, H.F. Page, N.C. Birkhead and K. Rodahl. The effects of physical conditioning on older individuals. I. Work capacity, circulatory-respiratory functions and work electrocardiogram. J. Geront. 21:182-191, 1966.

4. deVries, H.A. Physiological effects of an exercise training regimen upon men aged 52 to 88. J. Geront. 25:325-336, 1970.

5. deVries, H.A. Exercise intensity threshold for improvement of cardiovascular respiratory function in older men. Geriatrics 26:94-101, 1971.

6. Drinkwater, B.L., S.M. Horvath and C.L. Wells. Aerobic power of females ages 10 to 68. J. Gerontol. 30:385-394, 1975.

7. Gore, I.Y. Physical activity and aging--survey of Soviet literature. Geront. Clin. 14:65-69, 1972.

8. Getman, L.R., M.L. Pollock, J.L. Durstine, A. Ward, J. Ayres and A.C. Linnerud. Physiological responses of men to 1, 3, and 5 day per week training programs. Res. Quart. 47:638-646, 1976.

9. Gissal, M. A fitness trail for older adults. Master's thesis, University of Wisconsin, 1980.

10. Hodgson, J.L. and E.R. Buskirk. Physical fitness and age, with emphasis on cardiovascular function in the elderly. J. Am. Ger. Soc. 25:9,385-392, 1977.

11. Heinzelmann, F. and R.W. Bagley. Response to physical activity programs and their effects on health behavior. Publ. Hlth. Repts. 85:905-911, 1970.

12. Kasser, I.S. and R.A. Bruce. Comparative effects of aging and coronary heart disease on submaximal and maximal exercise. Circulation 39:759-774, 1969.

13. Lester, F.M., L.T. Sheffield and T.J. Reeves. Electrocardiographic changes in clinically normal older men following near maximal and maximal exercise. Circulation 36:5-16, 1967.

14. McPherson, R.K., F. Ofner and J.A. Welch. Effect of prevailing air temperature on mortality. Brit. J. Prevent. Soc. Med. 21:17-21, 1967.

15. Nagle, F.J., Balke, B. and J.P. Naughton. Gradational step tests for assessing work capacity. J. Appl. Physiol. 20:745, 1965.

16. Pollock, M.L. The quantification of endurance training programs. In: Exercise and Sport Sciences Reviews, edited by J. Wilmore. New York: Academic Press, pp. 155-188, 1973.

17. Pollock, M.L., H.S. Miller, A.C. Linnerud and K.H. Cooper. Frequency of training as a determinant for improvement in cardiovascular function and body composition of middle-aged men. Arch. Phys. Med. Rehab. 56:141-145, 1975.

18. Riley, C.P., A. Oberman, T.D. Lampton and D.C. Hurst. Submaximal exercise testing in a random sample of an elderly population. Circulation 42:43-52, 1970.

19. Rowell, L.B., H.L. Taylor and Y. Wang. Limitations to predictions of maximum oxygen uptake. J. Appl. Physiol. 19:919-927, 1964.

20. Saltin, B., B. Blomqvist, J.H. Mitchell, R.L. Johnson Jr., K. Wildenthal and O.B. Chapman. Response to submaximal and maximal exercise after bed rest and training. Circulation 38(7):1ff, 1968.

21. Sheffield, L.T., J.A. Maloof, J.A. Sawyer and D. Roitman. Maximal heart rate and treadmill performance of healthy women in relation to age. Circulation 57(1):79-84, 1978.

22. Sidney, K.H. and R.J. Shephard. Maximum and submaximum exercise tests in men and women in the seventh, eighth and ninth decades of life. J. Appl. Physiol. 43:2,280-287, 1977.

23. Sidney, K.H. and R.J. Shephard. Frequency and intensity of exercise training for elderly subjects. Med. Sci. Spts. 10(2):125-131, 1978.

24. Smith, E.L. and K. Stoedefalke. Aging and Exercise. Hillside, N.J.: Enslow Publishers, 1980.

25. Stamford, B.A. Effects of chronic institutionalization on the physical work capacity and trainability of geriatric men. J. Geront. 28(1):441-446, 1973.

26. Teräslinna, P.T., T. Partanen, A. Koskela and P. Oja. Characteristics affecting willingness of executives to participate in an activity program aimed at coronary heart disease prevention. J. Spts. Med. Phys. Fitness 9:224-229, 1969.

Charles E. Morse has been a graduate student at the University of Wisconsin-Madison since 1976, combining studies in exercise physiology with course work in gerontology. He holds a Bachelor of Arts degree in English Literature from Stanford University. He is a member of the American College of Sports Medicine and the American Association for the Advancement of Science.

EXERCISE FOR THE ELDERLY
WHAT ARE THE BENEFITS AND HOW DO WE GET STARTED?
Robert C. Serfass

Although no systematically collected data have been accumu-
lated on the phenomenon of the recent expansion of exercise
programs for the elderly, anyone who has been actively involved in the areas of exercise or sports medicine in the
past few years can substantiate the dramatic increase in re-
quests for information on program development for this age
group.  Program directors from nursing homes, senior citizens
organizations, YMCA's and YWCA's, community education programs and a myriad of other social service institutions have
become engaged in soliciting and, in many cases, developing
sound resource materials for the purpose of establishing effective physical activity and physical educational programs
for their elderly clientele.

This increasing degree of interest in geriatric exercise has been precipitated by an increasing number of pro-
fessionals, many of whom are participating in this symposium,
who are devoting substantially more of their time to research
and program development which focus on the aged.  These individuals in concert with professional organizations like
the American Alliance for Health, Physical Education, Recreation and Dance, the American College of Sports Medicine,
the National Association for Human Development, and the President's Council on Physical Fitness and Sports have generated
a significant amount of professional interaction and public
education in attempts to stimulate our intellectual curiosity
and our professional responsibility concerning a segment of
the population which has been relatively neglected by the

exercise sciences.

Whether or not the recent enthusiasm for the development and evaluation of exercise programs for the elderly will continue remains to be seen. In the face of their present expanding popularity, we must respond with an organized effort toward filling the gaps of knowledge which exist about the response of the aging organism to the stress of exercise if we are to insure that these programs will be optimally effective. The need for trained personnel to direct such programs will increase as the numbers of elderly citizens increases. Estimates suggest that people over the age of 65 will increase from 22 million in 1975 to approximately 30 million in the year 2000, and that they will then represent 12.5 percent of the total population (3). Many of these potential exercise program participants will be generally poorly motivated to initially enroll in and/or persist at regular exercise (23). The majority will have substantial restrictions on their income (26) and the older they are when they enter the program, the greater will be the chance that they will exhibit some type of debilitating condition which will necessitate adaptation of the normal exercise regimen (12). In order for us to serve their needs it will be incumbent upon us to continue to tax our adaptive ingenuity toward the development of programs which are medically and physiologically sound, economically feasible and motivationally attractive and magnetic.

Papers presented earlier in this symposium have been primarily directed toward identifying structural and functional aging characteristics of the major physiological systems which have considerable implications for the optimal development and maintenance of physical fitness in the elderly. It is our purpose in the upcoming series of manuscripts to provide information relative to our current knowledge about the adaptation of these systems in response to chronic physical activity.

When contemplating the benefits which might be derived from a program of exercise for the elderly one only has to consider their present preferred leisure pursuits and their perception of the factors which prevent them from engaging in those activities. McAvoy (18) surveyed the leisure time pursuits of a randomly selected state-wide sample of Minnesota elderly and reported that the eight activities which they most preferred to engage in were: sightseeing, walking for pleasure, fishing, reading, gardening, driving for pleasure, visiting friends and relatives and attending club and organizational meetings; certainly not an overly aggressive itinerary of activities. When asked, however, what they felt was the most prevalent problem which they encountered in the performance of these activities, they listed lack of physical ability three times more often than any other single factor.

It should not be surprising that we can often subjectively detect substantial physical and psychological improvement in chronically sedentary individuals who begin programs of moderate exercise. Experience with the dramatic effects induced by bed rest in young healthy subjects highlights the incapacitating effect of extended inactivity. A decrease in maximal work capacity of as much as 30 percent has been demonstrated with three weeks of bed rest and this effect is most dramatic in those who are initially more sedentary (25,33). Few people realize, however, that you do not have to go to bed for three weeks to exhibit similar debilitating symptoms. Lamb (15,16) has demonstrated that healthy, active young men who are subjected to 10-11 days of chair rest exhibit substantially diminished work capacity and symptoms of dizziness, fainting, circulatory collapse, nausea, and vomiting. It is easy to project that, as one gravitates toward greater degrees of inactivity in later years, the elicitation of these symptoms in even a mild form could become a catalyst in the sedentary elderly for further inactivity. Such a scenario often produces a vicious cycle from which it is difficult to escape and far too many of our senior citizens never come close to realizing their full physical potential. Participation in exercise programs on the other hand seem to have the opposite effect in the elderly resulting in an increase in other daily activities (6,28) and in the possible attenuation of other positive health behaviors (8,13,17).

The following presentations will consider only a limited number of beneficial physiological responses to exercise however, these areas of cardiovascular adaptations, muscular strength and endurance, flexibility, and aspects of body composition are considered by many to represent primary components of physical fitness which have considerable importance to the optimal development of healthy and physically active senior citizens.

There seems to be little doubt that elderly subjects can make significant gains in cardiorespiratory fitness in the form of improvement of the maximal oxygen consumption, whether measured directly (29) or predicted from physiological responses to standardized submaximal work (2,9,30,35). The implications of this ability to attain significant improvements in maximal work capacity and in submaximal cardiovascular response to work are especially important for those elderly in the lowest percentiles of cardiorespiratory fitness (34). The capability of even a moderate increase in these parameters could provide enough energy reserve for many who are at these lower levels of cardiorespiratory endurance to expand their daily activities out of the ordinary world of self-care and basic sustenance into a more enriching atmosphere of more satisfying leisure time pursuits. Indirect evidence that the elderly can maintain a relatively high level of physical capacity in later years is provided by studies of former athletes who have continued a life-long involvement in vigorous exercise (24) or by elderly people who train for Masters athletic competition (22,27). Further, Kasch and Wallace (14) have demonstrated that maximal oxygen consumption can be maintained at virtually the same level over a ten year span from age 45 to age 55 through an exercise program of running and/or swimming.

Chapman, deVries and Swezey (5) have demonstrated that exercising, elderly subjects can obtain increases in strength which are similar in magnitude to those which would be expected in much younger subjects and, more recently, Moritani and deVries (19) have suggested that much of the demonstrable strength gain in older individuals may be the result of learning to recruit a larger number of motor units. Regardless of the mechanisms involved it appears that the elderly can make improvements in muscular strength and endurance which will substantially improve their functional capacity.

The area of research relative to the effects of exercise on flexibility in the elderly has been sadly neglected considering the tremendous importance that adequate flexibility has in the maintenance of normal mobility. Those individuals who have attended to this type of research have generally found that exercise programs can be effective in the improvement of flexibility in older subjects (4,5,10). Munns (20) has reported that a program of dance related movement exercises three times per week for 12 weeks dramatically increased the range of movement in six major joints in elderly subjects with a mean age of 72 years.

Attempts to assess exercise induced changes of body composition in the elderly using traditional methods of skinfolds and hydrostatic weighing may present some difficulty as locations of major fat deposits may change substantially with increasing age (31) and relative shifts in major body components of water, protein, bone and minerals may make available predictive equations insensitive to the actual changes which may take place in later years (11). Current work in the area of bone mineralization research however, is extremely encouraging and, if preliminary results demonstrating increases (32) or stabilization (30) of bone mineral content with training can be confirmed in future more extensive trials, the participation in exercise programs by individuals who have a tendency towards osteoporosis will have far-reaching implications and benefits.

It is beyond the scope of this symposium to review all of the debilitating factors which typically affect the elderly and the extent to which they can be modified by exercise. Shephard (26) has presented an excellent review of this literature and reports that preliminary, and in many cases substantial, evidence is available which suggests that exercise may have beneficial effects in the areas of cardiovascular disease, chronic chest disease, maturity onset diabetes, arthritis, hormonal responses and psychological disorders among others. These observations should encourage those of us who have limited our involvement with exercise to programs for the young and middle-aged, to expand our efforts into the areas of programmatic development and research in geriatric exercise.

In order to provide assistance for those individuals who have not been previously involved in exercise programs for the elderly, several professional organizations have devoted a substantial amount of time and energy toward the development of exercise routines and educational materials specifically designed for the aged. One of the most useful resources is the AAHPERD News Kit on Aging (1) which is distributed twice per year in UPDATE, a professional newsletter of the American Alliance for Health, Physical Education, Recreation, and Dance. It provides excellent current information on national and regional conferences, printed and audio-visual materials, and legislative action related to exercise and aging. One of the most valuable features of this newsletter is a biannually updated directory of ongoing exercise programs throughout the country which provides the names and addresses of program directors along with a brief description of the objectives and important features of each program. The National Association for Human Development (21) has a variety of training manuals and exercise booklets on exercise programs for the elderly and, the President's Council on Physical Fitness and Sports has published a research summary on aging and exercise (7). The PCPFS has also recently cooperated in the completion of a packet of program materials entitled "The Good Life - Physical Fitness for Older Americans," which is available free of charge from the Travelers Insurance Company, Travelers Square, Hartford, Connecticut, 06115.

Several other useful resources are available and I have listed a limited number of these at the end of this manuscript. The materials listed under Background Books and Pamphlets have been selected on the basis of their value in developing sound foundational knowledges about the process of aging, the adaptation of the elderly to exercise and the formulation of sound prescriptive and programmatic guidelines. The other materials listed under Exercise Program Resources are materials which provide information relative to specific physical activities for the elderly and which represent a variety of successful approaches to programmatic development. It would be presumptuous of me to suggest that this list represents the best possible list or that it represents all of the successful approaches to programming geriatric exercise. These resources are only offered in the spirit of priming the pump in the hope that they may provide a fundamental foundation of current knowledge and a motivating stimulus toward the recruitment of interested individuals into a fraternity of colleagues who are committed to the premise that prudent exercise can make a significant positive impact on the quality of life of the elderly.

## REFERENCES

1. American Alliance for Health, Physical Education, Recreation and Dance. AAHPERD news kit on programs for the aging. Washington, D.C.: AAHPERD, March, 1979.

2. Barry, A.J., J.W. Daly, E.D.R. Pruett, J.R. Steinmetz, H.F. Page, N.C. Birkhead and K. Rodahl. The effects of physical conditioning on older individuals. I. Work capacity, circulatory-respiratory function, and work electrocardiogram. J. Gerontol. 21:182-191, 1966.

3. Brotman, H.B. Population projections - Part I. Tomorrow's older population (to 2000). Gerontol. 17:203-209, 1977.

4. Buccola, V.A. and W.J. Stone. Effects of jogging and cycling programs on physiological and personality variables in aged men. Res. Q. Am. Assoc. Health Phys. Educ. 46:134-139, 1975.

5. Chapman, E.A., H.A. deVries and R. Swezey. Joint stiffness: Effects of exercise on young and old men. J. Gerontol. 27:218-221, 1972.

6. Clark, B.A., M.G. Wade, B.H. Massey and R. VanDyke. Response of institutionalized geriatric mental patients to a twelve-week program of regular physical activity. J. Gerontol. 30:565-573, 1975.

7. Clarke, H.H. (ed.). Exercise and aging. Phys. Fit. Res. Dig. Series 7, No. 2, April, 1977.

8. Cooper, K.H., M.L. Pollock, R.P. Martin, S.R. White, A.C. Linerud and A. Jackson. Physical fitness levels vs. selected coronary risk factors. A cross sectional study. JAMA 236:116-169, 1976.

9. deVries, H.A. Physiological effects of an exercise training regimen upon men aged 52 to 88. J. Gerontol. 25:325-336, 1970.

10. Frekany, G.A. and D.K. Leslie. Effects of an exercise program on selected flexibility measurements of senior citizens. Gerontol. 15: 182-183, 1975.

11. Fryer, J.H. Studies of body composition in men aged 60 and over. In: Biological Aspects of Aging, edited by N.W. Shock. New York: Columbia University Press, pp. 59-78, 1962.

12. Hendricks, J. and C.D. Hendricks. Aging in Mass Society. Cambridge: Winthrop Publishers, p. 169, 1977.

13. Hickey, N., R. Mulcahy, G.J. Bourke, I. Graham and K. Wilson-Davis. Study of coronary risk factors related to physical activity in 15,171 men. Brit. Med. J. ii:507-509, 1975.

14. Kasch, F.W. and J.P. Wallace. Physiological variables during 10 years of endurance exercise. Med. Sci. Spts. 8:5-8, 1976.

15. Lamb, L.E., R.L. Johnson and P.M. Stevens. Cardiovascular conditioning during chair rest. Aerosp. Med. 35:646-649, 1964.

16. Lamb, L.E., P.M. Stevens and R.L. Johnson. Hypokinesia secondary to chair rest from 4-10 days. Aerosp. Med. 36:755-763, 1965.

17. Mann, G.V., H.L. Garrett, A. Farki, H. Murray and F.T. Billings. Exercise to prevent coronary heart disease: An experimental study of the effect of training on risk factors for coronary disease in man. Am. J. Med. 46:12-27, 1969.

18. McAvoy, L.H. Recreation preferences of the elderly persons in Minnesota. Doctoral dissertatation, University of Minnesota, 1976.

19. Moritani, T. and deVries, H.A. Neural factors versus hypertrophy in the time course of muscle strength gain in young and old men. Am. J. Phys. Med. 58:115-130, 1979.

20. Munns, K.M. The effects of a 12 week exercise and dance program on the range of joint motion of elderly subjects. Masters thesis, University of Wisconsin, 1978.

21. National Association for Human Development. Join the active people over 60. Washington, D.C.: Administration on Aging, 1976.

22. Pollock, M.L. Physiological characteristics of older champion track athletes. Res. Q. Am. Assoc. Health Phys. Educ. 45:363-373, 1974.

23. President's Council on Physical Fitness and Sports. National adult physical fitness survey. Newsletter, Special Edition, Washington, D.C.: PCPFS, 1973.

24. Robinson, S., D.B. Dill, R.D. Robinson, S.P. Tzankoff and J.A. Wagner. Physiological aging of champion runners. J. Appl. Physiol. 41:46-51, 1976.

25. Saltin, B., G. Blomquist, J.H. Michell, R.L. Johnson, Jr., K. Wildenthal and C.B. Chapman. Response to exercise after bed rest and after training. Circul. Suppl. 7:1-78, 1968.

26. Shephard, R.J. Physical Activity and Aging. Chicago: Yearbook Medical Publishers Inc., pp. 225-267, 1978.

27. Shephard, R.J. and T. Kavanagh. The effects of training on the aging process. Phys. Spts. Med. 6:38-46, 1978.

28. Sidney, K.H. and R.J. Shephard. Activity patterns of elderly men and women. J. Gerontol. 32:25-32, 1977.

29. Sidney, K.H. and R.J. Shephard. Frequency and intensity of exercise training for elderly subjects. Med. Sci. Spts. 10:125-131, 1978.

30. Sidney, K.H., R.J. Shephard and J.E. Harrison. Endurance training and body composition of the elderly. Am. J. Clin. Nutr. 30: 326-333, 1977.

31. Skerlj, B., J. Brozek and E. Hunt. Subcutaneous fat and age changes in body build and body form in women. Am. J. Phys. Anthropol. 11:577-600, 1953.

32. Smith, E.L. Physical activity and bone accretion. Paper presented at conference on exercise in the elderly--its role in prevention of physical decline and in rehabilitation. Bethesda: National Institute on Aging and PCPFS, 1977.

33. Taylor, H.L., A. Henschel, J. Brozek and A. Keys. Effects of bed rest on cardiovascular function and work performance. J. Appl. Physiol. 2:223-239, 1949.

34. Taylor, H.L. and H.J. Montoye. Physical fitness, cardiovascular function and age. In: Epidemiology of Aging, edited by A.M. Ostfeld and D.C. Gibson. Washington, D.C.: U.S. Department of Health, Education and Welfare, DHEW Pub. No. (NIH) 75-711, 1972.

35. Tzankoff, S.P., S. Robinson, F.S. Pyke and C.A. Brawn. Physiological adjustments to work in older men as affected by physical training. J. Appl. Physiol. 33:346-350, 1972.

RESOURCE LIST

### Background Books and Pamphlets

1. American College of Sports Medicine. Guidelines for Graded Exercise Testing and Exercise Prescription. Philadelphia: Lea and Febiger, 1975.
2. American Heart Association. Exercise Testing and Training of Individuals with Heart Disease or at High Risk for Its Development: A Handbook for Physicians. New York: AMA, 1975.
3. deVries, H.A. Vigor Regained. Englewood Cliffs, N.J.: Prentice-Hall, 1974.
4. Finch. C.E. and L. Hayflick. Handbook of the Biology of Aging. New York: Van Nostrand Reinhold Co., 1977.
5. Harris, R. and L.J. Frankel. Guide to Fitness After Fifty. New York: Plenum Press, 1977.
6. Shephard, R.J. Physical Activity and Aging. Chicago: Yearbook Medical Publishers, Inc., 1978.

### Exercise Program Resources

1. Addison, C. and E. Humphrey. Fifty "Positive Vigor" Exercises for Senior Citizens. Waldorf, Maryland: AAHPERD Publications, 1979.
2. Caplow-Linder, E., L. Harpas and S. Samberg. Therapeutic Dance Movement: Expressive Activities for Older Adults. New York: Human Sciences Press, 1979.
3. Frankel, L.J. and B.B. Richard. Be Alive as Long As You Live. Charleston, W. Virginia: Preventicare Publications, 1977.
4. Leslie, D.K. and J.W. McLure. Exercises for the Elderly. Iowa City: Department of Physical Education - University of Iowa, 1977.
5. Moran, J.M. Leisure Activites for the Mature Adult. Minneapolis: Burgess Publishing Co., 1979.
6. Peery, J. Exercises for Retirees. Oregon City, Oregon: Clackamas Community College, 1976.
7. Smith, E.L. and K.G. Stoedefalke. Aging and Exercise. Madison: Department of Preventive Medicine - University of Wisconsin, 1978.
8. Wear, R. Fitness Vitality and You, Serving the Elderly, The Technique - Part II. Durham: New England Center for Continuing Education, University of New Hampshire, 1977.

Dr. Robert C. Serfass is an Associate Professor and the Director of the Human Performance Laboratory within the School of Physical Education, Recreation and School Health Education at the University of Minnesota. He received his B.S. from East Stroudsburg State College and his M.A. and Ph.D. from the University of Minnesota. He is a former President of the Northland Chapter of the American College of Sports Medicine.

# CARDIOVASCULAR BENEFITS OF PHYSICAL ACTIVITY
## IN THE EXERCISING AGED
### Kenneth H. Sidney

The improvement of physical performance in the aged through regular participation in vigorous exercise involving rhythmical contractions of the body's major muscle groups represents a long-term adaptation to chronic stress. The first and foremost effect of such chronic endurance training is to improve and maintain the oxygen transport capacity of the cardiovascular system and the oxidative capacity of the skeletal muscle cells (11). Chronically well-trained older individuals will have an enhanced ability to transport oxygen and will show smaller displacements of metabolic and circulatory parameters from the resting state during the performance of submaximal work loads than untrained individuals (52,56). The fit person, compared to the untrained at any age, will sustain activity for a longer period of time before signs and symptoms of fatigue become limiting, while in recovery following exercise, equilibria will be restored more rapidly in the trained individual. On the other hand, a poorly trained individual will respond to exercise inefficiently and with great effort.

Recent reviews (11,56) have described the effects of physical conditioning on the cardiovascular adjustments to exercise for young adults, and other reviews (5,37,38,64,65) have summarized the effects of aging on the cardiovascular system and responses of the aged to exercise. This paper will review work on cardiovascular adaptations of healthy elderly persons to programs of endurance training, focusing primarily on longitudinal studies in which before and after training assessments of cardiovascular functions are made. However, most available longitudinal data provide information only on the effects of relatively short-term training (3 months or less). In order to determine the potential long-term effects of physical conditioning in the aged, cross-sectional data comparing well-trained persons (athletes) to untrained persons is examined.

The cardiovascular effects of training are considered under the following headings: (i) Changes at rest, (ii) changes in the response to submaximal exercise, (iii) changes in the response to maximal exercise and aerobic power, (iv) electrocardiographic changes, and (v) cross-sectional comparisons: The elderly athlete.

## CHANGES AT REST

In the young, it has long been recognized that resting heart rate is diminished following endurance training regimens (56). Surprisingly, a slowing of the resting pulse is not a common finding when people over the age of 60 years undergo conditioning (4,9,10,18,66,67) even though other variables indicate an improvement of cardiovascular performance. Only in three studies (1,44,58) were decrements (3-6 beats/min) of resting cardiac frequency observed.

In the healthy young adult it is doubtful whether exercise training can substantially modify systemic blood pressure (11,56). Reductions seem more likely in persons with elevated blood pressure, and most studies of older subjects (4,9,16,18, 30,52,58,66,67) but not all (1,44,72), have found significant decrements of resting systolic blood pressure. The mean change in one series was as large as 20 mmHg. A reduction of resting diastolic pressure has also been noted (9,16,18,30,58) with the decrement amounting to only 3-10 mmHg. One year of progressive endurance training was accompanied by a decrease of systolic pressure from 132 to 115 mmHg, while the diastolic pressure dropped from 87 to 81 mmHg (58).

In the above-mentioned experiments, it is difficult to rule out all possibility of habituation. Even where control groups were employed, the subjects in the experimental group necessarily have had more contact with the investigator and the laboratory environment. With respect to blood pressure, other factors contributing to the fall in values could include altered pulse wave reflections and improved fit of the measuring cuff concomitant with a reduction in adipose tissue (61).

Relatively few studies have investigated the effects of physical conditioning on other cardiovascular components of the oxygen transport system. Benestad (6) noted increases in both total hemoglobin and blood volume when his elderly subjects undertook 5-6 weeks of intensive training. However, training had no effect on hemoglobin concentration. In younger adults blood volume too can increase in response to training, but this is not a consistent finding (11,56); according to Clausen (11) hemoglobin concentration rather than the total amount of hemoglobin limits maximum oxygen intake.

In Benestad's study (6) there was also no change of heart volume. If such a 'dimensional' change were possible in the aged, a much longer period of time than 5-6 weeks would be required (28). Saltin (50) commented that changes of heart size were more difficult to achieve in middle-aged and older men, and Kindermann and Reindell (36) have noted that an increase of stroke volume with training can occur in elderly subjects without a corresponding rise in heart volume. In young and middle-aged persons, investigations have produced conflicting results. Some reports (48) have shown an increase of heart volume with conditioning, whereas others have shown a decrease (62) or no change (50).

Adams et al. (2) examined the effects of 10 weeks of bicycle training on resting and recovery systolic time intervals, including the total period of ventricular systole ($QS_2$), left ventricular ejection time (LVET) and the pre-ejection period (PEP = $QS_2$-LVET). An improvement of physical working capacity in the trained group was associated with an increase of LVET measured in the resting, sitting position. Lengthening of LVET and $QS_2$ may reflect increased stroke volume; lengthening of systolic time intervals has been previously described for middle-aged men following participation in various training programs (19,22).

## CHANGES IN THE RESPONSE TO SUBMAXIMAL EXERCISE

The majority of studies have found improvements in the cardiovascular responses of elderly persons to submaximal aerobic
exercise after physical conditioning.  The smaller increments
of most variables are suggestive of an increased economy of
effort and improved physical work capacity.

During exercise at a constant work load, there are reductions of heart rate (1,4,6,16,41,47,52,60,66,67) and blood
lactic acid levels (4,47,69), with little change of oxygen
intake (4,6,66,67) and diastolic blood pressure (4,6,16,47,
66).  There are thus parallel improvements of oxygen pulse--
the volume of oxygen transported per heart beat (1,4,16,66,
67)--and in physical work capacity and predicted aerobic power
(2,9,16,58,60,70).  Some authors have observed a decrease of
systolic blood pressure during exercise at a fixed work load
(4,66,67), but others (16,47) have not seen such a change.

A well-recognized index of cardiovascular conditioning is
a faster recovery of heart rate following physical exertion
(52).  Sidney and Shephard (60) found that after 7 weeks of
training the pulse rate during the first six minutes of recovery from a bicycle ergometer test averaged 6-10 beats/min.
less than values before training.  Following 14 weeks of
training, the total reduction averaged 9-17 beats/min.  Furthermore, the decrement in cardiac frequency was related to
the amount of training undertaken, with the largest responses
being evident in persons exercising at a high frequency and
intensity, and the smallest responses seen in persons exercising at a low frequency and intensity.

Few studies (30,40,41,47) have investigated the mechanisms by which the cardiovascular system adjusts to the
training stimulus in effecting an improvement of oxygen transport during muscular exertion.  deVries (30) found no change
of cardiac output, stroke volume, systemic arterial pressure,
total peripheral resistance or modified tension time index
(a measure of cardiac work load) when trained men were re-
tested at 75 watts on a bicycle ergometer.  Using a treadmill,
Niinimaa and Shephard (40,41) also saw no change in stroke
volume with conditioning, but because heart rate was lower,
they noted a trend for cardiac output to be reduced by 5-7%
at walking speeds of 40 to 80% of aerobic power.  Chronic

exercise failed to induce changes in the calculated arterio-
venous oxygen difference at constant work loads.

Rost and co-workers (47) investigated the hemodynamic
effects of endurance training in twenty 50-70 year-old men
whom they considered to have a high coronary risk. Following
3 months of training, there were increases of maximal $\dot{V}O_2$ and
decreases of heart rate during submaximal supine bicycle exercise. There were no changes of mean arterial pressure (measured directly) or cardiac output (measured by dye dilution
technique). The lowered heart rates were thus achieved by
increases of stroke volume. Furthermore, analysis of femoral
blood revealed no change in oxygen utilization, although
venous occlusion plethysmography revealed a decrease in post-
exercise hyperemia.

## CHANGES IN THE RESPONSE TO MAXIMAL EXERCISE AND AEROBIC POWER

The maximum oxygen intake or aerobic power ($\dot{V}O_2$ max) provides
a valuable index of the overall performance of the cardiovascular and respiratory systems (52). Thus $\dot{V}O_2$ max is normally
used as the standard of reference (training criterion) when
evaluating the effects of conditioning on the circulatory
adjustments to maximal exercise (56). The physiological interpretation and measurement of $\dot{V}O_2$ max have been previously
discussed in detail (51,52,53,55,59).

Endurance training of sufficient intensity, duration and
frequency elicits favorable changes of aerobic power and components of the oxygen transport chain in young and middle-
aged adults (11,52,56). Several studies have reported gains
in the directly measured $\dot{V}O_2$ max for men and women in their
sixth decade of life (29,33,34,35,44,50,72,73). However, in
view of the potential hazards of exhaustive exercise, few
investigators have examined the effects of training on the
maximal exercise responses of persons in their seventh decade
and older (55).

Benestad (6) found no gains in the directly measured $\dot{V}O_2$
max when 13 elderly men, aged 70 to 81 years, underwent 5-6
weeks of vigorous interval training. There were also no
changes of heart rate or oxygen pulse at maximal effort. The
absence of response may be explained by the relatively short
period of training and the fairly high initial level of

fitness (aerobic power 27 ml/kg·min). In contrast, Barry and colleagues (4) reported increases for both maximum oxygen intake (38%) and oxygen pulse (24%) in three men and five women (mean age 70 years) who completed 3 months of conditioning. At the initial test, however, the work tolerance was limited by local muscle fatigue, weakness or motivation in 4 of 8 subjects. In the remaining 4 subjects, effort was restricted by a physician because of abnormal ECG changes. Thus, in view of the low values for maximal heart rate (126 beats/min) and lactate concentrations (40 mg/100 ml) it is unlikely that Barry's subjects reached a centrally-limited (51) maximal effort on the initial tests. After training, the subjects either chose to push themselves harder, or were allowed to do so, so that the apparent gains of $\dot{V}O_2$ max were accompanied by increases of heart rate (24%), systolic blood pressure (10%) and lactic acid (43%). Although increases were in symptom-limited performance rather than plateau values of oxygen intake, the practical importance of their data should not be minimized. With training these individuals were able to perform what was a previously limiting load with less physiological disturbance, and also to perform at a 76% greater work load before effort became intolerable.

For reasons of safety, Sidney and Shephard (59) deferred direct measurements of $\dot{V}O_2$ max until their elderly volunteers had completed a 7 week program of conditioning. Unfortunately, most of the 'regulatory' components of training (27, 28) had already been completed at this stage. Nevertheless, subsequent gains of $\dot{V}O_2$ max totalled 7% (2 ml/kg·min) from the 7th to the 21st week of training. The greatest gains were evident in persons who selected a high intensity and frequency of training (15%, 4.6 ml/kg·min). No further gains of $\dot{V}O_2$ max were registered in 5 women and 4 men who continued training for the remainder of the year. In addition, Niinimaa and Shephard (40,41) found a 10% increase of $\dot{V}O_2$ max in old men and women who exercised at heart rates of 145-155 beats/minute for 11 weeks. In the Toronto investigations (60,41), there were no significant changes in maximal values for heart rate and blood lactic acid concentrations.

Predictions of $\dot{V}O_2$ max confirm that training can be induced in the aged given a suitable regimen of endurance exercise. Several authors have noted reductions of pulse rate at fixed submaximal work rates (1,66,67,68); assuming their subjects were habituated to the test procedure, this would imply an improvement of aerobic power. deVries (16) exercised 68 men aged 51 to 87 years for 6 weeks and reported a gain of predicted aerobic power averaging 5% (1.6 ml/kg·min); however, an almost equal gain was also noted in the control group. Eight of the exercise group continued their training for 42 weeks, and at this stage showed a non-significant 8% increase over their initial predicted $\dot{V}O_2$ max. More recently, Buccola and Stone (9) found 13% gains of predicted $\dot{V}O_2$ max in groups of elderly men (mean age 68 years) who either trained by jogging or cycling for 14 weeks. Comparable improvements were also reported by Suominen et al. (69,70,71) for male and female (mean age 69 years) Finnish pensioners following 8 weeks of physical training.

Sidney and Shephard (60) classified 42 men and women according to the intensity and frequency with which they participated in a program of brisk walking and jogging. After 7 weeks of training, gains of predicted $\dot{V}O_2$ max were related to both intensity and frequency of effort, with no response in persons who exercised less than twice a week at heart rates of 120 beats/min. On the other hand, persons who exercised 2 to 4 times per week with heart rates of 140-150 per minute achieved an increment of 9.8 ml/kg·min. Additional gains of aerobic power with a second 7 week period of conditioning were small. Ten men and 12 women (mean age 65 years) continued to train for one year; this group showed a 24% average increment of $\dot{V}O_2$ max, although 90% of this gain was realized during the first 7 weeks of training.

A rapid gain of $\dot{V}O_2$ max is in keeping with results of previous studies of young and middle-aged adults (34,35,48, 50,73). Early changes in cardiovascular fitness are likely 'regulatory' in type (27,28,50); 'dimensional' responses, that is, changes in body structure and composition, occur with more prolonged training (61).

It may be concluded that endurance exercise training can elicit increases of aerobic power in sedentary elderly men and women (Table 1). Moreover, the adaptive response to training is independent of one's sex. As in young and middle-aged subjects (23,39,46), the response of older women to conditioning programs is comparable with that of older men (40,60, 61,70).

## ELECTROCARDIOGRAPHIC CHANGES

The incidence of various abnormalities in the electrocardiogram of the elderly is high in asymptomatic individuals (12, 53,55). The proportion of the apparently healthy population with ST changes increases steadily with advancing age affecting at least 30% of both men and women in the 65 year old age group. In view of the association between ST changes and ischemic heart disease and sudden death, a reversal of abnormal ECG waveforms would seem a desirable outcome of exercise training. However, evidence regarding the influence of regular exercise upon ischemic ECG responses is conflicting. Some authors have observed no change in ST segmental deviation at a fixed work load (48,62). On the other hand, Bruce et al. (8) found a 10% decrease of heart rate during submaximal work accompanied by a 40% lessening of ST segmental depression; however, ST depression was unchanged when subjects performed at symptom-limited maximal effort. Several other authors (13,15,35) have noted lesser abnormalities at a given work load following physical conditioning, although ST changes at a fixed heart rate have remained unaltered. This would seem to imply that the beneficial effect of conditioning is attributable to a reduction of heart rate and, thus, cardiac work load at a given external effort.

One report (31), however, involving middle-aged post-coronary patients found some reversal of ST depression not only at a given work load, but also at a given heart rate. Sidney and Shephard (52) observed that endurance training involving apparently healthy men and women induced an elevation of the ST segment at rest, during bicycle ergometer exercise at a given heart rate (120 beats/min), and during recovery from effort. Moreover, the extent of the positive deviation seemed related to the intensity and frequency of training selected by the subject.

The significance of this ST elevation is not yet clearly understood. Saltin and Grimby (49) have suggested that endurance athletes show quite marked ST elevation, and Sjostrand

TABLE 1. THE EFFECTS OF ENDURANCE TRAINING ON AEROBIC POWER IN HEALTHY MEN AND WOMEN IN THE SEVEN AND EIGHTH DECADES OF LIFE.

| Investigator | Sex | Age (yr) | N | Frequency (per week) | Duration (min/total wks) | Intensity | Activity[a] | $\dot{V}O_2$ max Pre | Post | Δ | Δ% |
|---|---|---|---|---|---|---|---|---|---|---|---|
| Sidney and Shephard (60) | M&F | 67 | 8 | <2 | | HR~120/min | | 19.5[b] | 19.2 | -0.3 | -2(NS) |
| | | 63 | 5 | <2 | 45 min/14 wks | HR~140-150/min | W,J,Cal | 24.1 | 28.1 | 4.0 | 17 |
| | | 64 | 13 | 2-4 | | HR~120/min | | 21.7 | 24.8 | 3.1 | 14 |
| | | 61 | 8 | 2-4 | | HR~140-150/min | | 23.4 | 32.4 | 9.0 | 39 |
| | M | 65 | 10 | 1-4 | 45 min/52 wks | HR~120-145/min | W,J,Cal | 21.7[b] | 26.9 | 5.2 | 24 |
| | F | 65 | 12 | 1-4 | | | | 22.4 | 27.8 | 5.4 | 24 |
| Buccola and Stone (9) | M | 65 | 16 | 3 | 10-40 min/14 wks | HR<144/min | B | 23.7[b] | 26.9 | 3.2 | 14 |
| | M | 68 | 20 | 3 | | 6-7 mets→8-9 mets | J | 24.2 | 27.3 | 3.1 | 13 |
| Suominen et al. (70,71) | M | 69 | 14 | 3-5 | 60 min/8 wks | Submaximal | W,J,G,Cal | 28.9[b] | 32.0 | 3.1 | 11 |
| | F | 69 | 12 | 3-5 | | | | 27.9 | 31.3 | 3.4 | 12 |
| deVries (16) | M | 70 | 68 | 3 | 45-60 min/6 wks | HR<145/min | W,J,G,Cal | 33.9[b] | 35.5 | 1.6 | 5 |
| | | | 8 | | 45-60 min/42 wks | | | 33.7 | 36.5 | 2.8 | 8(NS) |
| Barry et al. (4) | M&F | 70 | 8 | 3 | 16-25 min/12 wks | Submaximal & maximal | B,Cal | 16.1 | 22.3 | 6.2 | 38 |
| Benestad (6) | M | 76 | 13 | 3 | 10-34 min/5-6 wks | Near-maximal | W | 27 | 27 | 0 | 0 |

[a] W = walking; J = jogging; Cal = calisthenics; B = bicycling, G = games/sports

[b] $\dot{V}O_2$ max predicted from the Astrand Ryhming nomogram

(63) has related the elevation to a slow heart rate. Kilbom (34) indicated that training leads to an elevation of the ST segment during both rest and work in middle-aged women, although two females with initial ST depression failed to improve.

In a group of 8 men and women averaging 70 years, Barry and co-workers (4) reported that of four subjects with initially abnormal ECG's, two demonstrated a definite improvement concurrent with training, and the other two showed possible improvements. Pollock and colleagues (44) initially observed 6 abnormal ECG findings in 22 sedentary men enrolled in a 20 week exercise program. On the post-training stress tests, three persons showed no change of ST segmental response, one subject increased the amount of ST segment depression but only after attaining a higher maximal heart rate, and the remaining two men showed no ischemic reponse on the post-tests at maximal effort; however, these individuals did not reach the same final heart rate. Sidney and Shephard (52) found that in 11 of 38 seniors who showed clinically significant ($> 0.1$ mV) ST depression on the initial stress test, five improved to the point where the depression was less than 0.1 mV at work loads up to 85% of $\dot{V}O_2$ max. Two men who had not resolved their abnormality at 14 weeks did so with another 35 to 40 weeks of participation in the exercise class.

Although ST depression induced by exercise is associated with an adverse prognosis, it has not yet been demonstrated that reversal of the ST change improves prognosis. It is, however, possible that the reduced depression is due to an improvement in collateral blood supply to the ischemic area of the myocardium. An alternative explanation is that a strengthening of the myocardial muscles and a reduction of mean ventricular diameter reduce the work load sustained by unit volume of cardiac tissue at any given external effort. This would reduce myocardial oxygen deficiency without any correction of underlying atheroma or development of new coronary blood vessels. An additional possibility is that the well-trained person releases less intramuscular potassium at a given intensity of effort (7), therby reducing ST segmental changes.

CROSS-SECTIONAL COMPARISONS:  THE ELDERLY ATHLETE

Many experiments involving the training of the aged have lasted three months or less (Table 1).  Therefore, it is important to compare the physiological characteristics of elderly athletes and other active seniors who have engaged in physical activities for prolonged periods with those of sedentary seniors.  Important limitations must be noted (55):  (i) Active persons and athletes are not necessarily typical of the 'normal' aging population; (ii) The athlete may not have persisted with his sport with the same degree of enthusiasm throughout his lifespan; (iii) Some older active persons do not actually commence sport participation until middle-age; and (iv) Most studies are cross-sectional in type, with increasing selection in the oldest age categories.

Hollmann (24) and more recently Dehn and Bruce (14) have suggested that maximum oxygen intake deteriorates more slowly in active people than in sedentary people.  However, the annual rates of decline cited for the active groups (0.70 and 0.56 ml/kg·min) are similar to rates reported in most cross-sectional studies of the general population (56).  Dill et al. (17) reported a loss of 0.67 ml/kg·min/year in still active champion runners.  Cross-sectional data for orienteers (49) and track competitors (3,32,43) show values of 50-57 ml/kg·min at age 45 years, with a total decrement of 6.1-8.3 ml/kg·min over the following 20 years.  Values of aerobic power for the physically active are higher than values for sedentary persons at all ages in both men (25) and women (42).  The 65 year old Masters athlete has a $\dot{V}O_2$ max close to that anticipated for a sedentary 25 year old adult.  Although the apparent rate of aging of active persons seems to be somewhat less than for the average person, this rate may reflect differences in changes of physical activity patterns between athletic and general populations, rather than a true retardation of aging in the endurance competitors.  Additional research is required to determine the possible contributions of differences in activity patterns and selective genetic sample attentuation to the apparent advantage of the athlete.

Systemic blood pressures of track competitors are marginally lower than published norms for sedentary persons of the same age (3,32,43).  While there is some evidence that regular exercise can lower arterial pressures, it is also possible that aging has brought about a selective elimination of hypertensive individuals from among the runners.

Heart volumes of the aging track contestants averaged 12-14 ml/kg of body weight compared to 10-11 ml/kg for sedentary males (32,54). Although the increased heart size of the athlete may be an expression of self-selection of running by well-endowed candidates, Shephard and Kavanagh (54) suggested that the increased size was probably a response to endurance training. Unfortunately, heart radiographs do not clarify whether the enlarged heart is attributable to cardiac hypertrophy or increased central blood volume.

The frequency of abnormal ECG's in endurance athletes of all ages is controversial. There have been reports of both a high incidence of ST segmental abnormalities (26) and reports of normal or lower than average incidence in former competitors (32,45,49,54). These differences among studies may relate to a wide variation in training intensities engaged in as the athletes became older.

Fardy and associates (20,21) recently studied the activity habits, aerobic power and systolic time intervals of 350 former athletes and 156 non-athletes ranging from 27 to 74 years in age. In general, their data show that former athletes have a higher $\dot{V}O_2$ max, lower heart rates, lengthened systolic time intervals ($QS_2$, LVET and PEP) and increased duration of diastole at rest and after exercise than non-athletes for all age groups. However, it is not certain whether the former athletes' advantages of cardiovascular fitness and cardiac functioning were due to differences in continued participation in physical activity (the former athletes engaged in more leisure activity than non-athletes) or to differences in heart rate, body weight and smoking history. The authors pointed out the need for controlled prospective studies in order to determine whether the apparent advantage of the former athletes is a result of environmental factors, the carry-over of physiological benefits from previous vigorous training, the result of current habitual activity patterns and attitudes, or the result of an inherited self-selection advantage.

## SUMMARY

Appropriate programs of regular vigorous physical exercise lasting 6-8 weeks can elicit cardiovascular adaptations in the elderly. Physical performance is improved by gains of aerobic power and appropriate adjustments of the cardiovascular system to muscular activity. Although additional study is required to determine the mechanisms responsible for the improved ability to transport oxygen, the extent and nature of the improvements seem similar to adaptations elicited in young and middle-aged adults. The question of which links in the oxygen conductance chain are strengthened by training has not been fully answered. A dearth of longitudinal studies investigating cardiovascular responses of aging persons to long-term training programs has also been noted. The extent of physiological improvement with endurance training is affected by personal factors such as motivation, attitude and initial health and fitness status, and by program factors such as the type of exercise employed and its duration, frequency and intensity. Additional research is required to establish the precise combination of intensity, frequency and duration needed to elicit optimal gains of cardiovascular fitness.

## REFERENCES

1. Adams, G.M. and H.A. deVries. Physiological effects of an exercise training regimen upon women aged 52 to 79. J. Gerontol. 28: 50-55, 1973.

2. Adams, G.M., H.A. deVries, R.M. Girandola and J.S. Birren. The effect of exercise training on systolic time intervals in elderly men. Med. Sci. Sports 9:68, 1977.

3. Asano, K., S. Ogawa and Y. Furuta. Aerobic work capacity in middle and old-aged runners. Proceedings of International Congress of Physical Activity Sciences, Quebec City, Canada, 1976.

4. Barry, A.J., J.W. Daly, E.D.R. Pruett, J.R. Steinmetz, H.F. Page, N.C. Birkhead and K. Rodahl. The effects of physical conditioning on older individuals. I. Work capacity, circulatory-respiratory function, and electrocardiogram. J. Gerontol. 21:182-191, 1966.

5. Bassey, E.J. Age, inactivity and some physiological responses to exercise. Gerontology 24:66-77, 1978.

6. Benestad, A.M. Trainability of old men. Acta Med. Scandinav. 178:321-327, 1965.

7. Blomqvist, G. Variations of the electrocardiographic response to exercise under different experimental conditions: deconditioning, reconditioning and high altitude. In: Measurement in Exercise Electrocardiography, edited by H. Blackburn. Springfield: C.C. Thomas, pp. 323-341, 1969.

8. Bruce, R.A., E.R. Alexander, Y.B. Li, N. Chiang and T.R. Hornsten. Electrocardiographic responses to maximal exercise in American and Chinese population samples. In: Measurement in Exercise Electrocardiography, edited by H. Blackburn. Springfield: C.C. Thomas, pp. 413-444, 1969.

9. Buccola, V.A. and W.J. Stone. Effects of jogging and cycling programs on physiological and psychological variables in aged men. Res. Quart. 46:134-139, 1975.

10. Clark, B.A., M.G. Wade, B.H. Massey and R. Van Dyke. Response of institutionalized geriatric mental patients to a twelve-week program of regular physical activity. J. Gerontol. 30:565-573, 1975.

11. Clausen, J.P. Effect of physical training on cardiovascular adjustments to exercise in man. Physiol. Rev. 57:779-815, 1977.

12. Clee, M.D., N. Smith, G.P. McNeill and D.S. Wright. Dysrhythmias in apparently healthy elderly subjects. Age and Ageing 8:173-176, 1979.

13. Costill, D.L., G.E. Branam, J.C. Moore, K. Sparks and C. Turner. Effects of physical training in men with coronary heart disease. Med. Sci. Sports 6:95-100, 1974.

14. Dehn, M.M. and R.A. Bruce. Effects of physical training on exertional ST segment depression in coronary heart disease. Circulation 44: 390-396, 1971.

16. deVries, H.A. Physiological effects of an exercise training regimen upon men aged 52 to 88. J. Gerontol. 25:325-336, 1970.

17. Dill, D.B., S. Robinson and J.C. Ross. A longitudinal study of 16 champion runners. J. Sports Med. 7:4-32, 1967.

18. Emes, C.G. The effects of a regular program of light exercise on seniors. J. Sports Med. 19:185-190, 1979.

19. Fardy, P.S. Left ventricle time component changes in middle-aged men following a twelve week physical training intervention program. J. Sports Med. Phys. Fitness 13:212-225, 1971.

20. Fardy, P.S., C.M. Maresh, R. Abbott and T. Kristiansen. A comparison of habitual lifestyle, aerobic power and systolic time intervals in former athletes and non-athletes. J. Sports Med. 18:287-299, 1978.

21. Fardy, P.S., C.M. Maresh, R.D. Abbott and T. Kristiansen. Myocardial function as influenced by age and habitual leisure time physical activity: A cross-sectional study. In: Sports Medicine, Vol. 5, edited by F. Landry and W.A.R. Orban. Miami: Symposia Specialists, pp. 85-91, 1978.

22. Franks. B.D. and T.K. Cureton. Effects of training on time components of the left ventricle. J. Sports Med. Phys. Fitness 9:80-88, 1969.

23. Getchell, L.H. and J.C. Moore. Physical training: Comparative responses of middle-aged adults. Arch. Phys. Med. Rehab. 56:250-254, 1975.

24. Hollman, W. Diminution of cardiopulmonary capacity in the course of life and its prevention by participation in sports. In: Proceedings of International Congress of Sports Sciences, Tokyo, 1964, edited by K. Kato. Tokyo: Japanese Union of Sport Sciences, pp. 91-93, 1966.

25. Hodgson, J.L. and E.R. Buskirk. Physical fitness and age, with emphasis on cardiovascular function in the elderly. J. Amer. Geriatr. Soc. 25:385-392, 1977.

26. Holmgren, A. and T. Strandell. Relationship between heart volume, total hemoglobin and physical work capacity in former athletes. Acta Med. Scandinav. 163:146-160, 1959.

27. Holmgren, A. Cardiorespiratory determinants of cardiovascular fitness. In: Proceedings of International Symposium on Physical Activity and Cardiovascular Health. Canad. Med. Assoc. J. 96:697-705, 1967.

28. Holmgren, A. Commentary. In: Proceedings of International Symposium on Physical Activity and Cardiovascular Health. Canad. Med. Ass. J. 96:794, 1967.

29. Ismail, A.H. and D.L. Montgomery. The effect of a four month physical fitness program on a young and an old group matched for physical fitness. Europ. J. Appl. Physiol. 40:137-144, 1979.

30. Jokl, E., M. Jokl-Ball, P. Jokl and L. Frankel. Notation of exercise. In: Medicine and Sport, Vol. 4, Physical Activity and Aging, edited by D. Brunner and E. Jokl. Baltimore: University Park Press, pp. 2-18, 1970.

31. Kavanagh, T., R.J. Shephard, H. Doney and V. Pandit. Intensive exercise in coronary rehabilitation. Med. Sci. Sports 5:34-39, 1973.

32. Kavanagh, T. and R.J. Shephard. The effects of continued training on the aging process. Ann. N.Y. Acad. Sci. 301:656-670, 1977.

33. Kiessling, K.H., L. Pilstrom, A.C. Bylund, B. Saltin and K. Piehl. Enzyme activities and morphometry in skeletal muscle of middle-aged men after training. Scand. J. Clin. Lab. Invest. 33:63-69, 1974.

34. Kilbom, A. Physical training in women. Scand. J. Clin. Lab. Invest. 28(119):1-34, 1971.

35. Kilbom, A., L.H. Hartley, B. Saltin, J. Bjure, G. Grimby and I. Astrand. Physical training in sedentary middle-aged and older men. I. Medical evaluation. Scand. J. Clin. Lab. Invest. 24:315-328, 1969.

36. Kindermann, W. and H. Reindell. Central hemodynamics in normal, well-trained and hypertensive subjects. In: Sports Medicine, Vol. 5, edited by F. Landry and W.A.R. Orban. Miami: Symposia Specialists, pp. 43-56, 1978.

37. Kohn, R.R. Heart and cardiovascular system. In: Handbook of the Biology of Aging, edited by C.E. Finch and L. Hayflick. New York: Van Nostrand Reinhold, pp. 281-317, 1977.

38. Lakatta, E.G. Alterations in the cardiovascular system that occur in advanced age. Fed. Proc. 38:163-167, 1969.

39. Massicotte, D.R., G. Avon and G. Carriveau. Comparative effects of aerobic training on men and women. J. Sports Med. 19:23-32, 1979.

40. Niinimaa, V. and R.J. Shephard. Training and oxygen conductance in the elderly. I. The respiratory system. J. Gerontol. 33:354-361, 1978.

41. Niinimaa, V. and R.J. Shephard. Training and oxygen conductance in the elderly. II. The cardiovascular system. J. Gerontol. 33:362-367, 1978.

42. Plowman, S.A., B.L. Drinkwater and S.M. Horvath. Age and aerobic power in women: A longitudinal study. J. Gerontol. 34:512-540, 1979.

43. Pollock, M.L. Physiological characteristics of older champion track athletes. Res. Quart. 45:363-373, 1974.

44. Pollock, M.L., G.A. Dawson, H.S. Miller, A. Ward, D. Cooper, W. Headley, A.C. Linnerud and M.M. Nomeir. Physiologic responses of men 49 to 65 years of age to endurance training. J. Am. Geriatr. Soc. 24: 97-104, 1976.

45. Pyorala, K., M.J. Karvonen, P. Taskinen, J. Takkunen and H. Kyronseppa. Cardiovascular studies on former endurance athletes. In: Physical Activity and the Heart, edited by M.J. Karvonen and A.J. Barry. Springfield: C.C. Thomas, pp. 301-310, 1967.

46. Roskamm, H. Optimum patterns of exercise for healthy adults. In: Proceedings of International Symposium on Physical and Cardiovascular Health. Canad. Med. Assoc. J. 96:895-899, 1967.

47. Rost, R., W. Dreisbach and W. Hollmann. Hemodynamic changes in 50- to 70- year-old men due to endurance training. In: Sports Medicine, Vol. 5, edited by F. Landry and W.A.R. Orban. Miami: Symposia Special-ists, pp. 121-124, 1978.

48. Saltin, B., G. Blomqvist, J.H. Mitchell, R.L. Johnson, K. Wilden-thal and C.B. Chapman. Response to exercise after bedrest and after training. Circulation 38:1-68, 1968.

49. Saltin, B. and G. Grimby. Physiological analysis of middle-aged and old former athletes. Comparison with still active athletes of the same age. Circulation 38:1104-1115, 1968.

50. Saltin, B., L.H. Hartley, A. Kilbom and I. Astrand. Physical training in sedentary middle-aged men and older men. II. Oxygen uptake, heart rate and blood lactate concentration at submaximal and maximal exercise. Scand. J. Clin. Lab. Invest. 24:323-334, 1969.

51. Shephard, R.J. Standard tests of aerobic power. In: Frontiers of Fitness, edited by R.J. Shephard. Springfield: C.C. Thomas, pp. 233-264, 1971.

52. Shephard, R.J. Endurance Fitness. 2nd edition. Toronto: University of Toronto Press, 1977.

53. Shephard, R.J. Physical Activity and Aging. London: Croom-Helm, 1978.

54. Shephard, R.J. and T. Kavanagh. The effects of training on the aging process. Physician and Sports Medicine 6:33-40, 1978.

55. Shephard, R.J. and K.H. Sidney. Exercise and aging. In: Exercise and Sports Sciences Reviews, Vol. 6, edited by R.S. Hutton. Philadelphia: Franklin Institute Press, pp. 1-58, 1978.

56. Sheuer, J. and C.M. Tipton. Cardiovascular adaptations to physical training. Ann. Rev. Physiol. 39:221-251, 1977.

57. Sidney, K.H. and R.J. Shephard. Training and electrocardiographic abnormalities in the elderly. Brit. Heart J. 39:1114-1120, 1977.

58. Sidney, K.H. and R.J. Shephard. Perception of exertion in the elderly. Effects of aging, mode of exercise and physical training. Percept. Motor Skills 44:999-1010, 1977.

59. Sidney, K.H. and R.J. Shephard. Maximum and submaximum exercise tests in men and women in the seventh, eighth and ninth decades of life. J. Appl. Physiol. 43:280-287, 1977.

60. Sidney, K.H. and R.J. Shephard. Frequency and intensity of exercise training for elderly subjects. Med. Sci. Sports 10:125-131, 1978.

61. Sidney, K.H., R.J. Shephard and J.H. Harrison. Endurance training and body composition of the elderly. Am. J. Clin. Nutr. 30: 326-333, 1977.

62. Siegel, W., G. Blomqvist and J.H. Mitchell. Effects of a quanti-tated physical training program on middle-aged sedentary males. Circula-tion 41:19-29, 1970.

63. Sjostrand, T. The relationship between the heart frequency and the ST level of the electrocardiogram. Acta Med. Scand. 138:200-210, 1950.

64. Skinner, J. The cardiovascular system with aging and exercise. In: Medicine and Sport, Vol. 4, Physical Activity and Aging, edited by D. Brunner and E. Jokl. Baltimore: University Park Press, pp. 100-108, 1970.

65. Sleight, P. The effect of ageing on the circulation. Age and Ageing 8:98, 1979.

66. Stamford, B.A. Physiological effects of training upon insti-tutionalized geriatric men. J. Gerontol. 27:451-455, 1972.

67. Stamford, B.A. Effects of chronic institutionalization on the physical working capacity and trainability of geriatric men. J. Gerontol. 28:441-446, 1973.

68. Strandell, T. Circulatory studies on healthy old men. Acta Med. Scand. Suppl. 414, pp. 1-44, 1964.

69.  Suominen, H., E. Heikkinen, H. Liesen, D. Michel and W. Hollman. Effects of 8 weeks endurance training on skeletal muscle metabolism in 56-70 year old sedentary men. Europ. J. Appl. Physiol. 37:173-180, 1977.

70.  Suominen, H., E. Heikkinen and T. Parkatti. Effects of eight weeks physical training on muscle and connective tissue of the M. vastus lateralis in 69 year-old men and women. J. Gerontol. 32:33-37, 1977.

71.  Suominen, H., E. Heikkinen and T. Parkatti. Effects of eight-week physical training on muscle and connective tissue of the M. vastus lateralis in 69 year-old men and women. In: 3rd International Symposium on Biochemistry of Exercise, edited by F. Landry and W.A.R. Orban. Miami: Symposia Specialists, pp. 279-284, 1978.

72.  Tzankoff, S.P., S. Robinson, F.S. Pyke and C.A. Brown. Physiological adjustments to work in older men as affected by physical training. J. Appl. Physiol. 33:346-350, 1972.

73.  Wilmore, J.H., J. Royce, R. Girandola, F. Katch and V. Katch. Physiological alterations resulting from a 10-week program of jogging. Med. Sci. Sports 2:7-14, 1970.

Kenneth H. Sidney received his initial experiences as a research and exercise leader of the elderly as a graduate student in the Department of Environmental Health at the University of Toronto. He earned his Ph.D. in applied physiology while studying under the supervision of Dr. Roy J. Shephard. He was a Research Fellow in the Department of Medicine at the University of Western Ontario. He is presently an Assistant Professor of Physical and Health Education at Laurentian University in Sudbury. He is also Program Director of the Sudbury Cardiac Rehabilitation Program and National Coach for Canada's Orienteering team. He is a member of the American Gerontological Society, the Canadian Association of Applied Sport Sciences, and a Fellow of the American College of Sports Medicine.

# TRAINING ADAPTATIONS IN THE MUSCLES OF OLDER MEN
Toshio Moritani

## AGING AND NEUROMUSCULAR SYSTEM

Atrophy and decrease of muscle strength are commonly seen in
the aging process (2,34). The decrease of muscle mass
(atrophy) has been shown to be due to decrease both in number
(26,59,64) and size (59,66) of the fibers. Recently,
Gutmann (25) has shown that the marked reduction of muscle
fibers is apparently associated with the progressive decrease
in number and size of myofibrils which proceeds very slowly.
Furthermore, a preferential atrophy has been reported in
animal studies (64) as well as in human studies (44) with
respect to different muscle fiber types. For example,
Tauchi, Yoshika, and Kobayashi (66) have reported that "white"
(fast twitch) fibers are characterized with a decrease in
both number and size while "red" (slow twitch) fibers decrease
in number. Similar results are also reported by Larsson,
Sjodin, and Karlsson (44) who have found a selective decrease
in type II fiber area with aging.

The deficiencies in motor performance in old age, i.e.,
slowness and decrease of muscle strength could be explained
in terms of physiological changes occurring in motor units
(MU) with advancing age. Recent animal studies (15,27,29,30)
have suggested that these motor disturbances might be due to a
primary disturbance of the neuromuscular junction with a progressive decrease in the trophic function of the nerve cells,
resulting in the random loss of muscle fibers and consequently
the decrease of the size of MU. There has been some evidence
suggesting that the decline of the trophic influence of the

nervous system is also associated with the metabolic changes taking place in the old mammalian muscles (25,67,63,16).

Enzyme activities concerning energy supply and utilization have been shown to decrease in fast muscles, more marked in the glycolytic than in the oxidative enzymes (25). The decrease in the ratio of glycolytic to oxidative enzymes in fast muscles may lead to a diminished capacity to utilize energy substrate anaerobically. On the other hand, this ratio does not seem to change significantly in slow twitch muscle (25). Therefore, it seems that there is a definite physiological trend toward a loss of metabolic differences of muscle fibers. This "dedifferentiation" (25) has also been demonstrated in ATPase activity in the animal (27,31,63). Damon (9) reported that in the human, age-related declines were observed in the various parameters of muscle strength tests, e.g., whether measured in isometric, concentric, or eccentric muscle contraction and also when measured as maximal instantaneous force exerted. Furthermore, it was demonstrated that the maximal velocity produced against any given mass was less for the old than the young; although the shapes of the observed force-velocity curve were quite similar (9).

The decrease in ATP, creatinephosphate (CP), glycogen, and ATP/ADP ratio in old age may result in a possible deficiency in energetics of muscular contraction (14,17,18). This is particularly manifested in the recovery phase after onset of muscular work. For example, the functional consequence of the decreased recovery of CP in old age leads to a diminished ATP recovery. Although there were no changes in the acute transfer of chemical energy into tension energy, the capacity for continuous work would be decreased since the recovery of CP was quickly exhausted in the aged (67).

An EMG fatigue study (19) indicated that fatigue rate (as determined by the rate of rise in the integrated EMG (IEMG)) was significantly greater in the old than in the young when holding isometric contractions at different fractions of maximal voluntary contraction. This result may be explained by the following chains of events in the light of recent findings. During an isometric contraction, a preferential recruitment of fast twitch fibers takes place due to a diminished blood flow and would bring about linear increases in lactate and decreases in CP (37,61). The increase in lactate and the decrease in tension are correlated, r = -0.99 (20). A reduced CP level and increased tissue lactate level with subsequent decreases in pH have been postulated to interfere with the excitation-contraction coupling, leading to a deficit in the developed tension (21,22,52,56). If the tension were to be maintained under these conditions, the recruitment of some additional MUs or increases in MU firing frequency must take place to compensate for the loss in contractility of some fatiguing MUs. In view of the age-related decrease in enzyme activities, delay in the CP recovery, and decreased size of MUs, a greater rate of increase in the IEMG as a function of time could be expected in the old.

## EFFECTS OF MUSCULAR TRAINING AND DISUSE DURING AGING

As discussed in the previous section, decreases in the neuronal impulse and nonimpulse (neurotrophic) activities have been shown to occur in experimental animals (25,26,28,29) and therefore a decline of the trophic function of the neuron could be assumed. According to Gutmann (25), this disturbance is caused by a decrease in the synthesis of neurotrophic agents and probably by a slowing of axoplasmic transport. This could lead to a slowly progressing disturbance of neuromuscular contact, resulting in a loss of muscle fibers (25, 26,27,59,64). Recent human studies (43,44) have indicated that histochemical changes in the muscle tissue such as decreased proportion of type II fibers and a selective atrophy of type II fibers do exist with increasing age. Furthermore, Larsson, Grimby, and Karlsson (43) showed that the strength decline in old age was correlated significantly with the type II fiber area. Electromyographic studies on humans (7,68) revealed that decreases in EMG amplitude and peak number resulted from a relative decrease in muscle fiber size and number and an increase in duration of action potentials. The significant increase in the polyphasic activity seems to suggest a delay in end plate transmission or muscle fiber response (7).

In considering the above-mentioned findings, trainability of old individuals may appear to decline in old age. In fact, some investigators (36,40) indicated that practically no observable improvement could be expected if training were started late in life. On the other hand, many investigators (3,4,12,32,41,60) reported that significant improvement in physical working capacity and muscle function could be obtained by training older people. More recently, deVries (12) and Adams and deVries (1) have furnished evidence that a physical training regimen could indeed bring about significant functional changes in older men and women, particularly those relating to oxygen transport capacity. Suominen, Heikkinen, and Parkatti (62) have shown that the mean $\dot{V}O_2$ max of 26 men and women (both aged 69 years) increased from 28.9 ml/kg·min before training to 32.0 ml/kg·min after training and 27.9 to 31.3 ml/kg·min, respectively. These results were further substantiated by the finding of an increased oxidative enzyme activity, thus leading to an enhanced capacity for aerobic metabolism in older subjects. It was also pointed out that the percentage of slow twitch (ST) fibers was nearly the same (in the m. vastus lateralis) in both groups.

Moritani and deVries (50) investigated the time course of muscle strength gain in young and old subjects under similar experimental procedures and training regimen. It was found that there was a significant increase in the maximal voluntary strength which was quite comparable to that of the young, when expressed as the percentage change with respect to the initial strength value. Furthermore, they observed an increase in the maximal level of muscle activation (as measured by the maximal IEMG) after 8 weeks of muscle training in the old.

On the basis of these studies, it seems that the trainability of old people does not greatly differ from that of young and middle-aged persons if compared on a percentage basis (12,50,62).

Disuse or "Hypokinetic Diseases," a term coined by Kraus and Raab (42), describing the whole spectrum of somatic and mental derangements induced by inactivity, may be of considerable importance as a factor associated with an age-dependent decrement in functional capacities (47). Disuse resulting in lack of mobilization of adaptive capacities can, a priori, be expected to cause marked regressive changes in the neuromuscular system (5,23,46,53). Booth and Seider (5) have recently shown that during an early stage of immobilization, there is a significant decline in the fractional rate of protein synthesis, suggesting very early changes occurring in molecular events that regulate protein synthesis in disused or immobilized skeletal muscle of rats. Similar results have also been reported by Goldberg and Goodman (23) who found the inhibition of α-aminoisobutyric acid (AIB) after section of the sciatic nerve. It was suggested that the amino acid uptake by muscle might be influenced by the amount of muscular activity since the AIB uptake was not affected in the diaphragm muscle which continued to function normally.

Histochemical (53) and biochemical (46) studies on human subjects seem to suggest that disuse resulting from immobilization of a limb can bring about losses in functional capacities, i.e., a decrease in fiber diameter, reduced CP concentration and reduced glycogen concentration. Thus, disuse or inactivity could produce functional deficiencies very similar to the progressive changes in the neuromuscular system seen in the older individuals. It seems apparent that the physiological changes which accompany the aging process might not be the result of aging alone (13). In this regard, it is interesting to note that Petrofsky and Lind (55) found no change in muscular strength or muscular endurance with age. It was suggested that the homogeneity of the subjects' (aged 22 to 62 years) occupations, in which all men were employed in a machine shop for an aircraft corporation, could be the primary factor for their findings. A decrease in motor activity associated with domestication of animals and data on "slower" aging in tissues of wild animals point out the fact that the aging process may not be the only important determinant for the physiological changes seen in the old (25).

According to deVries (13), one may hypothesize that the functional losses which have been observed and reported in the medical and physiological literature as age changes must be considered as resulting from at least three composite factors, only one of which is truly an aging phenomenon. Of the other two factors, unrecognized incipient disease process may or may not be causally related to aging. The third factor, disuse phenomena or "Hypokinetic Diseases," is the only one of the three factors which can be easily reversed (p. 263).

## NEURAL FACTORS VERSUS HYPERTROPHY IN THE TIME COURSE OF MUSCLE STRENGTH GAIN WITH SPECIAL REFERENCE TO AGE

De Lorme and Watkins (10) hypothesized the existence of at least two major determinants which influence the time course of muscle strength gain. They postulated that, "The initial increase in strength on progressive resistance exercise occurs at a rate far greater than can be accounted for by morphological changes within muscle. These initial rapid increments in strength noted in normal and disuse-atrophied muscles are, no doubt, due to motor learning." In support of this hypothesis there have been several studies (6,8,11,33) which indicated that an increase in muscle strength can be observed in the absence of measurable hypertrophy. On the other hand, a strong relationship has been shown both between absolute strength and the cross-sectional area of the muscle (57) and between strength gain and increase in muscle girth or cross-sectional area (10,35).

Ikai and Fukunaga (38), using ultrasonic measurement for assessing changes in the cross-sectional area of arm flexors, reported a 92% increase in strength with only a 23% increase in cross-sectional area after 100 days of ten-second isometric contractions. Since the significant gain in strength observed at the early stage of the training was not accompanied by any significant increase in the cross-sectional area, they have also hypothesized that there appear to be two primary mechanisms by which strength gain can be achieved through training: 1) the increase in the MU discharge to the acting muscles and 2) the morphological change in the contractile tissue itself (hypertrophy) brought about by tension induced through muscle training.

In our laboratory, we have developed EMG instrumentation and methodology which make it possible to separate muscle activation level (MU discharge and MU recruitment) from hypertrophic effects (morphological changes) (11,47,49,50). deVries (11) has shown that the ratio of muscle activation (as measured by IEMG) to the force developed (E/F ratio)

reflects the level of hypertrophy in skeletal muscles.
Furthermore, the level of IEMG attained during maximal voluntary contraction (MVC) is a measure of the maximal activation
of the muscle under voluntary contraction. The activation
level is necessarily the result of interaction of both facili-
tatory and inhibitatory phenomena which may act at various
levels of the nervous system. Since these factors are quite
complex and not yet clearly defined, we refer to them col-
lectively as "neural factors."

We have recently demonstrated that, under certain experimental conditions, the IEMG-force relationship for the elbow
flexors is linear throughout the entire range of forces up to
and including MVC, $r = 0.990$, $p < 0.0001$ (48).

Figure 1 illustrates the method for separation of the
proportional contributions of neural factors and hypertrophy.
If strength increase is achieved by "neural factors" such as
"learning to disinhibit" as suggested by earlier studies
(39,45), then we should expect to see increases in maximal
activation without any change in force per fiber or per unit
activation (MUs innervated) as shown in Fig. 1A. On the
other hand, if strength increase were due entirely to muscular hypertrophy, we should expect to see an increase in the
forces per fiber or unit activation by virtue of the hypertrophy without any change in the maximal IEMG as shown in
Fig. 1B. Fig. 1C illustrates our method for the evaluation
of the percent contributions when both neural factors and
hypertrophy are operant in the course of strength gain.

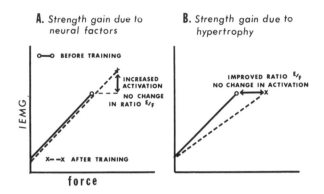

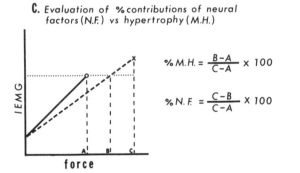

Fig. 1. Schema for evaluation of percent contributions of neural factors and hypertrophy to the
gain of strength through progressive resistance
exercise. From Moritani & deVries, <u>Am. J. Phys. Med.</u>
58:115-130, 1978 (49).

Using this method, we have investigated the time course
of strength gain with respect to the contributions of neural
factors and hypertrophy in seven young males (18-26, mean
22.0 years) during the course of an 8-week regimen of isotonic strength training. The EMG instrumentation, hydraulic
dynamometer, method for estimation of changes in cross-
sectional area of the muscle (elbow flexors), and testing
procedures have been described elsewhere (11,47,49,50).

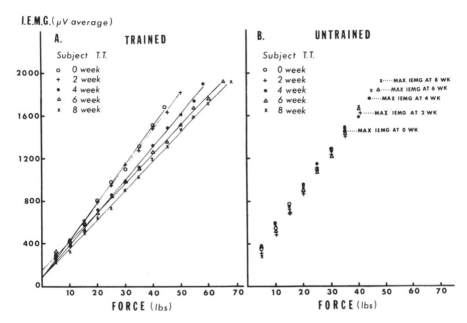

Fig. 2. Data plotted to show typical changes in the trained arm (A) as compared to the untrained arm (B). Both arms gained in strength but only the trained arm showed significant changes in the E/F ratio (hypertrophy). From Moritani & deVries, Am. J. Phys. Med. 58:115-130, 1978 (49).

The results indicated that highly significant training effects were brought about in the trained elbow flexor muscle groups in all parameters tested. It was shown that the significant strength increase (mean gain of 21.2 lb, $p < 0.001$) after the training was brought about by both neural factors and hypertrophy as demonstrated by the significant changes in the muscle activation level (mean increase of 223 µv, $p < 0.002$), the cross-sectional area (mean gain of 2.91 $cm^2$, $p < 0.004$) and the E/F ratio (EEA) (mean decrease of -6.36, $p < 0.007$).

The typical changes in the trained arm as compared to the untrained arm of the same subject with respect to the time course is shown in Fig. 2. It is interesting to note that even in the trained arm the EMG slope coefficient after two weeks of training remained almost identical to that of the pre-training (zero week) value, although the regression

line rose to higher maximal IEMG values. This of course
represents an increase in the muscle activation which
accounted for almost the entire strength increase seen at
this early stage of the training. However, the EMG slope
started to decline as the training proceeded, suggesting
that some degree of muscle hypertrophy gradually began contributing to the gain of strength, while the rapid increase
in the activation level was no longer maintained, but now
increased at a considerably diminished rate.

On the other hand, the same subjects' contralateral
untrained flexor muscle groups also showed a significant
strength increase (mean gain of 13.4 lb., $p < 0.001$),
supporting the findings of earlier investigators (8,33) who
studied the effects of muscle training of ipsilateral limb
on the strength of the contralateral limb. It seems most
likely that the resultant significant increase in strength
of the contralateral untrained arm was brought about by
"neural factors" in which the maximal activation level would
be expected to increase without any changes in the E/F ratio.
This was in fact the case in our study (see Fig. 2B).

Figure 3 shows the time course of strength gain with
respect to the calculated percent contributions of neural
factors and hypertrophy by using the method described
earlier. The results clearly demonstrate that the neural
factors played a dominant role in strength development at
early stages of strength gain and then the hypertrophic factor
gradually increased in importance in the contribution to the
strength gain.

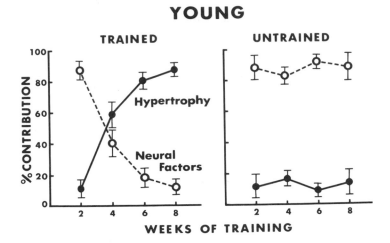

Fig. 3. The time course of strength gain showing the percent contributions of neural factors and hypertrophy in the trained and untrained arms of the young subjects. From Moritani and deVries, Am. J. Phys. Med. 50:115-130, 1978 (49).

NEURAL FACTORS VERSUS HYPERTROPHY IN THE OLD ADULT

Another experiment was undertaken in our laboratory so as to elucidate the difference, if any, between young and old subjects with respect to the percent contributions of neural factors and hypertrophy in an attempt to shed some light on the possible neurophysiological differences in the expression of human strength.

Five aged subjects (67-72, mean age of 69.6 years) who volunteered for this experiment were tested and trained under similar experimental conditions and training regimen as used in the first experiment described earlier. The results indicated that the significant increases in the maximal strength in the aged (mean gain of 13.8 lb., $p < 0.001$) were brought about by neural factors as demonstrated by the significant increases in the maximal muscle activation level (mean gain of 295 µV, $p < 0.001$) without any significant changes in the cross-sectional area (0.96 cm$^2$, $p > 0.282$) and EMG slope coefficient (-1.13, $p > 0.321$).

   Figure 4 illustrates the percent contributions of
neural factors and hypertrophy in the trained and untrained
arms of aged subjects.  It was demonstrated that increases
in the maximal muscle activation (neural factors) played a
dominant role throughout the training.  In the absence of
any significant muscle hypertrophy, it was suggested that
the effect of muscle training in the older subjects may
entirely rest on the neural factors which could be improved
by training and thus result in the higher levels of muscle
activation.

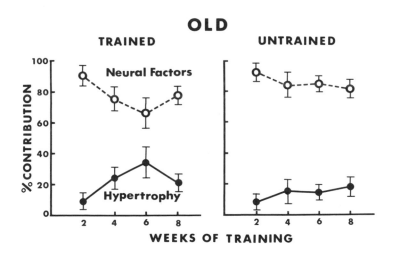

Fig. 4.   The time course of strength gain showing
the percent contributions of neural factors and
hypertrophy in the trained and untrained arms of
the old subjects.   From Moritani and deVries, J.
Geront., in press (50).

   The contralateral untrained arm also showed significant
strength gain in the aged (mean gain of 9.2 lb., p    0.004).
This increase appears to be the result of changes in the
neural factors in the light of significant gains in the
maximal IEMG of the untrained arms (270 $\mu$V, p < 0.002) with
no significant hypertrophy (0.76 $cm^2$, p > 0.266).

   It is interesting to note that the strength gain in the
aged induced by the changes in the neural factors was quite
comparable to that of the young, particularly when expressed

as the percentage gain with respect to the initial strength value (see Fig. 5). One could postulate the existence of some psychologically induced inhibitions influencing the initial strength level in which the older subjects might consciously or subconsciously restrict themselves from exerting maximal voluntary effort to a greater extent than the young. This psychologically induced inhibition might have been reduced by gradual "removal of inhibitory influences" (58) during the training period, thus elevating the level of maximal muscle activation by voluntary effort.

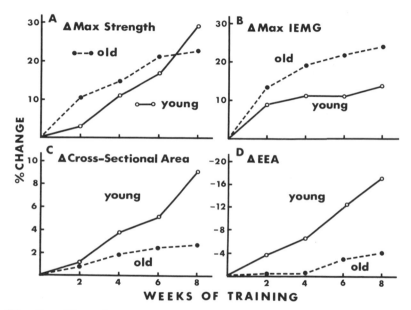

Fig 5. The time course of changes in the maximal strength, maximal IEMG (muscle activation level), cross-sectional area and EEA (EMG slope coefficient) when each value is expressed as percent change with respect to the initial values. From Moritani and deVries, J. Geront., in press (50).

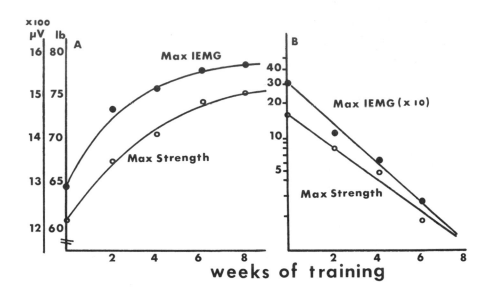

Fig. 6. Training curves of the maximal strength and maximal IEMG based on the data obtained from the old subjects' trained arms (A) and their plots on semi-logarithmic coordinates (B).

Another explanation for the small difference in the relative strength gains might be the difference in the initial strength level and the degree of hypokinesia which have been demonstrated to be important factors in determining the rate of strength development. Muller and Rohmert (51) pointed out that the closer one was to his theoretical maximum trained strength (termed "Endkraft"), the smaller the strength gain was likely to be. Thus, the sedentary person with a progressive hypokinesia and subsequent muscle atrophy would be expected to achieve the greatest gain through training.

With respect to the potential for muscle hypertrophy in the aged, Drahota and Gutmann (15) reported no apparent indication of compensatory hypertrophy or post-functional hypertrophy induced by electrical stimulation in old animals. On the other hand, some investigators (24,65) have shown that compensatory hypertrophy through a weight lifting regimen was not limited by age; although the extent of the hypertrophy was greater in the young animals. These differences in the experimental results may be due to the difference in the training intensity, duration and frequency used to induce hypertrophy. Our data seem to suggest that under the experimental conditions used in the present studies there may be no significant muscle hypertrophy in the aged subjects in response to the 8-week muscle training. It is also suggested that the training-induced increase in the maximal level of muscle activation (neural factors) through greater MU discharge frequency and/or MU recruitment may be the only mechanism by which the aged subjects increase their muscle strength in the absence of any significant evidence of hypertrophy. Data illustrated in Fig. 6 further support this assumption on the basis that there seems to be a very close association between the rate of increase in the maximal IEMG and the subsequent increase in the maximal strength in the aged subjects.

## REFERENCES

1. Adams, G.M. and H.A. deVries. Physiological effects of an exercise training regimen upon women aged 59-79. J. Geront. 28:50-55, 1973.

2. Astrand, P.O. and K. Rodahl. Textbook of Work Physiology. New York: McGraw-Hill Book Company, 1970.

3. Barry, A.J., J.W. Daly, E.D.R. Pruett, J.R. Steinmetz, H.F. Page, N.C. Birkhead, and K. Rodahl. The effects of physical conditioning on older individuals. J. Geront. 21:182-191, 1966.

4. Benestad, M. Trainability of old men. Acta Med. Scand. 178: 321-327, 1965.

5. Booth, F.W. and M.J. Seider. Early change in skeletal muscle protein synthesis after limb immobilization of rats. J. Appl. Physiol.: Respirat. Environm. Exercise Physiol. 47:974-977, 1979.

6. Bowers, L. Effects of autosuggested muscle contraction on muscular strength and size. Research Quarterly 37:302-312, 1966.

7. Carlson, K.E., W. Alston, and D.J. Feldman. Electromyographic study of aging in skeletal muscle. Am. J. Phys. Med. 43:141-145, 1964.

8. Coleman, E.A. Effect of unilateral isometric and isotonic contractions on the strength of the contralateral limb. Research Quarterly 40:490-495, 1969.

9. Damon, E.L. An experimental investigation of the relationship of age to various parameters of muscle strength. Doctoral Dissertation, University of Southern California, 1971.

10. De Lorme, T.L. and A.L. Watkins. Progressive Resistance Exercise. New York: Appleton Century, Inc., 1951.

11. deVries, H.A. Efficiency of electrical activity as a measure of the functional state of muscle tissue. Am. J. Phys. Med. 47:10-22, 1968.

12. deVries, H.A. Physiological effects of an exercise training regimen upon men aged 52-88. J. Geront. 25:325-336, 1970.

13. deVries, H.A. Physiology of exercise and aging. In: Scientific Perspectives and Social Issues, edited by D.S. Woodruff and J.E. Birren. New York: D. Van Nostrand Company, 1975.

14. Drahota, Z. and E. Gutmann. Long term regulatory influences of the nervous system on some metabolic differences in muscles of different function. Physiol. Bohemoslov. 12:339-348, 1963.

15. Drahota, Z. and E. Gutmann. The effect of age on compensatory and "post-functional hypertrophy" in cross-striated muscle. Gerontologia 6:81-90, 1962.

16. Ermini, M. Aging changes in mammalian skeletal muscle. Gerontology 22:301-316, 1976.

17. Ermini, M., I. Szelenyi, P. Mosen, and F. Verzar. The aging of skeletal (striated) muscle by changes of recovery metabolism. Gerontologia 17:300-311, 1971.

18. Ermini, M. and F. Verzar. Decreased restitution of certain phosphate in white and red skeletal muscles during aging. Experientia 24:902-903, 1967.

19. Evans, S.J. An electromyographic analysis of skeletal neuromuscular fatigue with special reference to age. Doctoral Dissertation, University of Southern California, 1971.

20. Fitts, R.H. The effects of exercise-training on the development of fatigue. Ann. N. Y. Acad. Sci. 302:424-430, 1977.

21. Fitts, R.H. and J.O. Holloszy. Lactate and contractile force in frog muscle during development of fatigue and recovery. Am. J. Physiol. 231:430-433, 1976.

22. Fuches, F., Y. Reddy, and F.M. Briggs. The interaction of cations with the calcium-binding site of troponin. Biochim. Biophys. Acta. 221:408-409, 1970.

23. Goldberg, A.L. and H.M. Goodman. Effects of disuse and dinervation on amino acid transport by skeletal muscle. Am. J. Physiol. 216: 1116-1119, 1969.

24. Goldspink, G. and K.F. Howells. Work-induced hypertrophy in exercised normal muscles of different ages and the reversibility of hypertrophy after cessation of exercise. J. Physiol. 239:179-193, 1974.

25. Gutmann, E. Muscle. In: Handbook of the Biology of Aging, edited by C. C. Finch and L. Hayflick. New York: Van Nostrand Reinhold Company, 1977.

26. Gutmann, E. and V. Hanzlikova. Motor unit in old age. Nature 209:921-922, 1966.

27. Gutmann, E. and V. Hanzlikova. Basic mechanisms of aging in the neuromuscular system. Mech. Age. Develop. 1:327-349, 1972/1973.

28. Gutmann, E. and V. Hanzlikova. Fast and slow motor units in aging. Gerontology 22:280-300, 1976.

29. Gutmann, E., V. Hanzlikova, and B. Jakoubek. Changes in the neuromuscular system during old age. Exp. Geront. 3:141-146, 1968.

30. Gutmann, E., V. Hanzlikova, and F. Vyskocil. Age changes in cross striated muscle of the rat. J. Physiol. 219:331-343, 1971.

31. Gutmann, E. and I. Syrovy. Contraction properties and myosin-ATPase activity of fast and slow senile muscles. Gerontologia 20: 239-244, 1974.

32. Hartley, L.H., G. Grimby, A. Kilbom, N.J. Nilsson, I. Astrand, J. Bjure, B. Ekblom, and B. Saltin. Physical training in sedentary middle-aged and older men. III. Cardiac output and gas exchange at submaximal and maximal exercise. Scand. J. Clin. Lab. Invest. 24:335-344, 1969.

33. Hellebrandt, F.A., A.M. Parrish, and S.J. Houtz. Cross education. Arch. Phys. Med. 28:76-85, 1947.

34. Hettinger, T. Physiology of Strength. Springfield: C. C. Thomas Publisher, 1961.

35. Hettinger, L. and E.A. Muller. Muskelleistung und muskeltraining. Arbeitsphysiologie 15:111-126, 1953.

36. Hollman, W. Changes in the capacity for maximal and continuous effort in relation to age. In: International Sports and Physical Education, edited by E. Jokl and E. Simon. Springfield: C.C. Thomas Publisher, 1964.

37. Hulten, B., A. Thorstensson, B. Sjodin and J. Karlsson. Relationship between isometric endurance and fiber types in human leg muscles. Acta Physiol. Scand. 93:135-138, 1975.

38. Ikai, M. and T. Fukunaga. A Study on training effect on strength per cross-sectional area of muscle by means of ultrasonic measurement. Int. Z. Angew. Physiol. 28:173-180, 1961.

39. Ikai, M. and A.H. Steinhaus. Some factors modifying the expression of human strength. J. Appl. Physiol. 16:157-163, 1961.

40. Katsuki, S. and M. Masuda. Physical exercise for persons of middle and older age in relation to their physical ability. J. Sport. Med. 9:193-199, 1969.

41. Kilbom, A., L.H. Hartley, B. Saltin, J. Bjure, G. Grimby, and I. Astrand. Physical training in sedentary middle-aged and older men. I. Medical evaluation. Scand. J. Clin. Lab. Invest. 24:315-322, 1969.

42. Kraus, H. and W. Raab. Hypokinetic Diseases. Springfield: C.C. Thomas Publisher, 1961.

43. Larsson, L., G. Grimby, and J. Karlsson. Muscle strength and speed of movement in relation to age and muscle morphology. J. Appl. Physiol.: Respirat. Environ. Exercise Physiol. 46:451-456, 1979.

44. Larsson, L., B. Sjodin, and J. Karlsson. Histochemical and biochemical changes in human skeletal muscle with age in sedentary males, age 22-65 years. Acta Physiol. Scand. 103:31-39, 1978.

45. Laycoe, R.P. and R.G. Marteiniuk. Learning and tension as factors in static strength gains produced by static and eccentric training. Research Quarterly 42:299-306, 1971.

46. MacDougall, J.D., G.R. Ward, D.G. Sale, and J.R. Sutton. Biochemical adaptation of human skeletal muscle to heavy resistance training and immobilization. J. Appl. Physiol. 43:700-703, 1977.

47. Moritani, T. Electromyographic analysis of muscle strength gains: Neural and hypertrophic effects. National Strength Coaches Assoc. J. 1:32-37, 1978.

48. Moritani, T. and H.A. deVries. Reexamination of the relationship between the surface integrated electromyogram (IEMG) and force of isometric contraction. Am. J. Phys. Ed. 57:263-277, 1978.

49. Moritani, T. and H.A. deVries. Neural factors versus hypertrophy in the time course of muscle strength gain. Am. J. Phys. Med. 58:115-130, 1979.

50. Moritani, T. and H.A. deVries. Potential for gross muscle hypertrophy in older men. J. Geront. in press, 1980.

51. Muller, E.A. and W. Rohmert. Die geschwindigkeit der muskelkraft zunakme bei isometrischen training. Int. Z. Angew. Physiol. 19:403-419, 1963.

52. Nakamura, Y. and Schwartz, A. The influence of hydrogen ion concentration on calcium binding and release by skeletal muscle sarcoplasmic reticulum. J. Gen. Physiol. 59:22-32, 1972.

53. Patel, A.N., A. Razzak, and D.K. Dastur. Disuse atrophy of human skeletal muscles. Arch. Neurol. 20:413-422, 1969.

54. Perkins, L.C. and H.L. Kaiser. Results of short term isotonic and isometric programs in persons over sixty. Physical Therapy Rev. 41:633-635, 1962.

55. Petrofsky, J.S. and A.R. Lind. Aging, isometric strength and endurance, and cardiovascular responses to static effort. J. Appl. Physiol. 39:91-95, 1975.

56. Portzehl, H., P. Zaoralek, and J. Gaudin. The activation by $Ca^{++}$ of the ATPase of extracted muscle fibrils with variation of ionic strength, pH and concentration of MgATP. Biochim. Biophys. Acta. 189: 440-448, 1969.

57. Rodahl, K. and S.M. Horvath. Muscle as a Tissue. New York: McGraw-Hill Book Company, 1962.

58. Roush, E.S. Strength and endurance in the waking and hypnotic states. J. Appl. Physiol. 3:404-410, 1951.

59. Rowe, R.W.D. The effect of senility on skeletal muscles in the mouse. Exp. Geront. 4:119-126, 1969.

60. Saltin, B., L.H. Hartley, A. Kilbom, and I. Astrand. Physical training in sedentary middle-aged and older men. II. Oxygen uptake, heart rate, and blood lactate concentration at submaximal and maximal exercise. Scand. J. Clin. Lab. Invest. 24:323-334, 1969.

61. Spande, J.I. and B.A. Schottelius. Chemical basis of fatigue in isolated soleus muscle. Am. J. Physiol. 219:1490-1495, 1970.

62. Suominen, H., E. Heikkinen, and T. Parkatti, Effect of eight week's physical training on muscle and connective tissue of the m. vastus lateralis in 69-year-old men and women. J. Geront. 32:33-37, 1977.

63. Syrovy, I. and E. Gutmann. Changes in speed of contraction and ATPase activity in striated muscle during old age. Exp. Geront. 5:31-35, 1970.

64. Tauchi, H., T. Yoshika, and H. Kobayashi. Age changes of skeletal muscles of rats. Gerontologia 17:219-227, 1971.

65. Tomanek, R.J. and Y.K. Wood. Compensatory hypertrophy of the plantaris muscle in relation to age. J. Geront. 25:23-29, 1970.

66. Tucek, S. and E. Gutmann. Choline acetyltransferase activity in muscles of old rats. Exp. Geront. 38:349-360, 1973.

67. Verzar, F. and M. Ermini. Decrease of creatine-phosphate restitution of muscle in old age and the influence of glucose. Gerontologia 16:223-230, 1970.

68. Visser, S.L. and W. de Ruke. Influence of sex and age on EMG contraction pattern. Europ. Neurol. 12:229-235, 1974.

Toshio Moritani came to the United States in 1973 after completing his B.A. degree in Physical Education at the Chukyo University in Nagoya, Japan. He obtained his M.A. Degree from the California State University at Northridge in 1975 and earned his Ph.D. under the direction of Dr. Herbert A. deVries from the University of Southern California. His major graduate work was directed toward physiology of exercise, particularly neuromuscular physiology and exercise physiology and aging. He is presently teaching at the California State University at Northridge.

# EFFECTS OF EXERCISE ON THE RANGE OF JOINT MOTION IN ELDERLY SUBJECTS

Kathleen Munns

One of the most pronounced changes associated with advanced age is the impairment of movement (25). Movement can be impaired and instability can result from a difficulty in balance, a loss in muscle strength and a decrease in flexibility or the range of joint motion. Simple daily movement (e.g., walking, climbing stairs) may even be avoided for fear of injury due to instability.

Modern conveniences and energy saving devices compound the problem of physical limitations by steering people away from the daily activity they need. Hypokinesis, meaning a low amount of movement and exercise along with an inadequate energy expenditure, has an adverse effect on people of all ages (17). Life long habits of inactivity combined with impaired movement and reinforced with society's "slow down and take it easy" advice to the elderly results in a large proportion of elderly people with the hypokinetic syndrome.

A sedentary life style may contribute to the tissue changes affecting the observed decrease in the range of joint motion in the elderly. Greey (9) and Jervey (13) cross-sectionally measured the age differences in flexibility. In a study involving 510 males, ages 18-71, Greey found flexibility for most joints greatest at 23.5 years. Jervey did a similar study with 407 females, ages 18-74. She found the greatest flexibility in most joints between the ages of 25 and 29. It was found from the cross-sectional data that flexibility is specific for each joint or muscle group in the body and that mean flexibility scores decrease with age for most movements.

Muscles, tendons and the joint capsule are the soft connective tissues responsible for the resistance to movement. It is difficult to determine how much each of these variables contributes to the impairment of movement, although the elastin component of connective tissue is more resilient during a joint motion than the collagen component (12). During the aging process the increase in the cross-linkage of collagen tissue (18) may contribute to some loss in joint mobility (23,26).

In addition to the normal age-associated changes in soft connective tissue, injury and disease can have deleterious effects on flexibility. Muscle tightness, arthritis and osteoporosis affect the mobility of their victims. Immobilization or lack of use shorten the joint's range of motion. The hamstrings, low back extensors, gastro-soleus, shoulder adductors and hip flexors are muscle groups that tend to shorten in advanced age (13). Knees, hips, shoulders, ankles and wrists are common sites for arthritis in the elderly, which adds to the restriction of movement. Tendonitis commonly strikes the supraspinatus muscles of the shoulder girdle and the point where the achilles tendon inserts into the calcaneous. A substantial amount of flexibility is also lost in the neck (3). Osteoporosis can result in the collapse of intervertebral discs. This has a definite effect on back mobility because one function of the intervertebral disc is to allow vertebral flexibility (16).

## REVIEW OF THE LITERATURE

Properly designed and conducted physical activity programs have the capacity to increase the range of joint motion in subjects of all ages. The soft tissues of the body are most easily modifiable through training. Since most of the stiffness in a joint is in the soft tissues of the muscle's tendons and joint capsule, exercises designed to work on those areas of the body associated with age related problems could potentially increase the range of movement by reducing stiffness (1).

There has been a limited amount of research testing the

effects of physical activity on the range of joint motion in the elderly. A study by Leslie and Frekany (22) involved 15 female volunteers, one age 55 and the others between 71 and 90, who exercised one-half hour two times a week for approximately 7 months. Subjects were measured before and after the 7 month exercise program at two sites: the ankle and hamstring/lower back. The Sit and Reach Test (15) was used to measure hamstring and lower back flexibility. Ankle flexibility measurements were taken with the subject in a long sitting position on the floor. A sheet of paper was attached to a clipboard and the subject would plantar flex and dorsiflex each foot. A line was drawn on the paper at the limit of each flexing motion and the angle created at the point of intersection was the recorded measurement. A significant improvement in flexibility was found in both ankles and in the hamstring/lower back. Apparent weaknesses in the study include the limited number of measuring sites and the lack of a control group.

Gutman et al. (11) studied elderly subjects ($\bar{x}$ = 73 years) comparing the effects of a Feldenkrais exercise program (slow therapeutic movement) with a conventional exercise program and with a non exercising control group. Measurements included height, weight, blood pressure, heart rate, balance, flexibility, morale, self-perceived health status and level of performance in daily activities. The only type of flexibility measured was rotational flexibility which was designed to measure how far the subject could turn to the right and left without foot movements. The exercise and Feldenkrais groups both met 3 times per week for six weeks. Members of the training groups responded favorably to the program and reactions at the end of the program were positive. The researchers saw some improvement in individuals, although none of the tests proved to be statistically significant. A major drawback in the study was an attrition rate of 50%. The attrition factor inevitably affected the significance of the results. Gutman et al., in discussing the study, stressed the necessity of medical screening of participants prior to the program with continual close medical monitoring during the exercise sessions. The researchers suggested the duration for study be extended in future investigations.

Chapman et al. (1) tested the effect of an exercise program on joint stiffness in 20 young (15-19 years) and 20 old men (63-88 years). Either the right or left index finger was used for the experimental procedure. The opposite index finger was used as a control. Stiffness was measured by a method described by Wright and Johns (26). All 55 exercised the experimental index finger by lifting weights ranging from 1/2 to maximum load three times a week, 10 finger lifts per exercise sessions for six weeks. Results showed significantly greater joint stiffness in the older subjects. In addition, an equal degree of reversibility of joint stiffness in both age groups with training was exhibited.

Lesser (21) studied the effects of rhythmic exercise on the range of motion in elderly subjects, age 61-89, with a mean age of 75. Thirty experimental subjects participated in the activity program 1/2 hour per session, two times a week for ten weeks. Thirty additional subjects served as controls. Flexion and extension range of motion at the shoulder, elbow, wrist, hip, knee and ankle were compared before and after the exercise program with a goniometer. Significant improvement was found at 8 of the 12 sites. The short duration and lack of specificity of the program were suggested as reasons for the lack of improvement in the 4 remaining joints.

## PROCEDURES

Forty subjects, ranging in age from 65 to 88 years ($\bar{x}$ =72) participated as volunteers in a 12 week study designed to test the effects of an exercise and dance program on the range of joint motion. Participants were free from serious illness and had a doctor's signed approval to participate in the program. Twenty of the 40 subjects were randomly assigned to the experimental group which met for a one hour duration, three times a week for 12 weeks and the remaining 20 subjects served as controls.

All 40 subjects were pre and post tested with a Leighton flexometer (19,20) at the following body sites: neck (flexion and extension), shoulder (abduction and adduction), wrist (flexion and extension), knee (flexion and extension) and ankle (flexion and extension). The Leighton flexometer consists of a weighted circular dial with a weighted needle enclosed in a metal case and measures the movement of body segments in degrees.

Three trials were taken on each joint action for each subject and the average of the three trials was used in computations. The temperature of the room was held constant at 72 degrees during pre and post testing. No warm-up exercises were done prior to the testing sessions.

## EXPERIMENTAL PROGRAM

The exercise and dance program designed for this study included movement activities that put each body joint through a full range of motion. These locomotor and non-locomotor movements were done:

A. In a variety of supported and free positions
    1. Sitting in chairs
    2. Standing, using a chair for support
    3. Free standing
    4. Moving
    5. Lying on the floor
B. To music
    1. Varying the beat
    2. Varying the tempo
    3. Adding syncopation
    4. Varying musical selections
    5. Live music
C. In different combinations
    1. Alone
    2. With a partner
    3. In small groups (N ≈ 3-8)
    4. As a class (N ≈ 20)
D. In different formations
    1. Random arrangements
    2. Circle formation
    3. Line formation
E. Using different degrees of force
    1. Slow, flowing movements
    2. Quick, staccato movements
    3. A combination of slow and quick movements
F. Changing body shapes, levels and dimensions
    1. Moving with the body high in space

      2.   Moving with the body low in space

      3.   Moving from one level to another, experiencing all the levels in between

      4.   Making the body small and compact

      5.   Stretching the body out and covering a maximum amount of space

      6.   Moving from one size and shape to another, experiencing all the other sizes in between

G.  In different directions

      1.   Forward

      2.   Backward

      3.   Sideways

      4.   Turning

      5.   Diagonals

Work loads generally ranged between 2.5 and 5.5 METS. The pace of the daily and overall program was geared to the ability and level of fitness of the participants and progressed in intensity over the 12 weeks. The number of repetitions and the degree of difficulty increased while the number and duration of rest periods decreased. Movements could be individualized, that is, made easier or more difficult in order to challenge each person and keep everyone actively involved. Heart rates were monitored by the subjects at rest and during the exercise sessions

## RESULTS

After the pretest data from both groups were collected, the distribution of scores was tested for normality, homogeneity of variances and equality of means. The distribution of the scores of both groups was found to be normal. Using Hotelling's $T^2$, a multivariate statistical test, at the .01 level, no significant difference was found between pretest means (see Table 1) of the six individual variables (measuring sites) (Table 2) or between the overall group means combining all six variables (6 dimensional vector mean (Table 3). Post test means of all six individual variables and the overall group means were significantly better in the experimental group at the .01 level (Tables 1-3).

Overall differences between groups were the main focus of the study. It is important to look at the six individual

TABLE 1

Pre- and Post-Test Range of Joint Motion Data of Experimental and Control Subjects Obtained with the Leighton Flexometer

| Measurement | | Neck | Wrist | Shoulder | Hip/Back | Knee | Ankle |
|---|---|---|---|---|---|---|---|
| Experimental Group | | | | | | | |
| - Mean | Pre | 98.9 | 88.9 | 138.5 | 99.2 | 114.3 | 26.2 |
| | Post | 125.4 | 110.3 | 150.1 | 125.9 | 127.6 | 39.1 |
| - Standard | Pre | 14.8 | 15.4 | 9.3 | 19.3 | 15.5 | 6.3 |
| Deviation | Post | 15.2 | 16.5 | 7.7 | 18.0 | 9.9 | 9.5 |
| - Variance | Pre | 221.3 | 239.5 | 87.1 | 375.5 | 241.3 | 40.4 |
| | Post | 233.7 | 274.8 | 60.2 | 325.6 | 98.0 | 90.9 |
| Control Group | | | | | | | |
| - Mean | Pre | 100.2 | 85.6 | 143.7 | 95.1 | 105.6 | 23.3 |
| | Post | 96.5 | 83.5 | 136.3 | 91.6 | 102.6 | 22.1 |
| - Standard | Pre | 16.8 | 18.3 | 11.2 | 16.8 | 14.4 | 5.4 |
| Deviation | Post | 14.4 | 16.2 | 16.4 | 15.2 | 16.2 | 4.9 |
| - Variance | Pre | 283.2 | 334.4 | 125.2 | 285.2 | 208.5 | 30.1 |
| | Post | 208.7 | 265.0 | 271.1 | 233.2 | 263.2 | 24.4 |

Scores are reported as the data from the flexibility tests by the Leighton Flexometer (unit of measurement degrees)

variables separately because of their assumed relationship to the overall aging process. Exercises for this study were designed to include movements specifically involving the six body areas to be measured. The significant post-test improvement on each of the six variables indicates that the program design was effective in increasing the range of joint motion. Table 4 reports the percent increase in range of motion at each measuring site.

When the post testing was completed, the experimental subjects were asked for their comments and response to the 12 week exercise and dance program. The self reports were favorable and fell into one or more of these three main categories: Absence of stiffness (N = 19), improvement in balance (N = 14) and increased movement independence (N = 16).

TABLE 2

T-Test Results Comparing Between Group
Means of All Six Variables Separately

| Measurement Variables | | T Value | P Value* |
|---|---|---|---|
| Neck | Pre | -0.26 | .70 |
| | Post | 6.14 | .01* |
| Wrist | Pre | 0.62 | .54 |
| | Post | 5.15 | .01* |
| Shoulder | Pre | -1.58 | .12 |
| | Post | 3.39 | .01* |
| Hip/Back | Pre | 0.72 | .48 |
| | Post | 6.49 | .01* |
| Knee | Pre | 1.84 | .07 |
| | Post | 5.88 | .01* |
| Ankle | Pre | 2.17 | .03 |
| | Post | 7.06 | .01* |

*All values are significant at the .01 level

TABLE 3

Results of Joint Range of Motion for Pre- and Post-Test Data
Showing Differences Among Group Means Using All Variables

| | Pre | Post |
|---|---|---|
| Hotelling's T-Square | 9.28 | 67.90 |
| F Value* | 1.34 | 9.831* |
| P Value | .27 | .01 |

*Significant F = 3.05 ($\alpha$ = .01)

Motivational levels remained high throughout the 12 week
program as evidenced by a 92% attendance rate with the majority of subjects missing less than 3 classes. There was no
program attrition.

## TABLE 4
Percent Change in the Range of Joint Motion Following
a 12 Week Exercise and Dance Program

|  | Experimental Group | Control Group |
|---|---|---|
| NECK | ↑27.8% | ↓3.6% |
| (flexion/extension) | | |
| SHOULDER | ↑ 8.3% | ↓5.1% |
| (abduction/adduction) | | |
| WRIST | ↑12.8% | ↓2.3% |
| (flexion/extension) | | |
| HIP/BACK | ↑26.9% | ↓3.7% |
| (flexion/extension) | | |
| KNEE | ↑11.6% | ↓2.7% |
| (flexion/extension) | | |
| ANKLE | ↑48.3% | ↓5.1% |
| (flexion/extension) | | |

## DISCUSSION

The results of this study demonstrate the ability to increase range of motion through a properly designed exercise program. Twenty subjects ($\bar{x}$ = 71.8 years) in an exercise and dance program met 3 times a week for 12 weeks. The experimental group exhibited a significant increase over the control group ($\bar{x}$ = 73 years) in the range of motion at all six body sites: neck, wrist, shoulder, hip and back, knee and ankle.

Results of this study contradict the finding of Gutman et al. (11). Both studies dealt with range of joint motion changes in the elderly before and after participation in specifically designed exercise programs. The program frequency of 3 times/week was consistent across both studies but the program duration varied from six weeks in the Gutman study to 12 weeks in this study. Gutman et al. found no significant post-test range of joint motion differences between the experimental and control groups. Although the difference in program duration could account for the discrepancy in results between the two studies, more probable factors could be the 50% attrition rate their study experienced, compared to a 0% attrition rate in this study. Other differences might include the number and type of measurements used and the specificity of the exercises done.

The significant improvement with the range of joint motion with the exercise group in this study was in agreement with the findings of Leslie and Frekany (22), Chapman et al. (1) and Lesser (21). While the studies differed in measurement technique, duration and frequency of design, the significant results in all these investigations indicate that an improvement of the range of joint motion with the elderly population is a realistic possibility. This finding contradicts a popular assumption of inevitable irreversible deterioration with age.

## SUMMARY AND CONCLUSION

Factors contributing to the loss of flexibility during the aging process are numerous. Inactivity is only one of them. This study attempted to reverse the habit of inactivity, and thereby show an increase in range of joint motion. The method used was a 12 week exercise and dance program designed to work specifically on the parts of the body to be measured. Twenty subjects over 65 years of age ($\bar{x} = 71.8$ years) participated in a 12 week exercise and dance program that met three times/week for an hour each time. Twenty additional subjects ($\bar{x} = 73.0$ years) served as control subjects.

The groups were pre- and post-tested on six single joint actions: flexion/extension of the neck, wrist, hip and lower back, knee and ankle and abduction/adduction of the shoulder. The Leighton Flexometer, a gravity-based instrument which measures the range of joint motion in degrees, was used to measure single joint actions.

Mean flexibility scores were not significantly different between groups at the pre-test level. The experimental group met three times/week for 12 weeks and participated in the exercise and dance class while the control group received no treatment. Both groups were post-tested and compared using Hotelling's $T^2$ at an alpha level of .01. At the end of the program, the experimental exercise group was significantly better on all six range of motion measurements.

The program experienced a 0% attrition rate, and attendance was excellent throughout the 12 weeks. A good indicator of the subjects' motivation was the unanimous decision to keep the program going once the post-testing was completed.

Within the limits of this study it may be concluded that:

1. The range of joint motion of elderly subjects was significantly improved after full participation in a carefully designed exercise and dance program.

2. Daily life practices and comfort in movement were affected as measured by the subjects' personal reactions at the end of the study.

## REFERENCES

1. Chapman, E.A., H.A. deVries and R. Sweezey. Joint stiffness and effects of exercise on young and old men. J. Gerontol. 27(2):218-221, 1972.

2. Conover, W.J. Practical Nonparametric Statistics. New York: John Wiley, 1971.

3. deVries, H.A. Physiological effects of an exercise training regimen upon men aged 52-88. J. Gerontol. 25(4):325-336, 1970.

4. deVries, H.A. Physiology of Exercise for Physical Education and Athletics, 2nd ed. Dubuque, Iowa: William Brown, 1974.

5. deVries, H.A. and G.M. Adams. Comparison of exercise responses in old and young men. II. Ventilatory mechanics. J. Gerontol. 27: 349-352, 1974.

6. deVries, H.A. Prevention of muscular distress after exercise. Res. Quart. 33:2, 1961.

7. deVries, H.A. Evaluation of static stretching procedures for improvement of flexibility. Res. Quart. 33:2, 1962.

8. Gardner, G.W. Effects of isometrics and isotonic exercise on joint motion. Arch. Phys. Med. 47:24-30, 1966.

9. Greey, G.W. A study of flexibility in selected joints of adult males ages 18-72. Doctoral dissertation, University of Michigan, 1955.

10. Gurland, J. and R.C. Dahiya. Statistical Papers in Honor of G.W. Snedecon. Madison, WI: University of Wisconsin, 1972.

11. Gutman, G.M., C.P. Herbert and S.R. Brown. Feldenkrais versus conventional exercises for the elderly. J. Gerontol. 32(5):562-572, 1977.

12. Holland, G.J. The physiology of flexibility - a review of literature. Kinesiology Rev. 49, 1968.

13. Jervey, A. A study of flexibility of selected joints in specified groups of adult females. Doctoral dissertation, University of Michigan, 1961.

14. Johns, R.J. and U. Wright. Relative importance of various tissues in joint stiffness. J. Appl. Physiol. 17:824-828, 1962.

15. Johnson, B.L. and J.K. Nelson. Practical Measurement for Evaluation in Physical Education, 1st ed. Minneapolis: Burgess Publishing Co., 1967.

16. Kazarian, L. Creep characteristics of the human spinal column. Symposium of the lumbar spine. Orthop. Clin. North Am. 6:3-18, 1975.

17. Kraus, H. and W. Raab. Hypokinetic Disease. Springfield: C.C. Thomas, 1961.

18. LaBella, F.S. and G. Paul. Structure of collagen from human tendons as influenced by age and sex. J. Gerontol. 20:54-59, 1963.

19. Leighton, J.R. A simple objective and reliable measure of flexibility. Res. Quart. 13:205-216, 1942.

20. Leighton, J.R. An instrument and technique for the measurement of range of joint motion. Arch. Phys. Med. 36:571-578, 1955.

21. Lesser, M. The effects of rhythmic exercise on the range of motion in older adults. Amer. Corr. Ther. J. 32:4, 1978.

22. Leslie, D.K. and G.A. Frekany. Effects of an exercise program on selected flexibility measures of senior citizens. The Gerontologist 4:182-183, 1975.

23. Long, C., B. Krysatofiak, I. Zamir, J. Lane and N.C. Koehler. Visco-elastic characteristics of the hand in spasticity: A quantitative study. Arch Phys. Med. Rehab. 49:677-691, 1968.

24. Schultz, P. Flexibility: Day of the static stretch. The Phys. and Spts. Med. 7(11):109-117, 1979.

25. Sigerseth, P.O. Flexibility. In: An Introduction to Measurements in Physical Education, edited by H.J. Montoye. Indianapolis: Phi Epsilon Kappa Fraternity, 1970.

26. Wright, V. and R.J. Johns. Physical factors concerned with the stiffness of normal and diseased joints. Bull. Johns Hopkins Hosp. 106: 215-231, 1960.

Kathleen Munns received her undergraduate degrees in Health Education and Physical Education from the University of Wisconsin-LaCrosse. She received her Masters Degree from the University of Wisconsin-Madison and is currently working toward her Ph.D. in exercise physiology. During the last three years she has worked on developing and leading activity programs for the elderly. She works at the Biogerontology Laboratory at the University of Wisconsin (Everett L. Smith, Director) and is involved with a four year research project investigating exercise and middle-aged women.

BONE CHANGES IN THE EXERCISING OLDER ADULT
Everett L. Smith

Bone mineral decline in the older adult is multifactorial in
nature. The 15 to 30% observed decline by age 70 results in
a skeletal system normal in mineral composition, but decreased
in bone mineral mass and strength. This bone mineral decline,
called osteoporosis, is the primary cause of increased hip
fracture by fifty fold between the ages of 40 and 70 (4) in
non-pathological subjects. One hypothesized cause of osteoporosis is inactivity. The dynamic balance between bone
apposition and resorption have been shown to result, in part,
as an adaptive response to the extrinsic environmental forces
on the bone. Bone adapts, like any other body tissue; when
stressed it hypertrophies, when unstressed it atrophies.

Vose and Kubala (19) stated that factors which effect the
strength of bone are not clearly understood, but any changes
in quality or quantity of the physical organic or inorganic
properties result in changes of bone strength. The physical
properties of any given bone may be expected to vary from
time to time under a variety of physical and biological conditions. The shape of a bone may be considered to result
from a series of forces acting in different areas, in different combinations, and under varying conditions of mechanical
efficiency. As early as 1917 Howell (8) stated that the
growth of bone is dependent, to some extent at least, upon
the amount of stress and strain exerted upon the bone. Wolff
in 1892 (21) reported that the mechanically adapted arrange-
ment of the trabecula and compacta, in the vertebra and bones
of the leg, is the result of the extrinsic forces acting upon

the bone.

Bone has two main extrinsic forces acting upon it: gravitational force due to the physical mass supported by the bone, and muscular force exerted by the contraction of muscles attached to the bone. These two forces result in a series of stresses on the bone during muscle contraction. The forces resulting from muscular contraction are applied on different areas and at different angles on the bone causing several combinations of varying lines of stress. Gravitational and muscular forces affect the mechanical organization of bone mineral and collagen which gives bone its strength to resist the forces acting upon it. If either of these forces are increased or decreased the bone will adapt to these forces through cellular and structural modifications.

Bone, at the cellular level, involves mineral homeostasis (serum calcium maintained constant), matrix formation and matrix maintenance, while at the structural level bone is observed to adapt in trabecular and osteon size and orientation. Bone adaptation like all other body systems is controlled by both genetic and environmental components.

Skeletal control is the combination of two homeostatic mechanisms, one concerned with blood calcium levels and the other with local bone structure. The skeleton functions as a chemical storehouse and contains ninety-nine percent of the total calcium in the body, eighty-nine percent of the phosphate, eight percent of the carbonates and seventy percent of the citrates. The level of blood calcium is well controlled by parathyroid hormone, calcitonin and growth hormone, vitamin D and gonadal hormones. Superimposed on this chemical homeostatic relationship between blood calcium levels and bone is the local homeostatic control. This is involved in the maintenance of the skeletal system in the support and protection of the organism.

Bassett and Becker (2) hypothesized that this localized self-maintenance adaptive mechanism is controlled by the conversion of mechanical to electrical energy within and along specific lines of stress applied to the bone. Bassett (1) demonstrated that bone acts like a piezo-electric crystal. When the crystal is deformed it produces a charge change. The compressed succession of the tissue results in a negative

charge, while the extended succession of the bone results in a
positive charge.   In the skeletal system the extrinsic and intrinsic forces deforming the bone tissue result in an electrical potential which is felt to control cell function (Figure
1).   Structures are altered, therefore, in a specific manner
appropriate to meet the demands of the extrinsic forces on the
bone tissue.

FIGURE 1

Bone Adaptation to Stress (1)

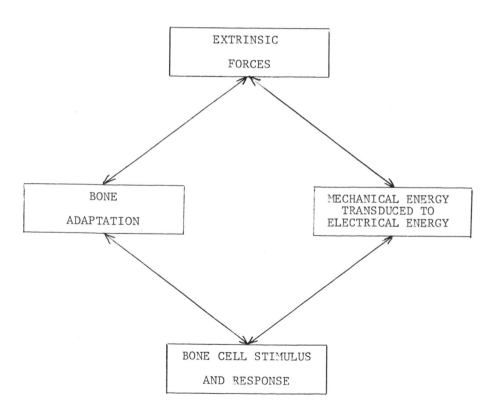

If bone is controlled locally by mechanical and electrical stimulation, one's occupation, sports activity and general
lifestyle should influence bone variation.

## INACTIVITY AND BONE

Hypodynamic states over extended periods of time, such as bed rest, immobilization, or weightlessness, should result in disuse osteoporosis. Mack et al. (10) demonstrated small, but significant, bone mineral loss in astronauts participating in the Gemini IV, V and VII flights. The astronauts of the fourteen day Gemini VII flight demonstrated less bone loss than the astronauts in earlier flights. The reasons given for this reduced bone mineral loss were greater food consumption and participation in an on-board isometric and isotonic exercise program by the Gemini VII astronauts.

It has also been shown that a negative calcium balance occurs in normal subjects during long-term bed rest where gravitational stress and muscle contractions are reduced. This reduction in external forces results in disuse osteoporosis. Donaldson et al. (6) studied three young males during six months of bed rest. They observed a bone mineral loss in the calcaneous of up to 39% using the photon absorptiometry system. Rambaut et al. (15) reported a decreasing bone mineral content in the calcaneous on the heel bone at a rate of 1.1%/week in eight subjects immobilized for 24 weeks.

## PHYSICAL ACTIVITY AND BONE

Prives reported the influence of specific life style in the form of physical labor and sports participation on the bone development of 3000 adult and senescent subjects (14). He concluded that characteristic bone shapes and structures exist for various occupations and sports and that these variables change with a change in occupation or sports activity.

Mashkara studied x-rays of the arms of 150 laborers in different trades and 80 office employees (11). He observed adaptational strengthening of the shoulder girdle, humerus, and of the radius and ulnar bones.

Ross (16) reported a specific example of bone adaptation to extrinsic forces in a construction worker. He observed metacarpal and phalanx hypertrophy in the fifth digit of the right hand in a worker who had lost the other digits in a shrapnel wound thirty-two years earlier. An x-ray of both hands demonstrated the fifth digit of the right hand to be similar in length and thickness to the third digit of the left hand. This response of the metacarpal and phalanx clearly demonstrates the extensive adaptability of bone to the extrinsic forces placed upon the tissue.

Dalen found that cross country runners between the ages of 50 and 59, compared to a control group of the same age, weight, and height, had a significantly greater bone mineral content of 20% in both the femur and the humerus (5). Nilsson and Westlin (13) used absorptiometry to measure the femur bone mineral content of sixty-four nationally ranked athletes and compared them to thirty-nine controls. The bone mineral content of the athletes was significantly greater than the controls. The athletes demonstrated bone hypertrophy in relationship to their specific sport activity: Weight lifters greater than throwers; throwers greater than runners; runners greater than soccer players and soccer players greater than swimmers. The control group consisted of an active and inactive group. The active group participated regularly in a physical activity program and demonstrated a highly significant greater bone mineral than the active group. Nilsson concluded that it seems possible to increase the bone mineral content above "normal" in man by physical activity; on the other hand, inactivity will result in bone loss.

Buskirk and co-workers studied bone and muscle hypertrophy in the forearms of tennis players (3). Their data revealed a significantly greater distal width of the ulna in the dominant arm and a radial midshaft width that differed significantly from that of the nondominant arm. A control group demonstrated no significant differences in any of the bone diameters. The anthropometric data reflected significantly larger wrists and forearm circumferences on the dominant side.

Similarly, the tennis players measured by Gwinup and associates showed significant muscle hypertrophy in the dominant forearm. The mean difference in circumference of the forearm was much greater than that of the upper arms (7). The humeri of the playing side showed a pronounced hypertrophy of 34.9 percent in men (N = 44) and 28.4 percent in women (N = 23) compared to the nonplaying arm. Jones observed an increase in humeral bone diameter and an increase in cortical thickness on the playing side compared to the control arm (9). Similar humeri bone hypertrophy has been reported by Watson using absorptiometry in a study of 203 baseball pitchers (20). He found a significant bone mineral content hypertrophy of the dominant versus the nondominant humerus in young males between the ages of 8 and 19.

## PHYSICAL ACTIVITY IN THE AGED

Smith studied changes of bone mineral content in residents of a nursing home as a function of exercise over a period of 8 months (17). The study population consisted of 21 subjects in a control group, 12 subjects in a physical activity program, and 6 subjects in a physical therapy program. Mean ages were 80.2, 74.8 and 82.3 years, respectively. An average increase of 7.8% was noted in the bone mineral content of the subjects in the physical therapy group. This was significant at the 5% level compared to the control group. The physical activity group demonstrated an average gain of 2.6% (p < .05); but when compared to the gain of the control group, the value was not significant at the 5% level. The control group showed a gain of 0.4%.

In a later study, 2 groups were matched for age, weight, and degree of ambulation (18). Bone mineral was measured by photon absorptiometry on 30 subjects aged 69-95 years at 3 month intervals for 3 years. Twelve subjects regularly participated in a 30-minute physical activity program consisting of light to moderate physical activity (2-4 METS), 3 times weekly while the remaining 18 subjects made no change in their daily routine. The bone mineral of the exercise group showed a significant increase of 2.29%. The control group lost an average of 3.28%. This increase in bone mineral of the exercise group is consistent with the concept that appositional bone growth is a function of adaptation to stress. This study demonstrated that physical activity plays an important role in maintaining and increasing bone mineral content in the aged.

Montoye and Smith (12) reported bone mineral hypertrophy in sixty-one male tennis players with a mean age of 64, whose average length of participation was 40 years. Measurements of bone mineral status were obtained by photon absorptiometry and x-ray on the dominant and non-dominant arms. Significant bone mineral hypertrophy of the dominant arm (p < .01) was observed in the radius (7.9%) and the humerus (13%) compared to the nondominant arm when measured by absorptiometry. Significant bone mineral hypertrophy of the dominant arm (p < .01) was observed for the second metacarpal length (.06%), total area (13.5%), and cortical area (15.2%) compared to the nondominant arm when measured by x-ray.

The exact mechanisms of increase in bone mineral due to physical activity are not yet clear, but possible mechanisms may involve increased circulation in the bone, improved subject nutrition, and/or the increased gravitational and muscular stress effecting bone cellular activity via the piezoelectric phenomena.

Physical activity, as a stimulus, affects human bone in two ways: First, there is an increased stress and strain on the skeletal system due to muscular contraction and gravity; and second, the increased metabolic demands of working muscles result in an increased blood flow and blood pressure in the cardiovascular system. Physical activity as a stimulus clearly produces bone mineral accretion in the young and old as the result of this increased stress and strain placed on the living bone tissue.

## REFERENCES

1. Bassett, C.A.L. Biophysical principles affecting bone structure. In: The Biochemistry and Physiology of Bone, edited by G.H. Bourne. New York: Academic Press, 1971.

2. Bassett, C.A.L. and R.D. Becker. Generation of electric potentials by bone in response to mechanical stress. Science 137:1063, 1962.

3. Buskirk, E., K. Anderson and J. Brozek. Unilateral activity and bone muscle development in the forearm. Res. Quart. 27:127-131, 1956.

4. Chalmers, J. Geographical variation in senile osteoporosis: The association with physical activity. J. Bone Jt. Surg. 52:667-675, 1970.

5. Dalen, N. and K.E. Olsson. Bone mineral content and physical activity. Acta Orthop. Scand. 45:170-174, 1974.

6. Donaldson, C., S.B. Halley, J.M. Voge, R.S. Hattner, J.H. Bayers and D.E. MacMillan. Effect of prolonged bedrest on bone mineral. Metabolism 19:12,1071-1084, 1970.

7. Gwinup, G., R. Chelvam and T. Steinberg. Thickness of subcutaneous fat and activity of underlying muscles. Ann. Int. Med. 74:408-411, 1971.

8. Howell, J.A. An experimental study of the effect of stress and strain on bone development. Anatomic Record 13:233-252, 1917.

9. Jones, H.H., J.D. Priest, W.C. Hayes, C.C. Tichenor and D.A. Nagel. Humeral hypertrophy in response to exercise. J. Bone Jt. Surg. 59A:204-208, 1977.

10. Mack, P., P. LaChance, G. Vose and F. Vogt. Bone demineralization of foot and hand of Gemini-Titan IV, V, and VII astronauts during orbital flight. Amer. J. Roent. 100:503-511, 1967.

11. Mashkara, K. Effect of physical labor on the structure of the bones of the upper extremities. Ark. Anat. Gistol. Embryol. 56:7-15, 1969.

12. Montoye, H.J., E.L. Smith, D.F. Fardon and E.T. Howley. Bone mineral in senior tennis players - unpublished data.

13. Nilsson, B. and N. Westline. Bone density in athletes. Clin. Orthop. 77:179-182, 1971.

14. Prives, M. Influence of labor and sport upon skeleton structure in man. Anat. Rec. 136:261, 1960.

15. Rambaut, P., L. Dietlein, J. Vogel and M. Smith. Comparative study of two direct methods of bone mineral measurement. Aerospace Med. 43:646-650, 1972.

16. Ross, J.A. Hypertrophy of the little finger. Brit. Med. J. 2:987, 1950.

17. Smith, E.L. The effects of physical activity on bone in the aged. In: International Conference on Bone Mineral Measurements, edited by R.B. Mazess. Washington, D.C.: DHEW Publication No. NIH 75-683, 1973.

18. Smith, E.L., W. Reddan and P. Smith. Physical activity and calcium modalities for bone accretion in the aged. In press.

19. Vose, G.P. and A.L. Kubala. Bone Strength--its relationship to x-ray-determined ash content. Human Biology 31:261-270, 1959.

20. Watson, R.C. Bone growth and physical activity. In: International Conference on Bone Mineral Measurements, edited by R.B. Mazess. Washington, D.C.: DHEW Publication No. NIH 75-683, 1973.

21. Wolff, J. Das Gesetz der Transformation der Knochen. Berlin: A. Hirschwald, 1892.

Everett L. Smith received his Master's Degree in Physical Education from the University of Minnesota in 1964 and his Ph.D. in Biodynamics at the University of Wisconsin in 1971. He is a clinical assistant professor at the University of Wisconsin, and teaches courses on aging for the Department of Preventive Medicine. The Biogerontology Laboratory, which is currently investigating osteoporosis, is directed by him. He has been a consultant in a number of programs to aid the aged, including a pilot television program. He is a fellow of the American College of Sports Medicine, and is a member of the Gerontological Society, The Wisconsin Educational Congress on Aging, the Faye-McBeath Institute for Aging and Adult Life and the New York Academy of Science.

189